COMMUNICATING FOR MANAGERIAL EFFECTIVENESS

SECOND EDITION

Phillip G. Clampitt

Sage Publications, Inc.
International Educational and Professional Publisher
Thousand Oaks ▪ London ▪ New Delhi

For information:

Sage Publications, Inc.
2455 Teller Road
Thousand Oaks, California 91320
E-mail: order@sagepub.com

Sage Publications Ltd.
6 Bonhill Street
London EC2A 4PU
United Kingdom

Sage Publications India Pvt. Ltd.
M-32 Market
Greater Kailash I
New Delhi 110 048 India

Printed in the United States of America

Library of Congress Cataloging-in-Publication Data

Clampitt, Phillip G.
    Communicating for managerial effectiveness / by Phillip G. Clampitt.—2nd ed.
        p. cm.
    Includes bibliographical references and index.
    ISBN 0-7619-2152-4 (alk. paper)
    ISBN 0-7619-2153-2 (pbk. : alk. paper)
    1. Communication in management. I. Title.
    HD30.3 .C52 2001
    658.4'5)—dc21   00-009550

This book is printed on acid-free paper.

            03 04 05 06 07 7 6 5 4 3

Acquiring Editor:	Marquita Flemming
Editorial Assistant:	Mary Ann Vail
Production Editor:	Diane Foster
Editorial Assistant:	Cindy Bear
Designer/Typesetter:	Marion Warren
Cover Designer:	Michelle Lee

COMMUNICATING FOR MANAGERIAL EFFECTIVENESS

SECOND EDITION

*To Laurey, the best partner in the world,
and to my parents, Dr. Bert and Betty Clampitt,
who provided all the physical, psychological,
and spiritual support a son could desire.*

CONTENTS

FOREWORD

The communication that takes place in an organization is an important influence in the success of that organization. Therefore, a good book on organizational communication can be a valuable resource for all kinds of students—managers who want to be effective communicators, as well as academic students who want to understand how organizations work. Phil Clampitt has written such a book.

Over the years, I have evaluated a number of manuscripts offered to various publishers, and many of them have good coverage of rather standard materials that are commonly covered about organizational communication. What Phil Clampitt has done, however, is to write a book that is original and interesting.

What strikes me most about his work is its freshness. The quotations with which he begins each chapter are not typical organizational literature; they demonstrate how well read he is, and how this breadth of resources has led him to think about organizational life in some innovative ways. He also demonstrates great originality in the way that he uses metaphor to explain how communication works. For example, although I love to dance, I would never have thought of using dance as a metaphor for the way organizational communication works. Yet Clampitt does so in a convincing way. Furthermore, he is able to coin new phrases that are rich in explanatory power.

I also like the way Clampitt makes this book a statement of his theory about organizational communication. It is not merely a report on the research about a topic. He includes basic propositions and clarifies some of his basic assumptions. He makes a major addition also by describing some common problem areas, and then telling his reader "what to do" about them. Finally, he adds some important areas that are often overlooked. His work with communication audits has prompted him to add major discussions of interteam communication.

One of the great rewards of being a university professor is being able to watch exceptional graduate students become major contributors to one's discipline. Phil Clampitt is doing this with his book. There are many gems in these chapters, and I am delighted to recommend it.

CAL DOWNS
University of Kansas

PREFACE

Since the first edition of this book, I have consulted with numerous organizations about many of the communication issues discussed in the original edition. Those experiences shaped this edition in two distinct ways. First, they reinforced my conviction that the notions discussed in the first edition can have a profoundly positive impact on the way organizations function and managers lead. I have seen poorly informed "subordinates" become knowledgeable team players, demoralized managers transformed into motivated ones, and dispirited organizations reinvigorated into organic learning systems. Second, I learned firsthand the difficulty many organizations experience translating seemingly simple and straightforward principles into action. In fact, a few of my projects were wonderful failures. Wonderful because they forced me to rethink and reshape some of these seemingly straightforward principles. After all, knowledge shaped in the crucible of experience ultimately proves the most enduring and valuable.

So what? This edition focuses on the same critical issues discussed in the first edition, but with a much greater emphasis on the successful implementation of the principles. Every chapter was revised in some major way. For example, this edition discusses a new way to manage the relationship between data, information, knowledge, and action. The first edition only touches on this concern. This edition also presents an improved way to communicate strategically about organizational changes. After leading dozens of change efforts in the past few years, I have grown to appreciate the difficulty and complexity of effectively implementing major organizational change. This edition analyzes many of those experiences.

Another force has also caused me to reshape this edition. The Internet has significantly changed the way organizations communicate. The book discusses "dot.coms" as well as the impact of the Internet on traditional brick-and-mortar organizations. The "dot" is the most significant aspect of the dot.com evolution, because dots can be easily connected. The ease of connecting employees, managers, and executives has not made organizational communication easier; it has only changed the nature of the challenge. This edition tackles this issue in a variety of ways. In fact, my consulting firm, MetaComm, developed a web site for the book intended to improve the connection between motivated readers and the material (see *www.imetacomm.com/CME*). The site contains chapter outlines, exercises, and case studies. I hope the book and web site provide the wisdom, insight, and advice necessary to enhance your communication effectiveness.

ACKNOWLEDGMENTS

C. S. Lewis once said, "Two heads are better than one, not because either is infallible, but because they are unlikely to go wrong in the same direction." Many wise minds steered me in the right direction. I'm profoundly grateful for the guidance of many friends and colleagues. First, I must again acknowledge Ann West for taking a chance on an "exciting idea" and originally shepherding this project through Sage. And she is still out there fighting for another one of my "exciting ideas." I have a new shepherd now, Marquita Flemming, and she has provided wonderful guidance throughout the project. I would also like to thank Stacey Shimizu, a wonderfully insightful and helpful copy editor.

Several colleagues provided provocative and illuminating comments on many of the core ideas in this edition, including Tim Meyer and Cliff Abbott at the University of Wisconsin—Green Bay, as well as two of my former professors, Lee Williams and Cal Downs. I also want to acknowledge a number of dedicated research assistants who did a great job of assisting and researching: Alida Al-Saadi, Holly Foth, Kristine Harring, Julie Sadoff, Amy Skaggs, Tracy Tesch, and Judy Thiel.

Finally, there is the unlisted coauthor of this book. She refuses to let her name appear on the cover, despite the fact that she read countless drafts, reworked major sections, and clarified my sometimes garbled thoughts. While listening to Vivaldi's concerti in beautiful Door County, we reshaped the manuscript into a work that we hope resonates with many people. I cannot imagine anyone having a better partner. In fact, she is mine—for life.

INTRODUCTION

❚❚The first principle is that you must not fool yourself . . . and you are the easiest person to fool," wrote the Nobel Laureate Richard Feynman. Physicists are not the only ones who must guard against self-delusion—managers must, as well. And the temptation of self-deception proves almost irresistible when it comes to the elusive business of communication. The purpose of *Communicating for Managerial Effectiveness* is to enable managers to view clearly their communication abilities, dilemmas, and challenges.

This is not an easy task for two reasons. First, our knowledge of the communication process is still unfolding. New and exciting theories have recently appeared on the horizon that allow us to see communication in a light never before possible. Only in the past few years have we started to discern the implications of these ideas. For instance, some scholars have challenged the traditional assertion that "understanding" should be the only goal of communication. Sometimes managers are purposefully ambiguous. What are the implications of this notion for managers? Can misunderstandings be useful in an organization? These are the types of questions entertained in these pages.

Second, there is what I call the *Everybody/Anybody Phenomenon*. Translation: Because everybody communicates, anyone can hold a seminar on the subject. Hence what often gets passed off as training for "communication excellence" consists of nothing more than warmed-over platitudes or rehashed pop psychology. That is unfortunate, not only because it misrepresents a rich field of scholarship, but also because managers encounter a host of communication challenges that are not addressed by the Everybody/Anybody speakers. They treat ideas like they are cotton candy: something fluffy and sweet, but not the staples of organizational life. Nothing could be further from reality. Ideas have consequences. Bad ideas have bad consequences. When the communication system breaks down, tragedy is often the result. A case in point: the space shuttle Challenger.

The impetus for this manuscript was research I conducted in over twenty-five organizations (see Appendix A). The methodology consisted of administering surveys and conducting interviews with employees (see Appendix B). As I conducted communication assessments, often in conjunction with students, I discovered a group of concerns that emerged as common themes in these organizations. For instance, executives were often dismayed at the seeming impossibility of getting departments to communicate effectively with one another. Employees were often frustrated by the lack of useful feedback from their managers. So the manuscript took shape around these concerns.

Figure I.1 provides the framework for the book. At the hub of managerial effectiveness lies communication and culture. The first two chapters are devoted to

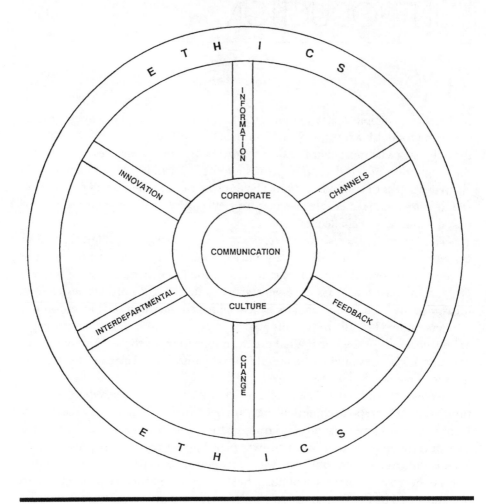

Figure I.1. "Wheel" of Communication Effectiveness

explaining the complex process of communication. The third chapter concerns the core issue of corporate culture, which has a pervasive impact on the communication climate. The spokes represent six critical communication challenges most managers face. In each case, I begin by analyzing the challenge, and then close with practical recommendations based on actual cases. These six chapters discuss how to

    ▷ manage information,
    ▷ select appropriate communication channels,
    ▷ develop an effective performance feedback system,
    ▷ communicate about organizational changes,

▷ foster interdepartmental communication, and

▷ create an innovative spirit.

The final chapter focuses on ethics and building trust through communication practices. And trust is the rim that holds an organization's communication system together. The wheel symbolizes wholeness as well as movement. I hope this book will provide a more complete picture of managerial communication effectiveness, while presenting an image of the ever-changing nature of that quest.

Examples are drawn not only from the business world, but also from a wide range of arenas, including politics, history, science, and art. The rationale is that communication is a concern in almost every arena of life. Many examples are drawn from my consulting experiences. Unless otherwise noted, I have changed the names and slightly altered the background in order to "protect the guilty." When particularly illuminating, I have discussed the findings of key scholarly studies. However, I focus on the practical implementation of the material in the organization. It is my hope that executives, managers, potential managers, training personnel, and students of business communication will find in these pages a way to abide by Professor Feynman's "first principle."

ONE

How Managers Communicate

Human communication permeates the human condition. Human communication surrounds us and is an in-built aspect of everything human beings are and do. That makes any effort to explain, predict, or to some extent control human communication a pretty big order. How does one get a handle on the totality of human communication?

Frank Dance

If, by a wave of a magic wand, managers could communicate perfectly, how would organizations change? Would the company be more productive? Employees more satisfied? The wand presents an intriguing dilemma for the manager. On the one hand, managers know that their success is largely a function of their communication skill. On the other hand, they are often unclear about what constitutes "perfect" or effective communication. Some argue, for example, that if employees completely understood their managers, organizations would function smoothly. Yet misunderstandings may prove useful, as in the case of an employee who misinterprets a manager's sarcastic criticism as a legitimate suggestion. Such a misunderstanding may temporarily preserve "the peace." How managers might use this magic wand proves revealing. It creates the illusions and reality of their world. Typically, managers choose to wave the wand in one of three ways: the Arrow, the Circuit, or the Dance approach, which are all discussed in detail below.

The Arrow Approach

Mr. Taylor almost perfectly, though unwittingly, articulated the Arrow philosophy during a presentation to a management team about communication problems in his organization. He managed the data processing department, and he asked the consultants numerous technical questions about how the data were analyzed. With each response he increasingly appeared more uneasy and antagonistic. When the consultant suggested that his employees were less than satisfied with certain aspects of the communication system, his technical questions assumed an almost acidic quality. The tone of the conversation became increasingly combative. Finally, he exploded with a fifteen-minute diatribe. As frequently occurs, the technical questions masked his actual concern. His remarks went along these lines:

> Why should I take my time to ensure that people understand? I spend my time putting the information together. I send memos, because then I know that I've communicated my message. Then I don't have to worry about it. I've done my duty. They got my message. These meetings you propose for our company may make people feel good, but I just see it as a waste of my time and the company's.

After this rather illuminating soliloquy there was a profound but understandable change in the atmosphere. An uncomfortable silence prevailed for a moment. However, there was also a sense of relief, because Mr. Taylor had laid all his cards on the table. His comments had some merit. He had clearly pointed out one of the greatest challenges in organizational communication: providing efficient methods of communication. Yet there were significant flaws in his thinking.

First, he assumed that messages sent via company mail would be received at the proper time. In some organizations, this is a dubious presumption at best. In fact, during a training session at a hospital, one participant revealed that in some cases it took two weeks to get mail from a seventh floor office to one on the eighth floor. Second, Mr. Taylor assumed that if the message was received, it was read. With information overload one of the facts of organizational life, this assumption may be suspect. Finally, he assumed that even if the message was read, it was understood in the way intended. This is probably the most tenuous of all his premises. Yet these are exactly the kinds of assumptions that all Arrow managers make.

Arrow managers tend to be straightforward and results oriented. They view communication rather like shooting an arrow at a target. Like the marksman, the speaker seeks to embed an intact message into the receiver so as to achieve the desired results—hit the bull's eye. They see communication as a one-way activity based primarily on the skills of the sender. The targets may move, but they never interact with the communicator. Hence the aim of communication for the Arrow manager is to select the proper words and organize the ideas effectively in order to hit the target. Arrow thinking focuses on the speaker or sender of the message.

Judging Effectiveness

At no time is this orientation more evident than when managers are asked about the meaning of effective communication. These are typical responses:

   ▷ "Being able to clearly and precisely put my thoughts into words."
   ▷ "Speaking with credibility and authority on topics I know about."
   ▷ "Getting the results I want by talking to my people."

Certainly managers should seek to speak clearly, concisely, and with credibility in order to achieve results. Yet reexamination of each of those statements in light of the underlying assumptions is revealing (see Table 1.1).

In short, the underlying premise is that managers are responsible for accurately encoding their thoughts into language, rather like selecting, aiming, and firing arrows at a target. Receivers of messages are viewed as passive information processors that react appropriately if the words are on the mark. Thus, feedback is not only improbable, but also unnecessary.

Explaining Communication Breakdowns

The problem is that communication does inevitably breakdown, in spite of "proper" encoding. Yet many managers tenaciously hold to the Arrow approach with explanations like these:

   ▷ "Why didn't they just follow my instructions?"
   ▷ "Why can't they get it right? If I told them once, I told them a thousand times."
   ▷ "How could this project get so fouled up? I told the idiots exactly how to do it."

In each case, the receiver is at fault for the foul-up. Hence, for the Arrow manager, lack of performance is caused primarily by the receiver's ignorance of the language or even, in some cases, a result of a malicious intent to undermine management objectives. After all, the meaning of the manager's words is self-evident and fixed; therefore, everyone should understand the message similarly. And certainly the workers heard what was said, because management repeated it "a thousand times." This type of reasoning inevitably leads some managers to the conclusions that their employees are inherently ignorant, lazy, or subversive.

But what if the manager fails to understand someone? Curiously, the onus of fault shifts from the receiver to the sender. The Arrow manager's likely responses are, "I should have been notified," "Why didn't you just say that?" or "You've just got to say it in plain English." In these cases, the sender clearly failed to "hit the target" because the "proper" words were not uttered. In sum, communication breakdowns are always the fault of the sender or the receiver. Arrow managers

TABLE 1.1 Evaluation of Arrow Manager's Assumptions

Communication Effectiveness	Underlying Assumptions
Being able to put thoughts into words clearly and precisely.	What is clear and precise to one person is clear and precise to another.
Speaking with credibility and authority.	Credibility is something the speaker possesses, not something given to the speaker by the audience.
Getting the results desired by talking to employees.	Communication is primarily a one-way activity.

never think that the problem, and hence the responsibility, might be mutual. They fail to see that effective communication is a shared commitment between both the sender and receiver.

Origins

Why would a manager adopt this orientation? It is probably not the result of a conscious decision. Rather, through countless individual experiences, an unconscious pattern forms that becomes the *modus operandi*. There are three major factors that appear to contribute to the process.

First, the technical training of many managers reinforces a stimulus/response orientation. On a number of occasions, I have had the opportunity to speak with engineers who have recently assumed managerial responsibilities. Many experience problems in managing people. For years, they have been trained to use precise formulas that exactly predict certain outcomes. If the design is developed according to standards, then it works and performs as expected. All competent engineers use basically the same formulas. Colleagues learn to interpret the drawings and specs similarly. Because the entire emphasis is on proper design and development, the results are inevitable.

Transferring such logic to management is as natural as it is problematic. Simply put, the communication effort is seen as a problem of proper design. After all, like the specs, everyone should interpret the message in the same way. Thus, communication is expected to be akin to engineering. Choosing the right language, as in selecting the proper materials, should lead to effectiveness. Of course, the problem is that people do not react like they are "supposed to" and human beings are not passive objects like girders, cable, and concrete. It requires great intellectual dexterity to get rid of these conceptions, built up through years of training and countless daily experiences.

The second contributing factor, strangely enough, is the "speech teacher." The very term *speech teacher* implies a one-way view of communication; why not *speaking and listening teacher* or just *communication teacher*? Historically, teach-

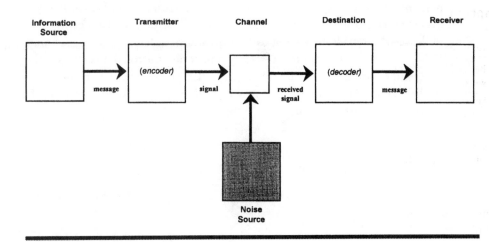

Figure 1.1. Shannon and Weaver Model

ers of public address have been profoundly influenced by Aristotle's remarkable work *The Rhetoric* (1960), which was one of the first truly systematic treatises on the spoken word. His genius was most fully realized in his penetrating discourse and explanation of the three canons or provinces of proof: *ethos* (the credibility of the speaker), *pathos* (the use of emotion), and *logos* (the use of logic). The canons have stood the test of time, for the system continues to be taught.

Aristotle emphasized the speaker, or the orator, arranging an appropriate message in accordance with general principles. If the communicator is effective, then justice and good triumph, and the speaker takes the credit. The hearers are passive and reactive rather than active and interactive. In short, communication is a one-way act of influence.

More recently, communication theorist have taken to model-building in an attempt to represent the communication process. An engineer at Bell Telephone Company, Claude Shannon, developed one of the classic and most influential models. This model, in Figure 1.1, was developed to help engineers decide how most efficiently to transmit electrical impulses from one place to another. Other models having a more social-psychological emphasis were developed based on Shannon and Weaver's (1949) basic premise (see, for example, Lasswell 1948; Gerbner 1956). As fascinating as these models are, my purpose is not to provide a thorough exegesis on them. Rather, the point is that in this class of models, communication is not only visually represented as a one-way activity, but also conceptually proclaimed to be so, just as Aristotle claimed.

Finally, certain people may have personality predispositions to communicate in this way. Treating communication as a one-way event allows the Arrow manager to avoid the complexities, ambiguities, and paradoxes of human behavior, thereby creating the illusion of permanence and finality in all that is spoken or written. Dynamic contexts, unique individuals, adjustable styles of discourse and multileveled conversations can prove not only bewildering but also deeply troubling to those who tenaciously cling to a simplistic worldview. The Arrow manager avoids all this, with seeming efficiency and total control. Thus, the origins may be a result of some sort of functional necessity for a manager's personal psychological makeup. After all, a world in which all elements are dynamic can be profoundly unsettling and deeply disturbing.

Evaluation

The Arrow approach has both strengths and weaknesses. These are examined below.

Weaknesses. The fundamental flaw of this approach lies in the belief that

Effective Expression = Effective Communication.

The problem, however, is that even if a person effectively articulates a position, this does not necessarily guarantee that it will be understood as intended, much less appropriately acted upon. Misunderstandings occur that may not be the fault of either party. Because feedback is not encouraged in this one-way approach, a corrective mechanism that might clarify a misunderstanding does not really exist. Ironically, Arrow managers may never know if they are "on target" or not. At the heart of the shortcoming are two critical assumptions that are simply inaccurate.

First, the receiver is seen as a passive information processor. Arrow managers typically communicate with people as information-processing machines, trivializing the listener's role. Although some Arrow managers recognize the difficulty of transforming an idea into a code and transmitting it, they usually fail to appreciate the listener's or reader's challenge of accurately reconstructing the message from the sender's signals. In short, they incorrectly treat communication as an event instead of a process. Often the net result is a work unit devoid of interpersonal warmth, sapped of the creative spirit, and soured by employee resentment. Taken to an extreme, this can be enormously debilitating to an organization. Consider, for example, the communication practices of top military leaders during the Vietnam War. Their Arrow style of communication prompted one distinguished pilot to remark,

> I didn't hate them because they were dumb, I didn't hate them because they had spilled our blood for nothing. I hated them because of their arrogance, . . . because they had convinced themselves that they actually knew what they were doing and that we were too minor to understand the "Big Picture." (Clancy and Horner 1999, p. 96)

He targets his anger and resentment at those leaders who would not treat fellow military personnel as thinking human beings. Creating this kind of ill will is exactly the risk that any Arrow manager runs. Fortunately, this particular pilot learned from others' mistakes; when Chuck Horner became a general and helped rebuild the Air Force, he operated in an entirely different way from his predecessors. He implicitly recognized that effective leaders treat communication as an *active,* not passive, process that is fraught with potential points of breakdown.

The second mistake is that words are viewed as containers of meaning. The language we use subtly works against us in this respect. The expressions we use everyday convey the notion that we put meaning into words, and the words act as carriers of meaning: "Capturing ideas in words," "Put that idea into writing," or "I have difficulty putting my thoughts into words." In fact, linguistics professor M. J. Reddy (1979) has made extensive studies of the metaphors used to describe the communication process. He conservatively estimates that about 70% of the English language is directly, visibly, or graphically based on metaphors that stress this perspective on communication. For example, phrases such as "I didn't get the meaning out of the memo," "Just read what it says," or even "Read my lips" create the illusion that meaning resides in the words themselves. Such is not actually the case. Rather, meanings are developed in a unique nexus that includes the words used, the context of the utterance, and the people involved. There is abundant evidence that people develop unique meanings for words and that words do not so much act as containers of meaning as they act as useful, although usually sloppy, stimulators of meaning.

Strengths. The fundamental weaknesses in the arrow theory should not obscure the benefits. **First, the Arrow approach encourages managers to clearly think out their ideas, accurately articulate their directives, and provide sufficient specificity in their instructions.** This emphasis on sender skills is certainly healthy for many managers. One of the common complaints of corporations hiring college graduates is the graduates' universal lack of basic communication skills, including the ability to make presentations, write a memo, and develop an agenda for a meeting (see, for example, Golen et al. 1989). Arrow managers tend to excel at such one-way communication tasks.

Second, the Arrow approach implies a strong link between communication behavior and action. Arrow managers discourage idle chatter, discussions of personal problems, and unnecessary information sharing. Thus, high productivity is encouraged because potential time-wasting communication activities are eliminated. Provided that subordinates do understand directives and management knows what is best, the Arrow approach may actually encourage maximum performance.

In short, although the Arrow approach is flawed in a number of significant ways, there are some redeeming aspects. The next approach reviewed attempts to rectify a number of the difficulties while emphasizing a new set of communication skills.

The Circuit Approach

If the language of the Arrow manager involves "targeting an audience," "attacking arguments," and "firing a volley of commands," then the discourse of the Circuit manager involves "networking," "going with the flow," and "making connections." The Circuit approach represents an evolution from the arrow to the circle. Circuit managers stress feedback over response, relationship over content, connotations over denotations, and understanding over compliance. Communication is seen as a two-way process involving a dynamic interplay of an active sender and receiver.

This interaction style is especially evident in conflict situations. We saw it at work when conducting a communication assessment at a car dealership. We discovered a strange split of opinion over the performance of the CEO, who had recently taken over the company from his father. Those in the sales department loved the new management style. Elton, as he like to be called, believed in participative management, and wanted to make sure that everyone was satisfied. However, employees in the service department had little or no respect for him. One service technician, nicknamed Bronco, explained that he was "elected" by his colleagues to confront the CEO about a problem. He did so. Elton was "delighted" with the chance to talk about the issue, but nothing changed. So Bronco went back to the CEO, and received the same enthusiastic reception and predictable results. Because the CEO seemed so open to these meetings, Bronco went back for one "final try." Bronco reported,

> He seemed like a nice enough guy. Then he starts questioning me about why I "really" came to see him. He started saying stuff like, "You don't really like me." He kept pushing. Finally, I got so mad that I told him that he was a lazy bum and he never would have gotten this job without his daddy. I thought that was it. You're history, bub. Pack your bags. But you won't believe what he did. He patted me on the back and said, "I knew we could get to the bottom of this issue." It was over. Problem solved. He didn't have the guts to fire me.

I asked the CEO about this incident. He explained, "I'm proud of that. Now my employees know that they can say anything to me and have no fears whatsoever." The employees may have had no fears, but problems were never solved either. Indeed, within a year, the organization was in such disarray that Elton's father, a classic Arrow manager, took over again. Elton went on to "bigger and better things." He is now a management consultant.

Elton's career track signals another intriguing characteristic of some Circuit managers. Consultants frequently command attention because of what they say, not what they do. Circuit managers often share this proclivity. Two insightful scholars, Jeffrey Pfeffer and Robert Sutton (1999b) call this the "smart-talk trap." Employees who "talk smart" sound confident, speak with eloquence, possess a

TABLE 1.2 Evaluation of Circuit Manager's Assumptions

Communication Effectiveness	Underlying Assumptions
Listening to employees in order to make them happy.	Job satisfaction is the goal of organizational communication.
Being sensitive to employees in order to adapt messages to each individual.	Messages are exclusively interpreted in the context of interpersonal relationships.
Being open and understanding.	Openness is useful in all circumstances. Understanding is always more acceptable than ambiguity.

good vocabulary, and share interesting ideas and information. But, as Pfeffer and Sutton note,

> smart talk tends to have other, less benign components: first, it focuses on the negative, and second, it is unnecessarily complicated or abstract (or both). . . . Unfortunately, such talk has an uncanny way of stopping action in its tracks. (p. 136)

Not all Circuit managers engage in smart talk, but the impact is much the same. Whether talking smartly or relating compassionately, the Circuit manager inspires little action but much conversation. This was Elton's only legacy.

Judging Effectiveness

Views of effectiveness prove to be so revealing because they expose individuals' goals and desires. To be effective, a manager must bring about a desired result. The critical question is, What are the desired results? Indeed, Circuit managers' responses to the effectiveness issue expose their ultimate aims:

▷ "Communication effectiveness is actively listening to my workers, so as to know what makes them happy."

▷ "I'm effective as a manager when I am sensitive to employees' needs and concerns. Then I try to communicate that sensitivity to them by adapting my message to each individual."

▷ "My communication is effective when I am open to my employees' ideas and suggestions. I want them to feel included and understood by me."

As seen in Table 1.2, there is an implicit perspective of the communication process in these comments. Circuit managers make conceptual leaps from communication behavior to job satisfaction to productivity. The research suggests that these leaps, particularly from job satisfaction to productivity, are dubious at best (Locke 1976). And the probability of successfully completing these leaps is about the same as one athlete completing the high jump, the broad jump, and the pole vault in one bound.

Explaining Communication Breakdowns

Unlike the Arrow manager who assumes that communication should always work, the Circuit manager recognizes the unavoidable certainty of communication breakdowns. According to this approach, there are four primary reasons for the breakdown.

First, the most frequently cited cause of communication breakdowns for Circuit managers is that people just "don't connect." That is, their values, ideas, or feelings are so dissimilar that they have difficulty relating to one another. Circuit managers are fond of saying, "Meanings are in people, not in words," which suggests that everyone has a unique interpretation for each message. Therefore, huge amounts of time must be invested in "reaching an understanding." The ODS Corporation of Japan, a research, consulting and advertising organization, seems to take the Circuit approach to the limit. There are meetings about everything, including a companywide meeting in which individual salaries are negotiated. In one instance this process lasted an entire workweek. Employees typically spend seven hours a week in meetings in which they may confess to treating clients inappropriately or critique other employees' wardrobes. Although the corporation is a booming success, there is a price—high turnover (Ono 1978). Most organizations are not willing to go that far. Thus, Circuit managers explain breakdowns by complaining about the lack of time available. Their underlying premise is that understanding is always possible, because everyone shares the same basic needs and desires.

Second, Circuit managers frequently cite poor listening as the reason for communication difficulties. Circuit managers often encourage their employees to develop active listening skills, such as paraphrasing others' remarks, giving feedback, and asking the appropriate probing questions. These skills help employees think about possible misinterpretations of their remarks as well as check for unintended messages. Therefore, employees involved in a misunderstanding are frequently reminded of the maxim, "You cannot not communicate."

Third, conflicts are explained in terms of "hidden agendas" or unarticulated goals. Circuit managers might seek to dissolve a tense situation with comments like, "Are you sure you are being completely honest with us?" or "You've got to share your true feelings." The obvious inference is that someone is hiding something or has a "hidden agenda." Circuit managers believe that trust comes from employees revealing their true motives, which in turn fosters an atmosphere of open and honest communication. Only then does the Circuit manager believe that conflict can be truly resolved.

Finally, like electrical circuits, the Circuit manager suggests that communication relationships can operate only under certain conditions. Circuit managers believe that many communication breakdowns occur because a proper climate has not been developed. Specifically, a defensive, as opposed to a supportive, climate inhibits communication effectiveness. Defensiveness is a result of evaluative comments, a dogmatic demeanor, and an attitude of superiority. Supportiveness is fostered through sensitivity to the connotative meanings of words, an emphasis on spontaneity, and a development of a climate of equality. When all other reasons fail to explain a communication breakdown, the Circuit manager suggests that there is a defensive climate. Ironically, it is rather perplexing to attempt to respond to the command, "Quit being so defensive." Either attempting to justify your behavior or an outright denial only proves your interlocutor's assertion. Perhaps a heartfelt laugh is the only appropriate response.

Origins

Managers develop a Circuit orientation to communication for a wide variety of reasons, but three tendencies appear to be particularly noteworthy.

First, in the not too distant past, business schools stressed a human relations orientation to management that harmonized with the Circuit approach. The well-known Hawthorne studies often provide the key arguments used to build the human relations case.[1] These studies began as an attempt to investigate the relationship between the levels of lighting in the workplace and worker productivity. Employees at Western Electric's Hawthorne plant increased their productivity in all instances: in the test group, when lighting was improved as well as made more dim, and even in the control group, where there were no changes in illumination. Therefore, it was determined that factors other than lighting influenced performance. The mistaken interpretation of the research often passed down in folklore was that employees thought management was interested in them, so they continued to increase their production regardless of the physical conditions. Hence the axiom, "Satisfied workers are productive workers." Therefore, great care is shown in keeping workers satisfied, and that means communicating in proper ways. The problem with these extrapolations is that the evidence shows that a satisfied worker can be a very lazy one (Downs and Pickett 1977). In fact, there is a fundamentally incorrect inference in the folklore. The key reason for the productivity increases was not managers' behavior, but the interpretations made by employees. That is where the emphasis should be placed, on employee interpretations, not on a manager's soothing communication style. These mythical interpretations of the Hawthorne study tend to encourage a Circuit orientation to communication.

Second, some communication teachers encourage a Circuit approach. Courses in Interpersonal Communication have been quite popular on campuses, and they typically focus on receiver listening skills, giving appropriate feedback, and relationship-building. Sometimes these courses are jokingly referred to as "Touchy-Feely 101," which is one way to characterize the emphasis on getting in

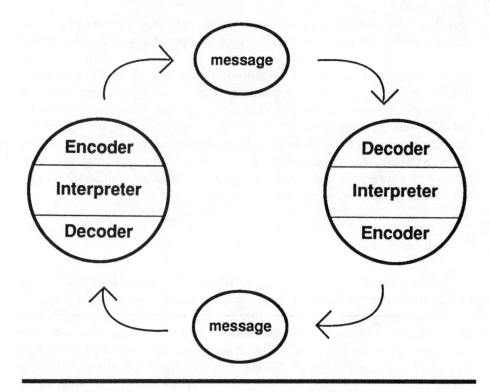

Figure 1.2. Schramm Model

touch with one's own feelings as well as others'. Even the models of communication used stress the circularity of the communication process. The Schramm model (1954) in Figure 1.2 is one of the classics of this type. It looks like a circuit diagram, and depicts the feedback portion of the communication event. Thus, such models lend theoretical justification to the Circuit perspective of communication skills.

Finally, some people seem to have a natural predisposition toward viewing communication like a circuit. They tend to focus on people's feelings and interpersonal relationships. People are naturally attracted to those who are sensitive to their feelings. It is one way to avoid controversy, build up self-esteem, or meet affiliation needs. Hence the Circuit manager may have a deep need to keep peace and harmony.

Evaluation

The fundamental assumption of Circuit managers is that

Understanding = Effective Communication.

But there are two flaws in this view.

First, there is an implicit belief that understanding will lead to agreement. Most problems between managers and employees are cast as "communication problems," which means that the parties do not understand one another. However, the problem may be that they understand one another all too well and simply disagree. The Circuit manager will often plead that they do not "really understand one another," yet, in this strange logic loop, the thought is never entertained that people could actually disagree. Unlike the Arrow manager, the Circuit manager acknowledges that people do not always understand a message in the same way. Therefore, it seems logical to assume that two people might not agree. Ironically, such thoughts are rarely entertained, because Circuit Managers will spend endless hours trying to ensure that their messages are "really understood."

Second, there is an error in assuming that understanding should be the singular goal of communication. People communicate for a wide variety of reasons. Effective managers, like politicians, may equivocate to induce creativity or give themselves room to change. Making sure that subordinates clearly understand everything is not always feasible or desirable. As Eisenberg and Witten (1987) write, "Ambiguous missions and goals allow divergent interpretations to coexist and are more effective in allowing diverse groups to work together" (p. 422). There are instances in which a manager may not have time to explain, just as a physician gives orders during an emergency. A sincere love of mutual understanding does not necessarily yield the best decisions. Accommodation strategies, although useful at times, do not guarantee solutions to difficult problems. Chris Argyris (1986) perceptively notes,

> The ability to get along with others is always an asset, right? Wrong. By adeptly avoiding conflict with coworkers, some executives eventually wreak havoc. And it's their very adeptness that's the problem. The explanation for this lies in what I call skilled incompetence, whereby managers use practiced routine behavior (skill) to produce what they do not intend (incompetence). (p. 74)

Paradoxically, an organizational culture in which "understanding" is the norm often breeds a reticence to bring up areas of disagreement. Employees become afraid to clearly articulate their views for fear of exposing how deep the gulfs really are. Therefore, differences—important and meaningful ones—are often glossed over in the name of "understanding."

Third, in spite of these shortcomings, there are some valuable insights that can be gleaned from the Circuit perspective. The emphasis on the relational aspect of communication and the importance of feedback are two noteworthy issues highlighted by this approach. Research has shown that competent communicators do pay attention to these aspects of interaction (see, for example, DiSalvo 1980), and these are precisely the kinds of issues the Arrow manager ignores. The proposition that messages can be interpreted in many ways is equally important. The Arrow manager focuses on constructing the best possible message, but the Circuit manager looks at the meanings imposed by listeners. This shift in perspective is enlightening and useful. Even though the link between job satisfaction and productivity has proven tenuous at best, the Circuit approach has persuaded many that job satisfaction is an important variable in its own right.

There is much to be learned from the Arrow and Circuit approach. However, there are gaps in both viewpoints. It is not so much that these approaches are wrong, as that they are incomplete. The lens of each perspective creates a somewhat distorted view of the communication process. There is a better point of view. I call it the Dance perspective on communication.

Communication as Dance

Some have argued that dance was the first form of communication. There are so many similarities between dance and communication that it is hard to disagree. Dance involves patterns, movement, and creativity; participants as well as observers can enjoy it; there are as many styles as there are people. Tastes vary, standards differ, styles change, and trends come and go, but dance has been and always will be part of the human community. Once a dance is performed, it can never be recaptured in the same way again; it is unrepeatable and irreversible. Even the simplest of dances involves thousands of intricate and complex maneuvers. It may well be one of the highest and most unique forms of human expression. So, too, with communication. The list of similarities could be quite lengthy indeed. A few of the more important ones are highlighted below.

Communication Is Used for Multiple Purposes

People dance for a wide variety of reasons: to entertain, to inform, to persuade, to incite, and even to seduce. Some dance for themselves, a form of self-expression, whereas some dance for others. The same can be said of communication. The famous physicist and poet Leo Szilard (1961) once commented,

> When a scientist says something, his colleagues must ask themselves only whether it is true. When a politician says something, his colleagues must first of all ask, "Why does he say it?" later on they may or may not get around to asking whether it happens to be true. A politician is a man who thinks he is in possession of the truth and knows what needs to be done. Scientists rarely think they are in full possession of the truth, and a scientist's aim in a discussion with his colleagues is not to persuade but to clarify. It was clarification rather than persuasion that was needed in the past to arrive at the solutions of the great scientific problems. (pp. 25–26)

Herein lies a problem. The scientist, the politician, the teacher, the salesperson, the philosopher, and the preacher all use the same language. It is like blurring the lines between entertaining dances and lewd ones; the purpose of communication is not always clear. In fact, communicators often have multiple goals for a single message. The effective teacher seeks to enlighten and motivate, the salesperson to inform and persuade, and the philosopher to clarify and question. In fact, effective managers at one time or another must perform each of these roles.

Therefore, communication effectiveness cannot be limited to either the "results" or "understanding" criteria as characterized by the Arrow and Circuit perspectives, respectively. For instance, the chairman of the Federal Reserve, Alan Greenspan (1995), once "explained" how he made decisions regarding interest rates: "If I say something which you understand fully in this regard, I probably made a mistake" (p. 6). Whether he was equivocating or simply saying, "This is too difficult to explain," is unclear. But it is clear that communicators can have any number of goals, including obfuscation, confusion, or deception. Whether these are legitimate goals is an ethical question, just as there will always be questionable forms of dancing. Hence there is no single measure of communication effectiveness, just as there is no one criterion to evaluate all dances.

Communication Involves the Coordination of Meanings

Dancers have to learn to coordinate their movements with one another regardless of the type of music. They must learn how to move together even though they do not necessarily share one another's reality. That is, dance partners see the situation differently, but they know their appropriate roles and responses. Communicators do as well. It is not always necessary or even desirable to totally share meanings to communicate, as long as participants know how to respond in their roles or according to the "rules of the game." In fact, there is a theory of communication, called the Coordinated Management of Meaning, based on this very premise. These theorists argue that

> communication is the process by which persons cocreate, maintain, and alter patterns of social order, but . . . the coordination of talk through which patterns of order emerge is not necessarily based on mutual understanding or a shared social reality. (Pearce, Harris, and Cronen 1982, p. 157)

Subordinates may not know why the boss asks, "How are things going?" but in time they learn how to respond. It may be interpreted as "intrusiveness" on the part of the subordinate and "concern" on the part of the boss. But, despite the vastly different interpretations, social order is maintained. Meanings are not necessarily shared, but they are coordinated.

So what? The point is that in order to understand the communication process, there is a need to look beyond the interpretations of messages. How messages facilitate social order, maintain structure, and set up patterns is of prime importance. The issue is, How does communication help or hinder the process of coordination in an organization? Couples who dance are evaluated, in part, on the degree to which their actions are coordinated with one another. The evaluation of communication effectiveness is similarly judged. Clumsiness, whether self-inflicted or induced by others, is not rewarded in organizations or dance studios.

Communication Involves Coorientation

In order to coordinate actions, dancers must learn to coorient. They must be able to sense one another's cues, anticipate their partner's possible actions, and know the appropriate responses. So, too, with communicators. When communication breaks down, it is not always the result of misunderstandings *per se,* but rather that people have failed to coorient; they have no adequate predictive capacity. Effective communicators are able to forecast with some accuracy the actions of others, their responses and interpretations. For example, the CEO of a paper-manufacturing firm was bewildered by rampant rumors about layoffs and plant closings circulated in the plant after his brief announcement about forthcoming pay freezes. In his speech, he had specifically noted that these were not considered to be alternatives to cope with an industry slowdown. When asked if he ever had a meeting like this before, he said, "I never had the need to." Even though he had personally hired most of these workers over a twenty-year period, he was so out of touch with their reality that he could not anticipate these possible reactions to his announcement. He did not effectively coorient.

The seeming ease with which professional dancers whirl, pirouette, and leap into one another's arms is deceptive. With long hours of practice, they can do this even when improvising because they are responding to one another's subtle cues. What is astonishing is that they can do all of this while both are constantly in movement. It is not like trying to get oriented while lost in a forest by calculating your position in relation to some fixed object. Rather, the "objects" are both moving, and they must simultaneously be orienting with one another. And this is precisely the complex and difficult challenge facing communicators who must simultaneously orient to each other while both are constantly changing. As the aforementioned CEO found out, people can change considerably over a twenty-year period. It takes time and energy to coorient, and there will inevitably be spills and mishaps along the way.

Communication Is Rule-Governed

How can dancers cope with the tremendous range of possible movements? How can all the possibilities be mastered? Communicators, like dancers, develop rules of thumb to cope with the uncertainties. In almost every style of dance there are rules of some sort, whether written or unwritten. Joan Lawson, who for seventeen years taught at the Royal Ballet School, wrote, "Principles and rules should all be studied by aspiring dancers and choreographers if they are to create the style and qualities of movement necessary to communicate the mood, emotion, theme, and story of classical dance" (Lawson 1980, p. 1). Years of experience are distilled in these rules, which allow the dancers to coorient.

Communicators, as well, develop a wide range of implicit rules that govern conversations. There are rules about who has the right to initiate or terminate a conversation, what topics are appropriate to speak about and under what conditions. The list could go on, but the point is that the rules affect the conversation in much the same way that rules of dance constrain movement. Conversational rules, too, are a way to handle all the uncertainty and distill the essence of learning into a few easily manageable units. It is by enacting these rules that people coordinate their actions in the organization.

There are basically two types of rules at work in conversations: interpretation and regulative rules (Pearce and Cronen 1980). Interpretation rules are the communicator's rules for abstracting the meaning out of a message.[2] For example, during a meeting about a new proposal, a manager might say, "Tell me more," to an employee, which is interpreted as, "You have a great idea; I want to hear the details." On the other hand, the same manager who says, "Tell me more," after an employee gives an unacceptable explanation for being late to work is communicating a very different message. The interpretation is, "This excuse is unacceptable; shape up." Even though the same words are used, the context has changed, and different interpretation rules apply. Regulative rules are those that regulate or guide the ongoing action of the communication event. Effective listeners, for example, often have these kind of regulative rules:

▷ Initiate conversations with questions about unrisky topics.
▷ If a person's comments are unclear, ask for clarification.
▷ If a person appears defensive, nod head.
▷ Terminate conversations by summarizing the conversation.

Note that in each case these rules help guide the conversation in a particular direction.

The rules vary from setting to setting, just as the conventions of dance change from the ballroom to the clubroom. To be an effective communicator, one must learn the special rules that apply in different settings. They, of course, vary from person to person, department to department, and organization to organization. That does not, however, mean that a whole new set of rules needs to be learned when experiencing a new situation. There are some common rules regardless of the situation, just as there are fundamental dance steps. However, effective communicators also learn the special rules of each setting. The rules do not exist on some unseen tablet waiting to be discovered. Rather, people are actively engaged in negotiating the rules, particularly during the first stages of relationships. This is why the orientation of new employees is so important. Negotiating over the rules, although usually implicit, is a fascinating process. There are even rules about making the rules—metarules. The important point is to recognize that the rules exist and to determine how they affect managerial effectiveness.

Communicators Develop a Repertoire of Skills That May Pass From the Level of Consciousness

Beginning dancers have to consciously think about each movement in executing a pirouette, for instance. Over time they no longer think about how to execute each movement; they become concerned less with body mechanics and more with artistry. The apparent naturalness and ease of execution come from years of practice, as movements that were once conscious submerge into the subconscious. Communicators learn in much the same way. When we learn a foreign language, we have to think more consciously about syntax and semantics. Over time, through trial and error, we learn the rules and can speak with apparent ease by relying on subconscious processes.

The same can be said of pragmatic rules of conversation. When first interacting with people, we may consciously have to think about appropriate behaviors, just as when we go to a first job interview. Over time, we no longer consciously focus on such concerns. Frequently, communication problems are the result of an unconsciously used rule, long ago "forgotten." For example, one manager reported that she was often accused by her employees of being a poor listener. She had difficulty understanding their perceptions. During a lull in a social conversation with her, I mentioned being involved in a minor car accident. Her response: "Really? But did I tell you about my new car?" Clearly, such episodes might cause her employees to infer that she was uninterested in them, and lead to the "poor listener" assessment. This manager apparently never learned the regulative rule, "When someone mentions an unusual event, probe for further information." Effective conversationalists utilize this rule all the time without any conscious thought of it. Unfortunately, this manager did not, and the result was that her employees were uncooperative. The manager's operative rule was, "When someone mentions an unusual event, talk about something that interests me." Even though these types of rules are unconscious, there are consequences of having them. In this case, the manager was eventually asked to step down and assume a lower paying job.

When training employees to become better negotiators, most individuals' existing set of rules need to be refined. For example, it is important to know that concessions should be offered slowly, not all at once (Gilchrist 1982). At first, consciously trying to do this seems awkward, but with practice it becomes natural. The same kind of procedure is effective in teaching interviewing, public speaking, and motivation skills. And this is precisely the technique used by dance instructors when they point out a motion that should be consciously attended to in order to execute a graceful maneuver.

Communication Can Be Viewed as a Patterned Activity

Choreographers map out patterns for their dances; a kind of circuit diagram drawn with arrows. Even with improvisational dances, a map can be drawn of the dancer's movements. Likewise, there are patterns of interaction in a conversation. The patterns are a by-product of the rules of interaction used by the communicators. In other words, the patterns are the net result of the way the enacted rules interlock with one another. The interaction rules are viewed through a telescopic lens, whereas the patterns are seen through a wide-angle lens.

Expert chess players, who are familiar with an adversary's style of play (i.e., personal rules), are frequently able to sense deep but recurring patterns in their opponent's games—not move by move—but in a more general sense. Communicators, like amateur chess players, may not be aware of their own patterns, but perceptive observers can see them. For example, a manager may jokingly insult an employee: "Hey, Pat! Has your golf game improved yet?" The employee may respond by placating: "I haven't been golfing lately." The manager could react to the placating with even harsher insults, to which the employee responds with more placating responses. The pattern repeats itself until either someone else steps in or the employee gets angry. The manager's regulative rule is, "Respond to placating with playful insults." The employee's regulative rule is, "Respond to insults with a placating reply." These rules interact to form a pattern in which the manager sees the employee as the problem, and the employee feels the manager is the problem (see Figure 1.3). Such problems are technically known as punctuation difficulties, in which each party sees the other as the source of the conflict (Watzlawick, Beavin, and Jackson 1967). Neither the manager nor employee sees the overall pattern resulting from their personal rules of interaction. This is a simple example; think about the complexity of group communication. Part of the challenge of an organizational communicator is to ferret out the destructive patterns while setting up constructive ones.

The Beauty of Communication Is a Function of the Degree of Coordination

The truly awe-inspiring dances are the ones in which the dancers flow as one with the music and each other. One dance that comes to mind is the "bottle dance" in the movie *Fiddler on the Roof,* in which the dancers begin by placing bottles on their heads. Slowly they start to move to the music, then the beat picks up with an ever increasing level of intensity. Step by step, beat by beat, the dancers move to the music and one another. The tempo and spirit of the music pick up even further, as do the dancers. The bottles waver but do not fall. One marvels at how everything can be so perfectly in balance and in step. The music beats faster still, and then precisely at the moment the music climaxes, the dancers flip the bottles off their heads and whirl into a rousing frenzy.

The aesthetic appreciation of the dance flows from the intricate patterns of coordination, the way in which it all fits together. So, too, with communication. The greater the coordination between communicators, the more effective it is. They learn to anticipate one another's reactions and possible meanings. They are able to

Manager's Interpretation (meaning rules)	Manager's Regulative Rules	Actual Conversation	Employee's Regulative Rules	Employee's Interpretation (meaning rules)
Greeting.	Initiate conversations with playful repartee.	**Manager:** Hey, Pat, has your golf game improved yet?		Insult. Manager doesn't care about my game or me.
Employee is ignoring me.		**Employee:** I haven't been golfing lately.	Respond to insults with placating reply.	Factual reply to a question.
Playful question.	Try to reestablish conversation with another playful comment.	**Manager:** Well, how's that clunker of a car running?		Another insult. What kind of game is the manager playing?
Employee is catching on, but still takes the conversation too seriously.		**Employee:** I sold it.	Respond to insults with a placating comment.	Another factual reply.
Joke.	Continue conversation with another playful insult.	**Manager:** I hope you didn't buy another lemon.		Another insult. Now the manager is questioning my decision-making ability.
What is the employee so upset about? I'm just trying to build some rapport. The employee is a poor conversationalist.		**Employee:** Why don't you just get off my back and mind your own business?	If placating doesn't work, then stand up for yourself.	My only alternative was to be assertive. The manager is insensitive and unprofessional.

Figure 1.3. Conversation Analysis

coordinate. They know the way in which the environment affects communication. This is what communicators aim for in organizations.

To be sure, there are some communication situations that require more specialized skills than others. Learning to negotiate effectively, for instance, requires more coorientation than does giving a speech. Employees have different levels of skill. For some, communication is easy. But, as with dancing, anyone can refine and improve his or her skills. Even natural dancers become more proficient with practice and training. The aesthetic thrill of an illuminating discussion or a scintillating meeting may prove elusive and rare, but there are few experiences more pleasing and fulfilling.

Conclusion

The anthropologist Mary Catherine Bateson (1989) once said, "There are few things as toxic as a bad metaphor" (p. 347). The Arrow and Circuit approaches mask the complexity of the communication process. Managers who view communication as a dance have a more vivid metaphor with which to analyze organizational situations. They see the complexities in the apparent simplicity of communication. They are concerned with patterns and unwritten rules. They look at the degree of coorientation between employees as well as departments. Unlike the Circuit managers, they are not exclusively concerned with what is best for relationships, but with what is best in a particular situation. Unlike Arrow managers, they are not solely focused on immediate results, but seek deeper patterns of sustained success. They do not expect to be understood at all times, and do not always see that as the goal of communication. Their communication style and choice of medium vary according to the goals and context. They do not share the Arrow manager's belief that humans are basically lazy, but neither do they believe that all are good. They recognize the organizational realities, but seek the ideal. Finally, they take comfort in the fact that there appears to be no relationship between their ability to communicate and their ability to dance.

Notes

1. For an insightful explanation of the Hawthorne studies, see Gabor (2000), pp. 110–120.

2. Pearce and Cronen (1980) call these constitutive rules. They also have an elaborate system that explains how meanings are abstracted at various levels.

TWO

What Is Communication, Anyway?

It requires a very unusual mind to make an analysis of the obvious.

Alfred North Whitehead

Understanding seems to be a very complicated notion.

Roger Schank

Describing communication as a dance can be illuminating. However, it is a more right-brain, holistic kind of illumination. The left-brain, linear orientation demands more precision. What actually happens in the mind of the sender? Of the receiver? Why do problems occur? Can communication breakdowns be described more specifically than to say that two people are not coordinating their actions? These are the issues considered in this chapter. Ten propositions about communication are presented and the practical implications of the notions are discussed.

Propositions

Proposition 1: Language Is Inherently Ambiguous

The inherent ambiguity of language can be seen in the words we use, the sentences we utter, and in the countless communication breakdowns we experience. One researcher says that for the 500 most frequently used words in the English language, there are over 14,000 definitions (Haney 1979). Take, for instance, the word *run*. A sprinter can *run* in a race. Politicians *run* races, but not exclusively with their legs. Although a horse *runs* with legs, it uses four of them, which is still a little different from a sprinter. A woman can get a *run* in her hose, which is troublesome, but having a *run* of cards is good. However, having a *run* on a bank is bad. For a sailor, *running* aground is not good at all, but a *run* with the wind can be exhilarating. To score a *run* in baseball is different from a *run* in cricket. Hence we *run* into the ambiguity of language at every turn even with a simple every day word like *run*.

The argument could be made that the context helps clarify the precise meaning of the word. In some cases, that may be true. Yet, in the long *run*, even the context of a sentence cannot guarantee precision. The seemingly innocent statement, "I'm going to run down to the bank," can be interpreted in at least two ways. Does the speaker mean a financial institution or a riverbank? A comment such as, "The chancellor ordered the professors to stop sleeping in class," can have a number of different meanings. Are students or professors the ones who are sleeping? Even the location of a pause in a conversation can radically alter the meaning of an utterance. Compare the following statements:

(a) People from Kansas who are industrious are well off.
(b) People from Kansas, who are industrious, are well off.

In the last sentence, all people from Kansas are considered well off, but in the first only those who are industrious are deemed to be well off. All of these examples could be seen as amusing little observations about the human plight, the kind of routine Andy Rooney does on *60 minutes*. Yet the ambiguity of language has deep implications that are right at the heart of understanding the communication process.

Proposition 2: The Communication Process Can Best Be Described in Terms of Probabilities

Given that language is inherently ambiguous, then it is reasonable to assume that the various interpretations can be assigned probabilities. The statement, "I am going down to the bank," when stripped of all contextual clues, could be seen as having a 50% chance of being interpreted as a trip to a financial institution and 50% chance as a journey to a river bank. Therefore, communication can be viewed as uncertainty reduction, in which the probabilities of one interpretation are in-

Conversation	Stage
Nurse: How much did you drink?	Stage 1
Patient: I haven't been drinking at all tonight.	
Nurse: No, no, I mean liquids.	
Patient: Oh, well, I'm not really sure. Normal, I guess.	Stage 2
Nurse: Ok.	
Patient: Why did you need to know about how much I drink?	Stage 3
Nurse: [caustically] I don't care how much you party! That's your business. But I see the results of you kids who drink and drive. It's not fair to those who don't.	
Patient: I didn't mean alcohol. I meant fluids, I meant. . . .	

Figure 2.1. Conversation Analysis

creased and others decreased. Context is the major implicit modifier of the probabilities. If the person is deep in the woods on a hunting trip, the chances are that the speaker is thinking of a riverbank. But it is not always that simple. In fact, a number of implications flow from this probabilistic view of communication.

Implication A: Typically, the message sender sees only one possible interpretation. Yet, for a receiver, there are three different options. First, the receiver may see the same possibility, in which case, the two individuals have understood one another. Second, the receiver may see a different possibility, which may go unnoticed or may even be amusing. Consider, for example, the newspaper headline, "Hershey Bars Protest." Are candy bars on strike? Third, the receiver may be unable to determine the correct possibility. At this point, a clarifying question may be asked. Or the receiver may choose not to inquire about the precise meaning, because the risk level may be too high. Fears of losing prestige, being ridiculed, ignored, or thought incompetent often stifle further understanding. In most large group situations, for example, the pressures not to ask for clarification can be immense.

Communicators who fail to understand the probabilistic nature of interpretations may encounter serious difficulties. An incident at a hospital provides an intriguing insight into the difficulty. A young woman from Green Bay, Wisconsin, was taken to a hospital's emergency room at 7:00 p.m. on a Friday night for a minor injury. After the usual name and address part of the intake process, the conversation continued (see Figure 2.1).

The nurse walked away in disgust. The patient limped away in pain. What is intriguing about this case is how the probable interpretations started out one way,

TABLE 2.1 Using Probabilities to Diagnose a Communication Breakdown

Meaning of term drink	Theoretical probability	Stage 1		Stage 2		Stage 3	
		Nurse	Patient	Nurse	Patient	Nurse	Patient
Alcohol	50%	0%	100%	0%	0%	100%	0%
Fluids	50%	100%	0%	100%	100%	0%	100%

flip-flopped, and reversed again. In the end, neither person recognized the true source of the conflict.

In the beginning (Stage 1), both people had different meanings for the question, "How much did you drink?" The nurse was referring to liquids (100% probability), the patient to alcohol (100% probability). Theoretically, both are plausible interpretations. For the nurse, the term *drink* "obviously" meant liquids in the normal context. After all, the amount of liquid in the human body is a crucial medical factor. But there is another context at work here, as well. For many people on a Friday night, the term *drink* typically means alcohol. This is particularly true in Green Bay, Wisconsin, which has one of the highest bar-to-person ratios in the country. Nevertheless, eventually each person recognized the "mistake" in the other's interpretation.

The relevant information was abstracted in Stage 2, with the patient adjusting to the interpretation of the nurse. Then, in Stage 3, each assumes the other's interpretation, still at a 100% probability, as the operating rule for the conversation. On the surface, this switch appears to be the source of the conflict. However, the real source of the problem is that neither the nurse nor the patient recognizes that *drink* has a probability of meaning either fluids or alcoholic consumption. In essence, both communicators considered only one possible interpretation (a 100% probability) throughout the entire conversation (see Table 2.1); hence, the communication totally breaks down in Stage 3, resulting in frustration for both nurse and patient.

Implication B: The sender of a message may purposely use language that has multiple interpretations. Speakers can use a kind of verbal Rorschach in which a phrase is used that can have many possible meanings. The famous Rorschach psychological test presents subjects with an ambiguous graphic, an inkblot. Then subjects are asked, "What do you see in this picture?" Theoretically, the interpretation of the inkblot reveals the subject's intellectual and emotional orientation. In the same way, statements can be designed that elicit different interpretations depending on the receiver's orientation.

Politicians provide a plethora of examples. Consider a statement like, "Our party wants to take the offensive on the drug war." The precise meaning of that

TABLE 2.2 Assessing the Value of Ambiguity

Potential Benefits	Potential Liabilities
Induces creativity	May not be useful with those desiring specific direction
Allows people to save face	May be used to deny personal responsibility
Resolves conflict through different interpretations of one message	May result in unwanted misunderstanding
Allows people strategically to delay making decisions	May delay conflict resolution
May enhance one's credibility in a conflict	May create ethical concerns
Allows diverse groups to work together	May gloss over meaningful differences
	Allows for plausible deniability

statement is practically opaque because there are so many possible interpretations. But it sounds good! Corporate executives are not above using such tactics, employing, for example, such statements as, "We are trying to develop a strong organizational base," or "People are the key to our success." Again, the precise meanings of these statements are difficult to ascertain. That does not imply, however, that such statements are void of meaning. On the contrary, such language can be extraordinarily powerful if the sincerity of the speaker is unquestioned. Even though every person who hears such a statement may have a different meaning for the message, the ultimate impact may be favorable. The receivers read their own meanings into the statements, yet none of the private interpretations can be confirmed. So, for the speaker, they are deniable.

Even less abstract language can be used in this manner. Sarcasm and jokes are often used in this vein to test how an individual may react. A disreputable salesperson who says, "Hey, you make this purchase order for your company and there will be a little something for you," may be coyly testing the waters. The receiver has to decide if this is indeed a bribe or a joke. The onus of interpretation lies with the receiver. If the receiver reacts negatively to the comment, then the salesman can say it was only a joke, and thus deny a clearly possible interpretation.

Is this kind of strategic ambiguity ethical? The question is, in a sense, moot. Ambiguity, whether we acknowledge it or not, is a part of the language. People who are both ethical and unethical use such tactics. Ambiguity can stir creative ideas, allow people to save face, or resolve a conflict. For example, scholars discovered that employees deemed effective do not have to actually agree with their managers on the regulative rules guiding conversation, yet they must be perceived by their managers as agreeing with these rules (Eisenberg, Monge, and Farace 1984). Hence ambiguity may serve to create the perception of unity, if not the reality. On the other hand, the unscrupulous do use such tactics for deception, power plays, and fraud (see Table 2.2). Although managers should assess their own personal ethics on this matter, it is equally important to detect such ploys when used toward illegitimate ends. The final chapter of this book deals with the question in more detail.

Implication C: The receiver may purposely misunderstand. In some circumstances, receivers exploit the probabilistic nature of communication in order to meet their goals. In short, they have a need to misunderstand. My favorite example involves the artist who sculpted figurines adorning the top of a prominent building in London. When city officials saw that the building was rimmed with statues of nude males, they ordered the artist to "cut off the offending parts." The artist complied, but in his own special way. He lopped off the heads of all the statues.

Employees often have a similar need to misunderstand communication they may find "offensive." For example, an employee was sent the following memo from his boss on a Wednesday afternoon: "I need the report first thing Monday morning." Then Monday rolled around and, lo and behold, no report. The angry boss confronted the employee, whereupon the employee remarked: "I thought you meant the following Monday." Sure enough, that is one possible interpretation. In fact, the memo could have been referring to any future Monday. Of course, the employee's interpretation conveniently fit in with his schedule. No doubt, the employee understood precisely which Monday the boss was referring to. But the extra week of preparation met his needs at the time. The employee needed to misunderstand. The probabilistic nature of communication allowed him legitimately to argue that there was a "communication breakdown."

Proposition 3: Context Shapes the Probabilities by Creating Default Assumptions That Solidify Interpretations

If communication is inevitably wrapped up in uncertainties, then how is it possible for two people ever to understand one another? Some scholars might argue that it is, indeed, impossible fully to understand another person, that there can never be 100% understanding. And in many ways that is true. However, people do seem to be able to understand each other well enough to get tasks done, communicate intentions, and effectively function in an array of situations. How? In part, the answer lies in the role that context plays in the communication process. The context freezes or predisposes certain probable interpretations

For instance, the acronym *IRA* has a multitude of possible interpretations. It could stand for the Irish Republican Army, Individual Retirement Account, International Rugby Association or even a person's name. Usually, it is not necessary to clarify how the acronym is being used. In a discussion on banking, IRA stands for an Individual Retirement Account. Likewise, two politicians on a subcommittee about British foreign policy can regularly use the acronym to stand for the Irish Republican Army. The exquisite ease and simplicity with which we understand the various uses of an acronym or term is astonishing. What happens is that the context of the discussion increases the probability of some interpretations, while decreasing others (see Figure 2.2).

Theoretical Possibilities

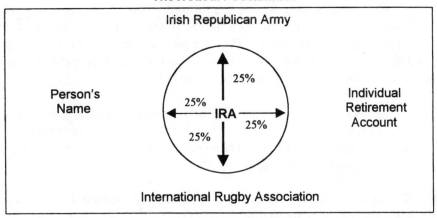

Talking to a banker at work

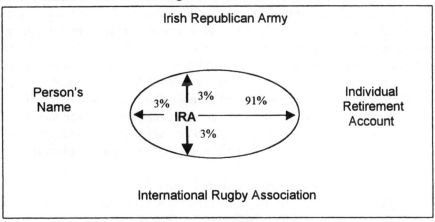

Talking about British foreign policy

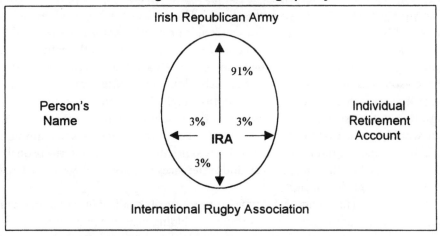

Figure 2.2. Probabilities Altered by Context

One of the great challenges for researchers working on artificial intelligence (AI) has been attempting to get a computer to "understand" human language. This has proved to be exceedingly difficult. Initial attempts sought to use the brute power of the computer by teaching it the meaning of a multitude of words. Yet this proved practically useless because of the ambiguous nature of even the most concrete of words. Douglas Hofstadter (1979) put it this way:

> It is probably safe to say that writing a program which can handle the top five words of English—"the," "of," "and," "a," and "to"—would be equivalent to solving the entire problem of AI, and hence tantamount to knowing what intelligence and consciousness are. (pp. 629–630)

The difficulty is that the precise meaning of those words depends heavily on unspoken assumptions that are part of the context.

What has proven more useful is constructing fairly restricted "scripts." Certain meanings and assumptions in specific situations, such as in a restaurant or hospital, are specified in advance. Thus, clearly specified interpretations are preprogrammed into the computer. For instance, one rarely says, "I want to eat," when ordering a meal in a restaurant. That is part of the context and must be programmed into the computer. When someone orders "chicken" in a restaurant, the context dictates that the chicken should be in an edible form, not live with wings flapping and feathers flying. Hence the computer can interpret the meanings of various phrases based upon assumptions about the context. Indeed, the context can be thought of as a series of hidden assumptions, which go unspoken and often unnoticed.

When the assumptions are not shared—that is, when the context is not shared—then the receiver fails to understand the sender's meaning. My favorite example of this occurs in a Peter Sellers movie. Sellers, as Inspector Clouseau, is standing at a street corner with a dog at his side when a stranger approaches him. The stranger asks, "Does your dog bite?" The always forthright Clouseau responds, "No." Then the dog at Clouseau's side promptly chomps on the leg of the bystander. The astonished man replies with justifiable anger, "I thought you said your dog does not bite." Clouseau calmly replies, "It's not my dog." The humor of this episode lies in the incongruity between Clouseau's context of interpretation and the other man's. The obvious assumption implied in the context is that the dog standing by Clouseau is his dog, which in this case proved inaccurate. Normally, one would assume that the "dog" being referred to is the dog that is in plain sight, even if the person standing next to the dog was not the owner. That is, the probabilities are shaped by the context to exclude references to all other dogs in the world and focus on the dog in sight.

However, all incidents of this type are not so easily chalked up to a comic's antics; some are quite serious. For example, a bidding deadline may be missed because the bidder assumes a different time zone than what was intended; or a party may assume the "final offer" is only a "firm offer" not the actual last offer that will terminate the negotiations. In both cases, the hidden assumptions—the contexts

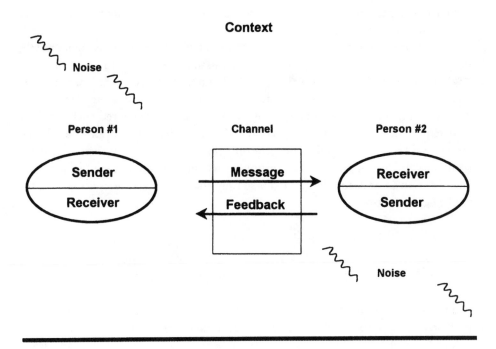

Figure 2.3. Typical Communication Model

of the sender and receiver—differ just enough so that different meanings are ascertained. The results are unintended, but very real and disturbing. The unspoken and the assumed can, by shaping the context, alter the probable interpretations in such a way that senders and receivers do not understand one another.

Proposition 4: A Context Is Developed Through the Dynamic Process of Individuals Interacting

One of the great myths about context is that it is something "out there." Typical models of communication look like the one seen in Figure 2.3. Note that the context is pictured as an element outside the communicators. The implication is that the two people share and operate in the same context. It is as if the context is like air; everyone breathes it, walks through it, and experiences it in a similar fashion. Therefore, many people assume that context exists independent of anyone's presence. This image is misleading. Situations may be commonly shared: contexts are not. There is not one context, there are many. A context is not walked into; rather, it is carried around in the minds of individuals. Context is not some kind of ever-present ether, but a function of complex interactions between people and the setting. Our culture clearly shapes our perceptions, but fundamentally, each individual has a personal and uniquely configured context. In short, context is a self-constructed image of the world.

Greeting behavior is one of the best examples of how contexts are dynamically developed. There is a limitless number of possible responses to questions like, "What's happening?" or "How ya doing?" In fact, the greeter is faced with an intriguing dilemma when someone actually proceeds to discuss in some detail "what's happening." Fortunately, most of the time we are spared such burdens. Past experiences in the "greeting contexts" make virtually certain that the responses will be quite limited. In fact, the only really important duty is to respond in some way, because ultimately, all responses are interpreted as a simple acknowledgement. In some cases, the context is so rigid that the greeter does not even listen to the actual response:

> *Greeting:* "How's it going?"
> *Response:* "Not so good. My dog just died and a truck ran over my foot."
> *Reply:* "Oh, great. Good to talk to you."

Creating a common context in the minds of communicators is a product of repetitive exposure to people in certain roles, under similar circumstances, and in comparable settings. Through repeated experience, a series of probable interpretations are highlighted and others deemed less likely. "What do you want?" is a statement that means something dramatically different in a restaurant and in an argument. "It's all your fault" can be a joke between friends or an accusation by a foe. One usually does not clarify such remarks. Indeed, the humor of a sarcastic comment is removed when explained. Rather, that secondary message, "This is a joke," is assumed from the context, which has been dynamically built up through numerous interactions.

This process of building contexts is a marvelously efficient way to communicate. All comments do not have to be clarified in precise detail in order for two people to interact effectively. As a result of certain interpretations being pushed into the foreground and others being pulled into the background, people can reasonably assume that meanings will be shared, except perhaps when talking to Inspector Clouseau. Hence there is rarely a need for a banker to fill in the IRA acronym or for two friends who are kidding around to clarify, "This is a joke." In short, the dynamic nature of context-building allows for a highly flexible but efficient method to reduce the interpretation probabilities.

Proposition 5: The Context Can Become So Powerful That It Acts Like a Black Hole

Astronomers, as well as science fiction buffs, have a fascination with black holes. These are places in space in which the heavens collapse into a concentration of supergravity that warps space-time to such a degree that light cannot escape from it. Celestial objects that get too close to a black hole can get sucked in and never return. Nothing, not even light, escapes from a black hole. In a similar but perhaps less dramatic way, a context can exert such a strong force that the probable interpretations can become severely warped. Indeed, the meanings that are inferred can have little or no relation to the actual realities of the situation or the intentions of the sender.

The proverbial tale of the boy who cried "wolf" once too often is a case in point. The first time he cried "wolf," everyone came running, only to find that it was a ruse. The second time, the same story. When an actual wolf appeared, no one believed him. The boy created a contextual black hole and was gobbled up by the real wolf. The context created by the previous incidents implied that the probable interpretation of "wolf, wolf" should be that of a joke. The shift of probable interpretations from the first incident to the final episode shows the powerful role that context plays in the communication process. In fact, any other comments made by the boy would have been tainted with doubts about their authenticity. The irony, as well as the moral, is that in the end the boy was actually being truthful, but, because the context was so strong, he had no means to communicate his message. In essence a black hole can destroy the capability for communication.

Unfortunately, the simple lesson of this child's tale goes unheeded in too many corporations. The situations vary in the particulars, but not in kind. Past communication builds a very powerful set of contextual cues. For example, the manager who continually criticizes and berates employees and then suddenly praises them may be seen as trying to placate or appease employees. His motives are suspect, when in fact he is giving honest praise.

Contextual black holes can also be a positive force. "Success breeds success" in part because useful meanings are accentuated by the context, while potentially negative ones are ignored. In many ways the reputation of Microsoft acts as a positive black hole. Even if a new Microsoft product may, in reality, be inferior to others, it is usually viewed positively. One purchasing agent for a major company, keenly aware of this "halo effect," said, "No one ever got fired buying a Microsoft product." The corporate philosophy, past successes, and image all serve to skew meanings in a positive way, regardless of more objective interpretations (see, for example, Fombrun and Shanley 1990). In sum, the black hole may act positively, as in the case of Microsoft, or it may function negatively, as it did for the boy who cried "wolf" once too often.

Proposition 6: Context Construction Is Uniquely Sensitive to Time Sequencing

The message in Figure 2.4 appeared on a marquee outside a church. If these two statements are read sequentially, as question and answer, then this church had a rather unusual approach to piety. Indeed, the humor comes from the fact that the first line was not intended to form the context for the second line. If the statements on the marquee were reversed (Figure 2.5), the faux pas no longer exists because the context does not necessarily suggest a sequential reading of the sign. This

Figure 2.4. Church Marquee A

Figure 2.5. Church Marquee B

amusing incident illustrates a more profound principle. Unlike basic mathematics, communication is not necessarily commutative: A + B = B + A.

Assumed links between events or comments may imply interpretations that are at odds with reality. Unfortunately, the receiver is not always able to discern this. Rosalyn Turek, the extraordinary pianist and harpsichordist, related a particularly delightful story that illustrates this principle. She tells of a famous, though unspecified, pianist who recorded Chopin's C minor étude in 3,000 takes. "What he did was to play four measures at a time about twenty or thirty times. And when he finished the four measures all that many times, then he went to the next four measures" (Turek 1985). In this way, he ensured that he performed each measure of the piece to perfection. Then the sound engineer had to find the best measures and sequence them properly. The supreme irony was that the recording was critically acclaimed, and the critics noted that the pianist's "endurance was phenomenal." In this case, the critics, like most people, naturally assumed that the piece was played in a complete sequence.

The timing of the messages can have a tremendous impact on the ultimate interpretations made by people. A major airline was uniquely affected by this on one of its flights. Fifteen minutes out of O'Hare airport, officials found out that half of the passengers on Flight 666 had tickets to go to New York City and the other half to Los Angeles. All was not lost. Passengers got to "vote" on whether they wanted to go to Los Angeles or New York. In the airspace over the plains of Illinois, democracy triumphed, and passengers raised their hands to vote on where they would spend the next twenty-four hours. So the plane flew to Los Angeles and the New York passengers immediately boarded another aircraft bound for Chicago, where they boarded yet another plane that actually did arrive in New York.

Most business travelers accept certain delays and mishaps as a normal part of the "travel package." Many travelers could even understand that the same flight number might be assigned to two different routes. But the timing baffles even the most seasoned traveler. If the problem had been noticed on the ground, then passengers might have blamed a computer malfunction and not have inferred anything negative about the airline. As it was, the problem was determined in the air, and passengers interpreted the oversight as managerial incompetence. If there were any doubts, the vote alleviated them: lunacy prevailed.

Such events are not unique. The manager who, while reading the *Wall Street Journal,* finds out about her organization's plans to restructure has a completely different perspective on the company than the manager who hears about the plans firsthand. Employees who depend on the grapevine first and the formal network second for accurate information come to different understandings than those who reverse the process. The tangle can become even more complex, however, when more than two messages are involved. And the problem of proper sequencing of messages will become more acute as employees make further use of the Internet and e-mail. Hence the wise manager is concerned about not only the messages employees receive but also their timing.

Each message forms the context for the next message, as one musical phrase does for the next. But it is not quite that simple. Some messages are seen as being connected to one another, whereas others are not. This, too, influences the interpretations. Why some messages are seen in the same context, as with the first church sign, and others are seen in different contexts, as with the second sign, is still somewhat of a mystery. Why do people connect some events or messages and not others? Future communication researchers will have to answer that question. For now, it is important to note that those with whom we communicate will not always sequence the messages in the same way we do. Many difficulties in communication can be traced to this very simple proposition. It is as if we all had the same musical notes, but arranged them into distinctly different melodies.

Proposition 7: Communicative Content and
Context Interact to Produce Meaning

Content is considered to consist of the actual words or behaviors of senders. This is the "stuff" that we normally think of as communication. But this is only part, and often a small part, of the picture. As discussed above, the context basically functions as the background on which the content is placed, like the canvas for a painting.

Content alone cannot produce any meaning except in a very rudimentary sense. "Ceci est un message de la part de cette société" is certainly a message. It has content, but does it have meaning? That depends, of course, on whether you can read French. Only then is a sufficient context provided to allow interpretation. Yet even if translated into English, can it then be argued that there is "meaning?" Only in a narrow sense. The sentence translates as follows: "This is a message from the organization." Now, that reveals a little more about the message, but still the "meaning" appears ambiguous.

However, this sentence, in a certain context, can have a very precise meaning. For example, one manager was given a lateral move in an organization. The manager was faced with the task of determining if this was a message from top management. In some companies, a lateral move is the kiss of death; an indicator of poor performance. In other companies, like Japanese corporations for example, a lateral move is not a message about performance at all; it is a normal corporate event. Even in the same company, a lateral move may or may not be a performance message. Hence the manager given a lateral move must determine if this is indeed a message or not.

Douglas Hofstadter (1979) provides a deeply penetrating explanation. He postulated that there are three layers of any message. Layer one, the frame message, says, "I am a message; decode me if you can!" In the example above, the manager had to decide if a lateral move was actually a message. In some cases, a manager may be unaware there is a message in the move, and hence not get the meaning. On the other hand, if the manager determines that there is, indeed, a message in the move, then a layer-two issue arises.

Layer two is the outer message, which tells how the message is to be decoded. What is the decoding mechanism for the manager? The corporate culture and the unwritten organizational rules determine how the message should be decoded. Yet a manager may be able to recognize that the lateral move is a message, but not know how to interpret it. The situation would be similar to someone recognizing that French is being spoken, but being unable to interpret the actual utterance.

The inner message, layer three, is the meaning as intended by the sender. In this case, top management may be saying, "Your performance has been lackluster. You had better shape up!" In essence, the top two layers provide part of the context so the actual meaning can be extracted.

Therefore, context provides two important pieces of information in order to reduce uncertainty. First, it designates what counts as a message and what does not. In one corporation, a lateral move may count as a message, whereas in other organizations it may not. Managers are continuously faced with some kind of ambiguity. Is being left off a circulation list an oversight or a message? What about not being invited to certain social events? Second, the context tells what decoding mechanism should be utilized. If, for example, an organization has gone through some radical changes to become "leaner and meaner," how should being left off a circulation list be decoded? Should the old interpretation rules be used or the new ones? Clearly the decoding mechanism significantly alters the interpretation. A message must have a context for interpretation to take place. Part of that context is provided by the message itself, but the most significant part is provided by the unwritten organizational rules.

Proposition 8: Meanings May Be Constructed
Without Any Message at All

The context can become so developed that the mere expectation of a message can "communicate" something. Take the case of nine-year-old Wendy Potasnik of Carmel, Indiana. She filed a lawsuit against Borden, Inc., because she did not get her free prize in her box of Cracker Jacks. She had written a complaint to the company, but failed to receive a reply within twelve days. A Cracker Jack spokesperson stated that a letter of apology and a coupon for another box was sent within thirteen days, but, by then, the suit had been filed.

In this case, the apparent "no response" created a meaning and, no doubt, an unsuspected reaction. The context exerted so much influence that the mere expectation of a message made certain that something would be "communicated to" Wendy. Unfortunately, these kinds of communication problems are not just cute, little human-interest stories that occasionally appear in the newspaper. Rather, such incidents occur with amazing regularity in most organizations. They have serious consequences and concern more critical matters than a box of Cracker Jacks. For example, how many valued employees leave organizations because management never gives them any feedback about performance? In most of these cases, the employees feel unappreciated, and that they can find more desirable working conditions elsewhere. And that is precisely what they do.

It is somewhat disconcerting to come to the realization that, to a large extent, message senders are at the mercy of the interpretations of receivers. That is, regardless of the sender's actual intent, it is the receiver who will determine "the meaning" of any given utterance. Some communication scholars extend the argument further and claim that "you cannot not communicate." In practical terms, that quip is nonsense. There are countless people with whom we do not communicate, with whom we do not intend to communicate, and who do not perceive an intent to communicate (Motley 1990). Rhetorically, however, this often quoted maxim is quite useful, because every person can be seen as a walking grab bag of *potential* messages that may be interpreted. The type of clothing worn, the briefcase carried, the haircut, the accent, the rate of speech are just a few of the potentially interpretable messages.

A manager who does not respond to a written request from a subordinate, whether by design or carelessness, "communicates" a very important message. The marketing representative who fails to return a phone call from a client "sends" a potentially negative message. But is it really proper to use such words as *sends* or *communicates* in these instances? Does the manager or marketing representative actually transmit a message as does one who sends a letter? Can "no communication" actually be "communication?"

At the heart of each of these questions is the role of intention in the communication process. A "no message" may actually be seen as a "sent message." The nonresponse to a subordinate's request may be an intentional strategy on the part of the manager to communicate the trivial nature of the request. But what if the manager simply forgot to respond? Is this nonresponse a "sent" message? But does it really matter? In either case, a meaning will be constructed in the mind of the subordinate because a response is expected. Therefore, "no communication," whether intentional or not, actually results in a communication of sorts. More precisely, meanings can be produced if there is the mere assumption of intent.

Using the term *receiver* implies that there is a kind of action on the part of some *sender*. The term *receiver* only derives meaning in relationship to the term *sender*. Therefore, even the language we use to communicate about communication obscures clear discussion of the issues. The point is that any action or nonaction can be thought of as having communication potential if there is a context present in the mind of someone. To extend the logic to the end of the line, employees could choose to attach any meaning they care to, to any act or nonact. Indeed, in every mental hospital there are those patients who suffer from just such delusions and who seem to operate exclusively on this principle. The restraining force on this kind of linguistic meltdown is that our culture and language do, in fact, severely limit the probable interpretations, and thus allow us to communicate with reasonable effectiveness. Two noted communication scholars, James Anderson and Tim Meyer (1988), discerningly point out that

> any piece of content limits the meanings that can be competently constructed from it. These limits are like the limits imposed in the phrase, "All the numbers between 1 and 2." Now we know that there is an infinite number of numbers between 1 and 2 (e.g., 1.000 . . . 00001, 1.000 . . . 00002); however, there is no 3. In a like manner, there is a large number of interpretations that can be given to any content, but there is an even larger number that can't. It's this larger number that makes communication work. (p. 26)

In short, even though there are limits on meaning construction, they are wide indeed. Meanings, in fact, may arise without any messages being sent at all; "something" actually can come from "nothing."

Proposition 9: There Are Secondary Messages in Every Communication Event

The discussion thus far has implied that a message has only one meaning. Actually, the process is much more complicated than that. With any given message there are countless secondary messages that can alter the context and change the interpretations. For example, to confirm a spelling for a name, people will often say something like this: "Mr. Arrow: *A* as in alpha, *R* as in rover, *R* as in rover, *O* as in orange, and *W* as in wagon." A functional equivalent that could be given by the stereotypical flirtatious man to a waitress could be: "*A* as in adorable, *R* as in rich, *R* as in really rich, *O* as in obliging, and *W* as in willing." To which the clever waitress might reply, "*N—O*; *N* as in never and *O* as in offensive." The secondary messages are quite obvious. The point is that the statements provide the same information on the surface—a redundant expression of the spelling—but carry vastly different secondary messages.

In a similar sense, it was no accident that the Arrow manager preferred to be addressed as Mr. Taylor and the Circuit manager went by his first name, Elton. When formal titles are used as a form of address, a more rigid and authoritative relational base is developed. The use of a first name implies a relationship of equality, openness, and flexibility. Peters and Waterman (1982) have perceptively pointed out that in the excellent companies, employees are called *associates, crew members,* and *hosts,* as opposed to simply *employees, subordinates,* or even *underlings* (p. 240). All of these names refer to the same basic role, but they express powerful secondary messages about the relationship between managers and employees. Forms of address are not the only ways to express secondary messages. The tale of the recently inaugurated university chancellor illustrates the point. He sent the memo in Figure 2.6 to all university employees. A number of employees, particularly long-term ones, were offended by the last point on the memo, which implied that they needed to be reminded about how to take care of their basic responsibilities. It was as if a parent were talking to a child. Indeed, one graffiti artist added, "And be sure to brush your teeth every night." Employees do not warm to messages, intended or not, that imply a relationship of superior to inferior.

Most professional speakers are quite skillful at exploiting the impact of secondary messages. Take the case of a management consultant addressing an audience of potential clients. While trying to illustrate the usefulness of a particular appraisal system, she reveals, "When I was working for IBM, Microsoft, and 3M, we used a similar system and recorded an immediate 10% improvement in production." Ostensibly, her statement provides evidence for her claim that the appraisal system works. Yet there are other messages implicit in that comment, as well:

1. I have used this system.
2. I have been a manager, just like you.
3. If the appraisal system is good enough for IBM, Microsoft, and 3M, it's good enough for your company.

Upper Midwest University

Walhain, Wisconsin 54321
Office of the Chancellor

7 November 2000

MEMORANDUM

TO: ALL UNIVERSITY EMPLOYEES

FROM: O.W. Caulder, Chancellor

SUBJECT: WINTER STORM PROCEDURES

1. Campus closings are rare.

2. The campus will be open unless you hear otherwise on
   your favorite local radio station.

3. Calls to the Information Center from students about
   specific classes will be referred to appropriate
   academic units.

4. If you commute by car, be sure it is properly equipped and
   maintained for foul weather driving.

Thank you for your cooperation.   *And be sure*
                                          to brush
OWC: pc   *your teeth*
                                             every night.

Figure 2.6. Example of an Unintended Message

Management consultants who use experiential examples to prove their points are more likely to be successful than those who rely exclusively on theoretical or statistical proof. The potent secondary messages provide a context—an aura of credibility—that makes the consultant more believable to listeners.

In many cases, people react as much to the secondary messages as they do to the primary message or, at least, to the ostensive reason for the message. Ultimately, the secondary messages, intended or unintended by the speaker, act as elements in forming the context of interpretation. That is, the secondary messages push or pull certain probable interpretations into the foreground or background. Often, secondary messages are not processed consciously, and speakers are often baffled as to why they are perceived in certain ways. Thus, the effective communicator pays attention to both the primary messages as well as the secondary ones.

Proposition 10: Even Though Interpretations Are Relative, the Process of Meaning Construction Is Not

One of the frustrations associated with this probabilistic approach to communication is that everything seems hopelessly relative. Can managers ever be completely sure their words or actions will be interpreted as intended? In a word, no. Indeed, Angela Laird's (1982) pioneering research on communication rules found that in one company, close supervision was regarded as "checking up" on the employee, whereas in another corporation it was thought of as "concern" on the part of the supervisor. Does this mean it is impossible to predict how a person will probably interpret a message? Absolutely not, but a manager must always realize that it is possible for a message to be understood in different ways. A manager cannot look for total certainty of interpretation, but rather must learn to live with the probable and plausible. There is a middle ground between absolute certainty and total uncertainty: This is the arena of communication. It may not be all that comforting to deal with communication in this fashion, but it is the most realistic.

How can managers achieve reasonable certainty that their actions and words will be interpreted as intended? They do so by fully understanding how people interpret messages. Although the interpretations people make are relative, the process is not. Every dancer has a different style, but there are certain fundamentals that all dancers learn. The meaning construction process is similar for everyone; context and content interact to yield an interpretation. A manager achieves reasonable certainty by realizing that the context of communication is equally as important as the content of the communication. Inferring how the context and content will interact in the minds of the receivers is at the heart of effective communication. The more the manager knows about both facets of the communication process, the greater the chance of predicting the likely reactions to the messages. Likewise, the more a dancer is familiar with a partner's capabilities and the music, the greater the likelihood that she can predict the movements of her partner.

Implications of the Propositions

The implications of the basic propositions discussed above are woven into the fabric of the following chapters. However, several deserve to be highlighted at this point.

Explore the Employees' Context

The more managers know about the context in which employees interpret actions and messages, the greater the likelihood that they can accurately predict the probable interpretations. Meaning is a product of the interaction of context and content. It logically follows that the more managers know about both variables, the greater the chance they will know how their employees will react to a communication episode. In fact, Peters and Waterman (1982) found that excellent companies often practice MBWA (Management By Wandering Around). By learning about employee attitudes, environment, needs, and desires, managers develop an understanding of the employees' context of interpretation. This kind of knowledge can help the manager implicitly, if not explicitly, structure communication so it will be interpreted as intended. The mistake most managers make, especially the Arrow managers, is to assume that, because they know what they mean, others will as well. That is, they assume that the context is stable and that knowledge of the content alone is sufficient. They need to think again. Perhaps William H. Peace (1986), the vice president and general manager of KRW Energy Systems, summarized it best:

> Perceptions form around tiny bits of data and become stronger as supporting evidence accumulates; they are never completely accurate, nor are they completely wrong. Staying in touch with others' perceptions is difficult, however, partly because these may not be wholly conscious and partly because only the tip of what may be a large threatening iceberg will be known to any one employee. So managers must piece together the overall picture for themselves by listening for the tone, or context, or shading that doesn't quite match their own perceptions. Moreover, managers (particularly those at high levels) must consider carefully how their decisions will be perceived. If a decision is right in some business sense but wrong (for whatever reason) from the employees' perspective, its implementation will be erratic at best. (p. 65)

Think About the Possible Interpretations (and Misinterpretations) of Messages, Events, and Symbols

Typically, managers think only about how to best structure their messages to get their points across. They rarely think, How might my message be misunderstood? Because communication is probabilistic in nature, it seems reasonable to try to lessen the possibility of likely misinterpretations. Osmo Wiio (1978), a former Finnish parliament member turned organizational communication scholar, put it this way, à la Murphy's Law:

> ▷ If communication can fail, it will!
> ▷ If you are satisfied that your communication is bound to succeed, it is bound to fail.

> ▷ If a message can be understood in different ways, it will be understood in just that way that does the most harm.

With tongue only partly in cheek, he makes the fundamental point that no manager can be 100% certain that his message will be understood as intended.

Clarify Potentially Ambiguous Comments With the "Blackout" Tactic

Occasionally, a speaker will make a statement and follow it up with a series of "I am not saying *X*; I am not saying *Y*" statements. This may seem a bit odd, for certainly most speakers know what they are saying. Yet, upon closer examination, this tactic can be exceedingly useful for the audience, because it clarifies the precise meaning of the speaker. In essence, the speaker has blocked out certain probable interpretations of his remarks. When the original remark is made, it is as if seven spotlights turn on to illuminate the stage. As the speaker says "I do not mean," each light is extinguished one by one until only one light remains illuminated. This is the speaker's precise meaning. Of course this strategy could be modified to black out only a few possibilities and still leave a number of possible meanings highlighted, like illuminating only a sector of the stage.

Pay Attention to Secondary Messages

Sometimes, employees unwittingly undermine their credibility by sending inappropriate secondary messages. Consider this scenario: One manager spent close to an hour interviewing a potential employee, and the interviewer was suitably impressed by the candidate's experience, skills and education. That changed in an instant. At the end of interview, the manager asked the interviewee if she had any questions. Her response was, "Tell me more about the vacation schedule." Fair or not, the manager concluded that the candidate did not have the right work ethic. Was this a legitimate question? Sure. But not for the first question. It signaled an inability to focus on important issues. After all, the candidate could have asked about the performance appraisal system or mentoring programs. To the manager's credit, she picked up this important secondary message and made the appropriate decision; the candidate was not offered the job.

Be Aware of the "Law of Large Numbers"

Statistician Persi Diaconis as quoted in Paulos (1998) observed that "if you look at a big enough population long enough, then 'almost any damn thing will happen'" (p. 162). Likewise, any message sent to enough people could be interpreted in almost any conceivable way. In fact, we should expect wacky interpretations from at least a few people. Several years ago, Pepsi ran a commercial campaign in which consumers collected points in order to purchase "Pepsi Stuff." As a humorous clincher, the ad suggested that anyone collecting seven million points could redeem them for one Harrier jet. How could anyone think this was a serious offer? Well, someone did. A Seattle man even convinced several investors to help him collect the required number of points. Of course, when he went to redeem his prize, Pepsi shot down his dreams. The whole mess ended up in court. Fortunately, sanity prevailed, and Judge Kimba M. Wood ruled that "no objective person could reasonably have concluded that the commercial actually offered consumers a Harrier jet" ("Attempt to sue Pepsi" 1999). Pepsi had fallen victim to the "law of large numbers" by communicating to millions of reasonable people, but also to some unreasonable ones.

Frame Messages Carefully

Gail Fairhurst and Robert Sarr (1996) describe framing in the following way:

> The essential tool of the manager of meaning is the ability to frame. To determine the meaning of a subject is to make sense of it, to judge its character and significance. To hold the frame of a subject is to choose one particular meaning (or set of meanings) over another. When we share our frames with others (the process of framing), we manage meaning because we assert that our interpretations should be taken as real over other possible interpretations. (p. 3)

The frame acts as a lens through which the other issues are viewed, highlighting certain images and refracting others. The frame alters the probable interpretations. Consider Tom Cashman, who adeptly manages a large and complex unionized plant that manufactures paper products. He is also a skillful framer. After months of grueling decision making, the corporate headquarters decided to make a $25 million capital improvement at his plant. Unfortunately, this also meant shutting down a sister plant in Pennsylvania—good news for his plant, bad news for the other plant. Announcing this news required a deft touch. He had to simultaneously signal his excitement at winning a difficult corporate battle, his resolve to meet the new challenge, and his sadness for workers (also unionized) at the sister plant. What to do? He began his address to the hundreds gathered by asking this question, "How many of you guys remember when you proposed to your wife?" Hands shot up all over the room. He continued,

> Do you remember your emotions at the time? Perhaps you recalled all the crazy things you did to woo her. Possibly you were even thinking about how you were going to make this work in the future. Maybe you remember wondering whether she would accept the offer. And you might even feel a tinge of guilt because you wooed her away from your best friend.

That was the frame. Now the message: "That is how I feel today. . . . " He went on to explain why, over the last few years, he asked the plant to do some "crazy things" like taking on new projects: "They might not have made sense then, but we were positioning the plant for the future." He expressed concern over the sister plant by comparing the news to the guy who marries his best friend's girlfriend. The entire presentation was designed to set the tone for the coming challenges, and to help employees make sense out of a stressful situation filled with conflicting emotions. One wonders how the news would have been received without this frame. Would employees have been as motivated to meet the new challenges? Would they have focused on positive aspects of the announcement? Would they have understood the significance of the decision? Would they have felt honored? I doubt it.

Sculpt the Proper Context

Build enough frames, and a context emerges. Skilled managers and companies carefully craft contexts by artfully accentuating certain interpretations while chiseling away others. Consider Johnson & Johnson, a company that routinely tops the "Best Corporate Reputations" list. No single incident accounts for their stellar image. Johnson & Johnson is passionate about putting customers first. Their credo says it all: "We believe our first responsibility is to the doctors, nurses, and patients, to mothers and fathers and others who use our products and services. In meeting their needs, everything we do must be of high quality." And the credo is everywhere: web pages, sides of buildings, posters, and so forth. It is even the basis for training programs and performance appraisals (Alsop 1999). The result is that customers learn to expect this level of commitment and employees feel obliged to meet those expectations. In other words, Johnson & Johnson carefully crafts the context so that employees pay attention to the right things—customer needs. The context shapes interpretations such that employees become accustomed to viewing events from the customers' perspective. This is the underlying reason why, years ago, Johnson & Johnson deftly handled the Tylenol scare. The CEO from a cruise line, who almost defiantly proclaimed that the fire on the ship "wasn't that bad, because the smoke wasn't toxic," clearly worked from a different context than the folks at Johnson & Johnson. And this is why we will not see that cruise line's name at the top of the "Best Corporate Reputations" list.

Conclusion

A probabilistic view of communication does not provide the certainty that most Arrow managers want. The propositions highlighted in this chapter point to a far more fluid and dynamic situation than may seem comfortable. Even Circuit managers may find it disconcerting to find that meanings are not simply the product of interpersonal relationships, but are influenced by a broader context that includes the organizational rules, corporate environment, and culture. Yet effective managers are more comfortable with a realistic view of communication than a convenient one.

THREE

Communicating the Corporate Culture

> Culture includes the entire symbolic environment. Culture defines reality: what is, what should be, what can be. It provides focus and meaning. It selects out of the myriad of events and interactions in the world those we pay attention to. Culture tells us what is important; what causes what, how events beyond our lives relate to us. Culture gives us values and standards of value. What we may distinguish analytically (and at our peril) as fact, value, and goal is existentially integrated in culture—in identifications, expectations, and demands of individual persons.
>
> *Jeane Kirkpatrick*

As historians cull through the artifacts of our culture and read the chronicles of our times in an attempt to discern the myths of this century, they will come to many startling conclusions. I believe one that they will expose is our unadulterated faith in numbers and statistical reasoning.

"The numbers don't lie . . . ," "The polls predicted that . . . ," "The stats show that . . ." are the incantations of twentieth-century Western culture. Anything that can be measured is measured. Many people believe that everything that is really important can be measured. But numbers do not always tell the whole story. The easiest distinctions to make are not always the most important. A number can do many wonderful things, but it cannot relay the beauty, the tragedies, the hopes, and the dreams of a people. It cannot embody culture.

Companies, like societies, have cultures. Values, myths, rituals, heroes, and devils are all parts of corporate life. As Jeane Kirkpatrick, the former UN ambassador, perceptively suggested above, culture structures our view of reality. Consequently, employees are deeply influenced by corporate values. Managers ignore these facets of corporate life at their peril, because they are as real and important as any profit and loss statement.

What Is Culture?

The origin of the word *culture* is revealing. The term has agricultural overtones, as in the word *cultivation*. It meant to prepare the ground, to develop or foster a particular kind of growth. Weeds have to be destroyed and the soil tilled in order to refine or improve growth. To the early Christians, culture involved a kind of worship (*Oxford English Dictionary* 1989).

Culture still encompasses both definitions. Organizational cultures foster certain types of growth, provide fertile ground for certain types of enterprises, and weed out other types of behaviors. Although an organization's culture does not cause growth, it does cultivate the conditions of growth. Cultivation of the "organizational soil" allows for the reproduction of compatible and beneficial behaviors, practices, and policies. And in many companies, there is a kind of zealous religious guardianship of the organizational culture. In some companies, "worship" may not be too strong a word to describe the culture. In some Japanese organizations, employees ritually chant corporate slogans, and certain employees are afforded an almost sacred status because they symbolize the beliefs, values, hopes, and dreams of the culture.

The *Oxford English Dictionary* (1989) defines culture as "the training, development, and refinement of mind, tastes, and manners; the condition of being thus trained and refined." Note that culture can be thought of as a process or a condition. Actually, it is both. An organization's culture is simultaneously both somewhat stable and constantly evolving as new challenges are encountered. Judgment lies at the core of the concept. Implicit or explicit decisions are made to encourage some values and discourage others. Jacob Bronowski (1978), a twentieth-century Renaissance man, said, "For the values rest at bottom on acts of judgment. And every act of judgment is a division of the field of experience into what matters and what does not" (p. 132). These choices or "ways of being" become so thoroughly ingrained that other ways of doing things are precluded.

Organizations, like countries, have styles of action and typical patterns of thought that slowly evolve. If there is "an American way," then we can also say there is the "Microsoft way." In short, culture consists of the fundamental values and beliefs of a group of people. *Corporate culture,* then, is the underlying belief and value structure of an organization collectively shared by the employees that is symbolically expressed in a variety of overt and subtle ways. Few organizations begin with the corporate leaders philosophizing over the "appropriate" values.

Out of a host of individual practices emerges a company style, which ultimately reflects "how things are done around here" (Deal and Kennedy 1982, p. 4). Faced with the frenetic pace of corporate life, few managers can take the time to contemplate what the organization has become and is becoming. Although they may not be able to clearly articulate the values, they certainly function by them.

Why Do Organizations Have Culture?

Culture acts like music for dancers. It does not strictly determine movement, but it does constrain the options. In the long and intimate history of dance and music, there has evolved a symbiosis between the two, such that changes in dance result in changes in music, and changes in musical traditions alter the structure of dance. Think about the impact of MTV on the music of the 1980s. One musicologist, Will Staw (1988), has forcefully argued that music videos have encouraged the "generic stabilization" of popular music. There is less musical experimentation now than in the past, and rhythms have become standardized to fit into the three- to five-minute dance format. Likewise, culture does not create communication patterns, but does foster certain types of interactions. The communication practices of employees contribute to and change the harmonies and rhythms of an organization. The driving beat of a march suggests a rigid cadence and a strict adherence to a rhythmic structure such as the Arrow manager enjoys. Yet a melody can have such powerful emotive overtones that sentimentality almost drips off each note. Form becomes more important than substance. Such are the tendencies of the Circuit manager's culture. Furthermore, music can express discord, confusion, turmoil, or even randomness, just as many employees stumble to the beat of an erratic culture. To harmoniously and creatively blend form and substance, rhythm and melody, is the cultural challenge for the Dance manager.

Regardless of the precise form of culture, what is abundantly clear is that all organizations have some kind of culture. Why? There are three basic reasons.

1. Employees Need Focus

The human mind is capable of innumerable ideas and beliefs. We must select a few to live by in order to cooperate with one another. The alternative is disconcerting. If individuals did not have some kind of semipermanent belief structure, their behaviors would be governed by randomness. Communication would be almost impossible, because the context would be continually shifting, like talking to a person with multiple personalities. Community, cooperation, coorientation, and coordination would all suffer. Chaos and anarchy would be the likely results. In athletic leagues, the "cellar dwellers" in the standings are often populated with teams in which players and coaches have different philosophies. Teams cannot function effectively when players have different beliefs about how the game is played. A semistable set of beliefs and values allows athletes, as well as employees, to develop a "role on the team," a unique self-identity, a self-"valuableness," if you will.

2. Culture Provides an Efficient Mechanism to Coordinate the Activities of Employees

There are basically two ways to control behavior: inductive and deductive approaches. Inductive approaches outline the specific rules, regulations, and job descriptions for the employees, with the expectation that they will conform to those stipulations. The problem is that employers cannot possibly specify every contingency that may occur, even in the most mundane of jobs. Even if the supervisor could be that specific, few employees could remember all the rules and regulations. The supreme irony is that managers try to use this approach with just the employees who have the least intellectual capacity to process the overload of information. This is not to argue that rules, regulations, and job descriptions are useless. Rather, the point is that the inductive approach must be balanced with the deductive.

Coordinated actions can also result from more deductive strategies, in which general approaches or ways of doing things are specified. Policies such as "Treat the customer with respect" or "The customer is number one" are of this ilk. Of course, a manager might specify certain rules, such as greeting each customer with a smile or finishing a sales transaction with a comment such as "Thank you for shopping at our store." Although useful, such rules are potentially innumerable and clearly do not allow employees creatively to implement strategies that achieve the same objective. In fact, a strict insistence on rule-governed behaviors can act like a psychological straitjacket on the employee.

Cultural approaches focus on teaching employees a few underlying values and why they are important. For example, Disney World has a legendary culture of customer service. Rick Johnson, who conducts seminars about the Disney culture, explains:

> You can't force people to smile. Each guest at Disney World sees an average of seventy-three employees per visit, and we would have to supervise them continually. Of course, we can't do that, so instead we try to get employees to buy into the corporate culture. (McGill 1989, F4)

Then employees are expected to behave according to these general principles as unique situations occur. Employees usually prefer to work with a manager who has a set of values rather than a set of rules, who challenges others to share values instead of enforcing regulations, and who believes in people over procedures. The cultural or deductive approach offers a unique and expedient method of coordinating activities within the organization.

3. Managerial Power Is Limited

Ultimately all managers necessarily derive their power from their ability to control the livelihood of their employees. To be blunt, managers can fire employees and control the purse strings. Yet this power can only ensure conformity in the short run. With the level of litigation over wrongful firings running high, even these traditional power levers are being eroded (Geyelin 1989). There are only so many times a manager can threaten to fire someone. Although rewards may be somewhat more motivating, even these have limitations. The challenge for the manager is to transform power into duty and conformity into desire. Indeed, culture is a necessity for this very reason—it allows workers to be self-motivated by a set of internalized beliefs and values. The culture holds the organization together in the absence of threats or rewards. Without a healthy culture, we are merely beasts. Without music, there is merely movement.

In sum, all companies have some sort of culture, but this does not mean that all corporate cultures are equally successful. Some companies implicitly encourage too many conflicting values. Others seek to manage primarily with inductive techniques, and some even rule through the ruthless use of power. These strategies send their own brand of cultural messages to employees. Fundamentally, such approaches rob the company of the beauty, grace, and even the *power* of an evolving culture, much like comparing some dull musical cadence to a stirring Tchaikovsky ballet.

What Are the Consequences of Culture?

Because organizational culture is a given, why should a manager be concerned with it? Of what consequence is it? Corporate culture influences the organization in a variety of ways. This section highlights four of the more notable consequences.

1. Culture Affects the Bottom Line

James Kotter has devoted much of his scholarly life to investigating the habits of visionary and value-oriented cultures. In a study of 207 companies over an eleven-year period, he and his colleague found that the companies that lived by their stated values experienced four times more growth in revenues than their counterparts (Kotter and Heskett 1992). Two other well-regarded researchers, Collins and Porras (1994), concurred that the fit between the stated and actual values was critical:

> In short, we did *not* find any specific ideological content essential to being a visionary company. Our research indicates that the *authenticity* of the ideology and

the extent to which a company attains consistent alignment counts more than the *content* of ideology. (p. 67)

This should not be surprising. The right culture coupled with the correct strategy provides employees with focus, purpose, and motivation. In a sense, a strong culture allows employees to read the minds of executives, efficiently coordinating actions. The result is less waste, more innovation, higher productivity, and ultimately higher profits.

2. Culture Influences How an Organization Analyzes and Solves Problems

Few business activities have more significance on the profit and loss statement than how decisions are made and carried out. Paul Bate (1984), a noted scholar from University of Bath, England, wrote in a thought-provoking article,

> People in organizations evolve in their daily interactions with one another a system of shared perspectives or "collectively held and sanctioned definitions of the situation" which make up the culture of these organizations. The culture, once established, prescribes for its creators and inheritors certain ways of believing, thinking, and acting which in some circumstances can prevent meaningful interaction and induce a condition of "learned helplessness"—that is, a psychological state in which people are unable to conceptualize their problems in such a way as to be able to resolve them. In short, attempts at problem solving may become culture-bound. (p. 44)

His research confirms that culture can, and in fact does, restrain organizational thought.

Indeed, poor decisions can result from such cultural restraints. Meaningful alternatives are not explored because "that's not how things are done around here." For instance, one small but growing company had several problems with how various departments interrelated. The normal procedure was to forward all such problems to the president and let him resolve the issue. After all, such procedures worked well in the past, and the president, a corporate hero, was legendary for his ability to solve problems equitably. The difficulty was that as the firm grew, it became increasingly difficult for the president to know the necessary facts in order to make appropriate decisions. A simple and obvious solution was to have a middle manager's meeting to solve many of the problems and coordinate activities. Strangely, no one in the company had thought of this idea. Why? Because of the "way things are done around here." To put it another way, the value of respect for the chain of command precluded even thinking about such a solution. The culture had put perceptual blinders on the entire management team. The consultant who suggested the change was not constrained by these blinders, and was widely praised for this "revolutionary idea." Once the meetings began to take place, many of the problems were quickly and easily resolved.

In another company, a manager boldly admitted during a meeting that she did not meet her quarterly goals. The vice president's response was, "I would have lied." His statement set in motion a "shoot the messenger" type of culture in which accurate information is not valued in the organization. Effective decision making was compromised from that point onward.

3. *Culture Influences How the Company Will Respond to Change*

Culture can actively encourage quick and decisive change when conditions demand it. Many high-tech firms realize that, to keep pace, there is a constant need for change and development. Consider Amazon.com, run by the disarmingly understated Jeff Bezos. His goal is "universal selection, the earth's biggest river, earth's biggest selection." Some of Amazon.com's innovations, such as purchase circles, which allow customers to see what books colleagues in the same "circle" are buying, are legendary. Others are complete failures. No matter; few traditional companies would take such risky, costly, and bold steps, particularly when, well into the late 1990s, the company had not shown a profit. Yet this is exactly what the culture demanded of its employees.

On the other hand, the organizational culture can act as an impediment to necessary change. Universities are almost legendary for such resistance. If the need arises to develop a program that crosses departmental boundaries, the budgetary and bureaucratic obstacles are almost overwhelming. Why? In a word, inertia. The entire system conspires to maintain the traditional departmental structure. Fundamentally, it is an expression of the belief that knowledge can best be compartmentalized. Hence barriers are developed to ensure that this belief is not violated. In some ways, such barriers to change may be beneficial, but the benefits should be weighed against the costs. All organizations should closely examine the environment to determine how much change is actually needed. Then the question becomes, Does the culture foster the necessary degree of change? The answer has critical consequences for the organization's long-term survival.

4. *Culture Affects Employee Motivation*

There can be no greater motivation for employees than when they believe in what they are doing, what the company does, and what the company stands for. Excellent companies are motivating because of their corporate cultures. When a company espouses one philosophy but practices another, employees become disheartened and disillusioned. An organization with a corporate philosophy that says all employees should be respected, but does not respond to employee inquiries and unfairly rewards employees, is doomed to an unhealthy culture. Likewise, the corporation that says it believes in offering a "fair pricing system" to its customers, and then regularly deceives clients as to the actual price of goods and services, fosters disrespect among employees. When practice and belief are incongruent, the culture is de-motivating. Hypocrisy has its price.

In short, culture does have consequence. George Gilder, in his book, *Wealth and Poverty* (1981), summarized it best:

> Matters of management, motivation, and spirit—and their effects on willingness to innovate and seek new knowledge—dwarf all measurable inputs in accounting for productive efficiency, both for individuals and groups and for management and labor. A key difference is always the willingness to transform vague information or hypotheses into working knowledge; willingness, in Tolstoy's terms, transferred from the martial to the productive arts, "to fight and face danger," to exert efforts and take risks. (p. 26)

How Can the Culture Be Discovered?

Reflect on the Type of People in the Organization

Employees, particularly those at the highest levels, are at once creators, carriers, and consequences of culture. The people hired, their backgrounds, biases, prejudices, and styles shape corporate culture. In turn, these employees carry or embody culture. The daily rituals, the inside jokes, the taken-for-granteds are all reflections of the values (Pacanowsky and O'Donnell-Trujillo 1982). Employees are also consequences of the culture, because even as they are shaping the culture, they are being shaped by it. The entire past, present, and future of the company are reflected in the employees, just as a broken corner of a hologram reflects the imagery of the entire picture (Smith and Simmons 1983).

To be more specific, by questioning, probing, and observing the behavior of others, one can get a vision of the corporate values. Why are certain individuals hired, fired, or promoted? What makes a person successful in the organization? Unsuccessful? What does top management value in an employee? How are decisions made? Why?

The "why" questions are the most difficult and revealing, because the answers disclose the underlying thought patterns, beliefs, and values of the organization. More often than not, the "whys" are implicit and unconscious. For instance, why do most organizations go through the ritual of asking for more information than they can possibly use? Many managers are abundantly aware of the practice, but the critical question is, Why? The practice is in part a reflection that most companies want to believe they make informed decisions. Of course, the underlying assumption that more information equals more knowledge is a bit dubious. Why would a company take time to interview a number of people it has no intention of hiring? A silly practice? Perhaps. But it may reflect a corporate value of giving everyone "a fair chance." Thus, a thorough examination of why people do what they do proves exceedingly useful in uncovering corporate values.

Pay Attention to Corporate Symbols

Corporate heroes frequently provide a rich source of information on organizational values. For example, during one seminar with bank employees, the discussion turned to some typical difficulties tellers had in dealing with "uncooperative" clients. In the middle of the discussion, the president stood up and told a story. In a rather lengthy soliloquy, he told how he had handled a similar situation when he was a teller, and went on to explain with great relish how he had become president from his modest beginnings. Although I was a bit surprised, the employees were not. In subsequent discussions it became apparent that such an event was not without precedent. Marvin, as the president liked to be called, was one of the corporate heroes, and those stories were common knowledge among employees.

What purpose did Marvin's story serve? Fundamentally, the message reiterated the value that top management was "employee-centered" and that anyone can "make it." The president, whom they all knew on a first-name basis, was a coworker who understood their difficulties and troubles. Most of all, he cared. He communicated, consciously or unconsciously, the secret to this organization's success. For most employees at this seminar, the significance of this little event was short-lived. After all, it was common knowledge. Yet the wise manager understands the deeper meaning of the commonplace and finds significance in everyday events. As the insightful scholar George Gerbner (1990) has said, "The control of any culture is dependent on those who control the stories that are told."

Examine the Corporate Slogans, Philosophies, and Value Statements

"All the news that is fit to print" has been the rallying cry for the *New York Times* for years. The Aid Association for Lutherans (AAL) is a successful life insurance company with a corporate slogan of "Common concern for human worth." The slogan reflects the beliefs of the founders that life insurance should be provided at a reasonable cost. Even the employee publication, *Common Concern,* in both name and editorial policy, reflects the corporation's values. Issues frequently contain articles describing how AAL meets the needs of members and how members show concern for their community. Concern is the consistent theme and rallying cry for the organization. It provides meaning and purpose. Slogans may appear to be simpleminded and trivial, yet there is an elegance in simplicity; the farsighted manager never underestimates the power of the simple.

Corporate philosophies can also be clues into corporate values. They provide a brief and concise view of how the organization views itself and its mission—a sort of corporate self-image. Imperial, Inc., a nationwide telemarketing firm, has

MISSION

Through the development of our people,

Imperial, Inc.

intends to be the recognized national leader
in TeleServicing™ that provides quality products
and is committed to unequaled customer service
and state-of-the-art distribution systems, while
meeting our profitability and growth objectives.

MAJOR CORPORATE GOALS:

Increase retention and penetration of current accounts.

Complete transportation and agriculture specialization.

Complete investigation and testing of industrial and
heavy-duty markets.

Figure 3.1. Imperial, Inc., Corporate Mission

consistently grown despite economic fluctuations. Part of its secret lies in a clearly
stated and easily internalized corporate mission, as seen in Figure 3.1. Not only are
employees instructed on the philosophy, but customers are made aware of it

through publication of the credo in the product manual. Therefore, internal and external pressures act to preserve the value of customer service. Such practices must be having an effect. Over a nine-year period, sales per employee nearly doubled.

Contemplate the More Subtle Indicators of Culture

At Imperial, Inc., they use an intriguing rhetorical device to further transmit the value of customer service. The organizational chart is "upside down," with the customer at the top as the "chairman of the board" (see Figure 3.2).

Company newsletters can be equally revealing, as we discovered in a study on employee publications. Of the 100 samples we gathered from various organizations, we noted the styles ranged from one-page photocopies to elaborate magazines (Clampitt, Crevcoure, and Hartel 1986). Champion International Corporation's newsletter had beautiful pictures and graphics that looked like they were plucked from the pages of *National Geographic*. The firm, an industry leader in the production of high quality paper products, no doubt uses this publication to showcase their prowess. The implicit message is abundantly clear to employees and their families: Champion is a high quality organization. One of my colleagues examined a publication from another business and remarked that it reminded him of a high school yearbook. Indeed, the proliferation of pictures of the company bowling team, softball teams, and company parties would tend to confirm such an evaluation. Discussions with several company employees revealed that top management wanted to instill a "family atmosphere." The newsletter was one vivid manifestation of the value.

In brief, symbolic clues into corporate values abound. Some are more explicit, such as corporate heroes, slogans, and philosophies. Others are more implicit, such as symbols, graphic designs, and company newsletters. This is not to suggest that the culture exists in the symbols themselves. Rather, it is the way in which employees come to understand, react to, and relate to symbols that create the culture. Through a dynamic interplay of symbols and reactions, culture evolves. In this way cultural symbols refine or cultivate certain values and beliefs.

How Can the Culture Be Evaluated?

This issue perplexes many because of the inevitability and pervasiveness of culture. Yet wise managers often find that the roots of fundamental problems are buried deep within the culture. The three tests discussed below can reveal fundamental troubles with the culture.

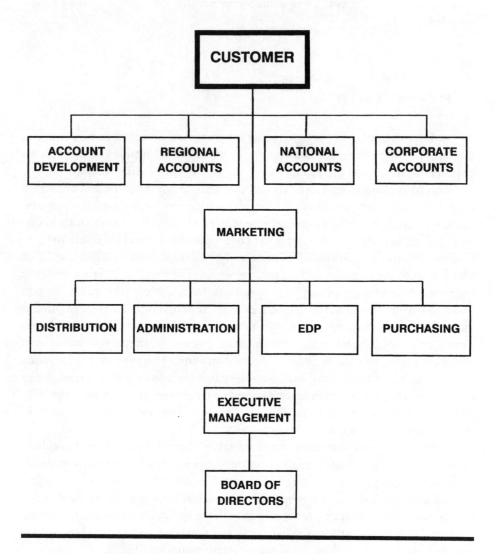

Figure 3.2. Imperial, Inc., Organization Chart

1. *Is the Organization Trying to Close the Gap* *Between the Stated Culture and Actual Culture?*

The stated culture always differs from the unstated one. No one, not even a preacher, can entirely practice what he or she preaches. The important question revolves around the nature of the gap between the two. Large gaps can promote cynicism, discouragement, and poor performance. Consider the following situation.

A small university prided itself on its commitment to teaching. Prospective students were told of the stellar teaching qualities of the faculty. Even new faculty recruits were indoctrinated about the importance of quality teaching. And it worked, for awhile. Then, one day, a new dean became enamored with seeking a special certification for one of the largest departments on campus. This particular certification required that the department's professors have terminal degrees. The only problem was that some of the best and most experienced teachers in the program had masters degrees, not Ph.D.s.

What to do? Here was a real test of values. If teaching really mattered, then the leadership would either seek a way around the certification requirements or abandon the quest. But that did not happen. The dean decided to terminate the contracts of those with masters degrees, one by one as their contracts expired. He also terminated any pretense that teaching really mattered. Image was all that counted. Even that was tarnished, as it became clear years later that the certification would never materialize. As many predicted, the initiative failed for lack of resources and commitment. In fact, a few of the faculty members with masters degrees were not even replaced and almost half of the newly hired Ph.D.s ended up leaving anyway. Student complaints about the quality of teaching increased dramatically for awhile, but abated when they realized they just had to "jump through the hoops" to get the degree. They learned this critical lesson from leadership that persisted in jumping through the certification hoops. But, at least the students received a diploma. The department never received its certification. This is typical. Cynicism, apathy, and pretense prevail because the chasm between the stated and actual culture is too wide to bridge.

2. Is the Actual Culture Suited to the Organizational Challenges?

A strong culture can actually be a bad thing for an organization, because it can create resistance to other ways of doing things. Allan Kennedy coauthored the book *Corporate Cultures: The Rites and Rituals of Corporate Life* (Deal and Kennedy 1982), which popularized the notion of culture in the early 1980s. He spoke to *Inc.* magazine about the misuse of the concept:

> [The companies profiled in the book have been] successful, not because they created particular cultures but because they created cultures that are consistent with their business strategies. A culture may help or hinder a company, but if you get the strategy wrong, you're dead in the water no matter what you do culturally. ("The culture wars" 1999, p. 108)

Different cultural values are required to compete in the age of e-commerce. Traditional "brick-and-mortar" companies, like Sears, Wal-Mart, and Sony, transitioning to the e-economy, learned this lesson the hard way. "Click-and-mortar" companies like Amazon.com work at the speed of light, eschewing formal airs. For example, one home furnishing company, GoodHome.com, went from business plan to venture capital funding to startup in a mere ten weeks (Stepanek 1999). When Procter & Gamble was investigating how to break into e-commerce, they sent a delegation to Silicon Valley for a field trip. They talked to the twenty-something "veterans" in the field. One Procter & Gamble official, astounded at the pace, offered this insight: "Silicon Valley speed is different from Fortune 500 speed" (Useem 1999, p. 104). They were culture shocked. But this may be the only way to bring the culture in line with the competitive pressures.

Organizations with cultures that are not compatible with the competitive pressures cannot survive for very long. Some companies are wise enough to know it. In the late 1990s, Merrill Lynch, a full-service brokerage, decided to break with tradition because they saw the proverbial handwriting on the wall. Only it was not "the wall" they ran into: it was the net. The growing power of the Internet, discount brokerages, and day traders signaled a major market shift. The old Merrill Lynch culture prided itself on fostering close relationships with customers through well-trained full-service brokers. This kind of enterprise could not survive in the e-commerce age. Consequently, they decided to reinvent the culture before it was too late and to break from their tradition by offering discount brokerage via the Internet. Many Merrill Lynch veterans bristled at the cultural changes, but they were necessary to remain competitive. In short, when the competitive situation dramatically changes, so must the culture.

3. Does the Actual Culture Fit the Employee's Beliefs and Values?

Most company mergers and acquisitions fail to live up to their promise. In fact, researchers have consistently found a 50% to 60% failure rate (Cartwright and Cooper 1993, p. 57; see also *Reed: Reflections* 2000). This makes perfect sense, because employees from one company do not often share the values of the other company. In one instance, a large regional financial firm acquired a local banking chain that prided itself on its unique culture. The local chain offered highly personalized customer service, even serving tea to clients as they entered the bank. When the regional firm took over, the tea parties stopped. So did the personalized service. They were replaced by standardized procedures and formalized relationships. The result was that employee turnover went sky high while customer satisfaction hit a new low. No wonder mergers rarely live up to their promise. Executives cannot expect that employees will assimilate a new culture without major repercussions.

How Can the Culture Be Communicated?

The effective manager teaches employees what the corporation values, why it is valued, and how to transform values into action. This is no simple task. Employees, like students, do not always see the value of what they are doing until after they have done it. They may tire, get discouraged, or even resist. Yet the farsighted manager overcomes these hindrances while engendering commitment to corporate values and inspiring employees to enact them. Ultimately, the values must move from objective statements to subjective realities. That is, employees must transform corporate rhetoric about values into personal commitments and experiences. How can managers facilitate this process? In a word, communication.

Most organizations construct their culture through an unplanned, haphazard, and trial-and-error process. Effective corporations with healthy cultures contemplate, plan, and manage their corporate values. Every manager creates a kind of subculture in the organization as well. Effective managers consciously construct cultural cues for their employees. Reviewed below are ten useful strategies for communicating the values.

1. Craft Actionable Cultural Statements

Organizational value, mission, and purpose statements are inherently ambiguous, and with good reason. This bit of equivocation can inspire a variety of creative but disciplined responses. If the cultural statements are too narrow, they straitjacket employees, inspiring only the automatons. If the statements are too ambiguous, they unleash employees, inspiring the disruptive elements. Consider the following statements:

> ▷ "We are in the business of serving customers."
> ▷ "Our employees are our number one resource."
> ▷ "Our mission is to make the best damn product we can."

They may sound nice, but a proper employee discussion would quickly expose their banality and insipidness. For example, how well should customers be served? Resources can be bought, sold, and bartered. What about employees? And what if the "best damn product" the company makes is not what the customer wants? In short, the statements do not motivate, inspire, or compel the right action. Overly ambiguous statements dominate the organizational landscape. Why? Probably because writing purpose, value, and mission statements has become fashionable. Companies can even purchase fill-in-the-blank "tailored-made" mission statements—no doubt guaranteed to inspire even the indolent. This boggles the mind; it is akin to plagiarism and has the same degree of authenticity.

Cultural statements should be carefully contemplated. Ideally, get as many people as possible involved in crafting and even wordsmithing the statements. This allows everyone to understand the nuances, test out examples, and discuss implications. A group of consultants specializing in these issues expressed it this way:

It pays to spend more time in the planning and gathering and discussing of the analysis, mission and vision, because the buy-in will be substantially stronger and the implementation phase will just be a continuation of the process, rather than a disjointed hand-off from planners to doers. (Scott, Jaffe, and Tobe 1993, p. 13)

Consider the experience of our consulting team with one dairy plant. We spent hours discussing the implications of one value statement, "Purpose directed energy." We discussed what it meant and what it did not mean. We also developed a secondary list of statements designed to clarify the value (see Figure 3.3). Milking the statement for all it is worth, we even created a PDE index for meetings (e.g., "On a 0 to 10 scale, how much of our energy in the meeting was 'purpose directed?'"). The discussions about the values were always rated a 10 on the PDE index. It is ideal to link cultural statements directly to measures. When it is not possible, other methods such as those discussed below will have to be used to make the values actionable.

2. Socialize Employees Appropriately

From the first moment potential employees enter the organization, they begin to develop a picture of the corporate values (Jablin 1987). The manner in which they are treated, the way employees talk to one another, the office design, and even the selection process are all indicators of the corporate cultures. After being hired, the training procedures, the daily rituals, and practices further reinforce "what this company is all about." So the socialization process slowly and steadily builds the pieces of the corporate value structure for the new employee.

Through this process managers can actively encourage the appropriate values. The hiring process itself can render messages to potential employees that the company is serious about hiring the best. Who does the hiring and interviewing can send equally powerful messages. Admiral Hyman Rickover, the founder of the nuclear Navy, was notorious for his rigorous interviews of all cadets who wished to serve on the submarines. In fact, the title of President Jimmy Carter's book *Why not the best?* came from a comment by Rickover during one of those interviews (Carter 1976). Here was one of the most powerful men in the world interviewing a cadet, and asking him if he always did his best. Rickover thus set in motion the standard of excellence he expected from all those in his charge. In fact, his legendary commitment to quality was so great that his programs were usually considered "untouchable" during defense budget cutting days (Polmar and Allen 1982).

Research indicates that the initial weeks of employment are a critical period for the manager to exert influence (Clampitt and Downs 1993). Supervisors, to some extent, lose their power to shape the values, beliefs, and behaviors of employees after the first month or so. This makes the initial training period extremely important, because managers are not only teaching specific skills but also the corporate philosophy. Detailed discussions of corporate history, successes, and fail-

Purpose Directed Energy

▷ What *we* do is *directed* at set targets.
▷ *Everyone* has a clear picture of the plant's objectives.
▷ *Our* time and efforts are *directed* at things that matter.
▷ *Everyone* understands *why* we do *what* we do.
▷ *All* employees meet defined *expectations*.

Figure 3.3. Actionable Value Statement

ures help instill corporate values into employees. Some companies, such as IBM, go through extensive discussions of corporate values—not just the "whats," but also the "whys" of policy. One IBM employee remarked, "After you're done with their training, you know what they believe, why they believe it and you end up believing it."

Thorough explanations of corporate philosophy or plans can also help embed the value system. These recitations can act as a kind of organizational mantra, in which repeating the words weaves a magic incantation (Broms and Gahmberg 1983). Employees not only need to *think* about values, but also *feel* them. It is silly to recite over and over again a fact like "The speed of light is 186,000 miles per second." Once is enough. Yet a value only once recited is stillborn. We do, in fact, listen to the same music over and over again. It replenishes our strength, focuses our spirit, and energizes us, similar to the effect of such statements of value as "Why not the best?" or "Quality is job one."

3. Develop Symbolic Reminders of the Core Values

Employees should live in a symbolic environment dominated by the core values. Appleton Papers, a producer of specialty coated papers, does more than paper the walls with its core values. Walking around the company, you see the letters *CFQ* everywhere: on posters, work shirts, letterhead, pens, you name it. CFQ stands for Customer Focused Quality, and translates into "meeting or exceeding customer expectations in all aspects of every transaction with Appleton Papers." This is not merely some kind of political campaign slogan; it is deeply ingrained into the very fabric of the organization. For instance, departments measure their performance against CFQ standards, which are then linked to compensation and bonuses. Symbols attached to real dollars cast a powerful spell. CFQ provides a unique point of identity and commonality for all Appleton Paper employees. It is what distinguishes this paper company from the others. Besides the traditional communication tools, they have some unique ones as well. Customers can park in specifically designated CFQ spots close to the office buildings and plants. My favorite example involves a special program that compensates employees for purchasing designer license plates that contain the CFQ acronym. On the streets of Appleton you cannot help but notice CFQ license plates with gems like "IM4 CFQ" and "FORE CFQ." One almost senses a religious sect casting a magic spell. In fact, one citizen wrote to the local newspaper inquiring about the "CFQ cult." Appleton Paper's prayers were certainly answered with publicity like that.

Prayers of a different sort were answered for one minister who practiced what this principle preaches by developing a clever anagram. He believed that, instead of the usual practice of "begging" various church members to serve, they should *volunteer* for church responsibilities. Not only did he preach from the pulpit that "God calls people to serve," but he also signaled the value through a simple rhetorical device. Instead of a "nominating committee" that sought volunteers for various church functions, he reversed the spelling to coin the term "ETANIMON Committee," in which members applied to serve the church. Here, in this deceptively simple act, he reversed the nominating process in both spelling and deed. The pastor also reversed the trend; the church had more applicants than they knew what to do with.

In each of these cases, the symbols reinforced the critical values, acting as continual reminders of what the organization stood for. The creative powers of many managers would be well spent in thinking of such simple and novel methods to symbolize critical corporate values.

4. Link Values With Specific Behaviors

Values are necessarily abstract concepts. Hence there are countless specific behaviors that could spring from one value. Wise managers not only encourage certain behaviors, but also link those behaviors to a specific value. Thus, the value becomes the focal point, which in turn encourages other novel behaviors that also express the value. One classic example occurred during the 1984 Olympic trials for the USA basketball team. Leon Wood, a standout offensive player at Cal State Fullerton, was a leader in scoring and assists, but was not known for his defense. That was bound to change when Mr. Wood met Coach Bobby Knight, who was known for the prowess of his devastating defense at Indiana University. Not one to disappoint, Coach Knight gave Mr. Wood a lot of "personalized" instruction on how to play defense. At one point, Leon reported that "Coach Knight came over to me and said, 'Leon, you took a charge, didn't you? That's your first one in camp, isn't it?' I said it was, and so he told me to go to the spot on the floor where I took the charge and sign the court." As requested, Mr. Wood autographed the basketball floor in the Indiana fieldhouse ("Wood shows signs" 1984).

The event must have made a deep and lasting impression on Wood and the other players. Here is an exquisite example of linking the person (Wood) to the value (defense) and to a specific action (taking a charge). The genius of the act of Wood autographing the floor is that it created a permanent symbolic representation of the value. There must have been times when Leon was racing down the court that he looked over to that place on the floor and remembered the incident that was indelibly etched in his mind. This memory, no doubt, had the desired effect of encouraging him to play aggressive defense. It must have worked, because the team won the Olympic gold medal that year. Employees, like basketball players, need to have experiences that act as reminders of corporate values, and they need to be praised for manifesting them (see, for example, Feinstein 1986). Incidents like this show that the organization takes its values seriously and expects the values to be lived out on a day-to-day basis.

Moving from the hardwood to the office floor, we can find other compelling examples. For instance, Imperial, Inc., the telemarketing firm mentioned before, has a "Two rings is plenty" policy. Whenever a phone rings at Imperial, someone always answers within two rings. Frankly, it is a refreshing departure from the typical practice. An unanswered phone or continually ringing phone annoys most customers. Yet focusing on the practice itself misses the point. Simple in design, but powerful in effect, the policy symbolizes a central corporate value of "serving the customer." The policy clearly links Imperial's corporate value of customer service to a tangible behavior. Employees are encouraged to dream up other ways to better serve the customer, but senior management sets the tone. Customer service is not just a fuzzy idea in the heads of management at Imperial, Inc., but a daily commitment and practice of all employees.

5. *Filter Information Through the Values*

Employees can pay attention to an infinite array of information sources, ranging from listening to the latest gossip to reading the employee manual. Effective organizations use the values to structure information in order to provide both a focus and a reminder: focus, because the values should tell employees what is important, highlighting the most critical information while de-emphasizing less salient issues. Structuring information this way also provides a reminder to employees that the values permeate everything the organization does. Consider how one task force restructured a plant's monthly production report. The original version of the thirty-plus page report (organized by departments) consisted of a mass of statistics wrapped in a morass of tangled and jumbled commentary. All too often employees read only what was going on in their own unit. The committee cut through this thicket of information by reorganizing the report around the core values, disposing of pages of data, and slicing the report by twenty pages. For instance, one core value was safety. All the safety data from various departments were grouped together in an easy-to-read chart designed to highlight the progress from month-to-month. Below the statistical data, various important safety incidents and issues were described. A similar strategy was used for all the other core values.

Focus groups revealed that employees liked the new format and were more inclined to read the entire report. Executives were particularly pleased by the emphasis on plantwide issues, because, in the past, they were frustrated at the lack of interdepartmental learning. For example, when an employee sustained a peculiar injury in one department, the supervisor would dutifully write it up in the report so that other employees would learn from the incident. But, because no one read the old report, a similar incident would occur in another department. This all changed with the newly formatted report: Employees began reading it, and learning started to occur.

6. Tell the Right Stories

If employees know the stories of the culture, they know the culture. If they do not know the stories, they will not abide by the cultural values. Roger Schank (1990) may know more about storytelling than anyone in the world. Why? Because he leads a team of scholars trying to teach computers to "tell the right stories." This daunting task goes to the very core of human experience: "We are the stories we tell. We not only express our vision of the world, we also shape our memory by the stories we tell" (p. 170). The storyteller's simple tale diverts our attention from its power and complexity. As Roger Schank put it, "If we all share the same stories, we feel part of a common group. Moreover, when we believe that our most intimate stories are shared by our listeners, communication feels most intense" (p. 194). The wise manager seizes the power of the story, and uses it as a tool to regularly communicate the core values. What happens if a manager *cannot* think of a good story that illustrates a critical organizational value? Nothing at all. Employees will not understand the values, much less try to abide by them.

A good story has a moral, and that is what employees should remember and act on. In fact, in a wonderfully titled book, *Managing by Storying Around,* David Armstrong (1992) describes how his company uses stories:

> We have found stories to be so effective, they've replaced our policy manual. . . . Storytelling is a much simpler and more effective way to manage. I don't have to make thousands of individual decisions—is it okay to have a drink during [a company] dinner? how about charging an in-room movie to the hotel bill [during a company trip]? . . . The story gives people our guidelines, and then it is up to them. Storytelling promotes self-management. (p. 11)

Self-management is the critical point. The stories provide the mechanism to move the values from stale statements written on a piece of paper to a fresh testament written in the hearts and minds of employees.

7. Use Financial Resources as Powerful Reminders

If you want to know what an organization really values, watch how it spends money and resources. A lot of companies say they believe in customer service, but few actually put their money where their espoused values are. L. L. Bean, the legendary mail-order company for the adventurous, is one exception. They had a goal of achieving $1 billion dollars in sales in 1992. But this objective was sacrificed and growth purposely slowed so that the company could focus on customer service. Indeed, the company lost the coveted National Quality Award as a result of their slowed growth, by deciding to invest $2 million to improve customer satisfaction (Pereira 1989). The net result was that consumers now routinely rank L. L. Bean at the top of the customer service charts (Mardesich 1999).

It is easy to say that a company values employees, but the message is taken to heart when employee compensation is at stake. For instance, Herman Miller, Inc., the office furniture manufacturer, credits their growth to treating employees fairly and engendering a commitment to corporate goals. One unusual method they have used to communicate this message was to limit the CEO's salary to twenty times the average wage of factory workers. Thus, in 1989, the CEO earned only a little over $465,000, including bonuses, which was a far cry from what many CEOs earned that year (Labich 1989).

Employee stock ownership plans, or ESOPs, are another way to link corporate values to compensation. Stock in the company is bought for the employee by the ESOP trust: employees do not invest their own funds. At many companies, ESOPs become a substitute for a pension plan. When the employee retires or leaves the company, he or she often has the option of taking the ESOP payment in stock or in cash. The ESOP at PepsiCo, Inc., is part of a "SharePower" program meant to build team spirit and send a clear message to all employees that they are important (Solomon 1989b). The premise is that workers have incentive to do better, because part of their retirement benefit is directly influenced by the performance of their company's stock. Indeed, Corey Rosen, head of the National Center for Employee Ownership, believes that the key to improved organizational performance lies in using ESOPs to encourage employees to participate in the company. He has found that companies with ESOPs grow at a rate of 8% to 11% faster than those that do not (McCormick 1989). Putting the money where the values are usually pays off. How an organization spends its capital may tell employees more about corporate values than any other symbol.

8. Manage Conflict Through the Values, Not the Hierarchy

Managing conflict through the values routinely happens at Appleton Papers. The following incident nicely illustrates the point.

An hourly employee was arguing with a mid-level manager about how to pack a semitrailer with a paper product. The hourly worker invoked CFQ: "This is the way the customer wants us to pack it. I thought we believed in focusing on the customer." As a result, the trailer was loaded the way the customer wanted. In many companies the hourly worker would quickly acquiesce to those in authority. The story rapidly spread throughout the plant. On the surface, the story circulated by employees may appear to highlight the "victory" of the union worker over one of the "suits." But, on a deeper level, it signals that Appleton Papers tries to "walk the talk." Incidents like this more powerfully communicate the values than a thousand pep talks.

Unfortunately all organizational conflicts are not resolved as easily. Organizational conflicts often arise because of clashes between competing values. Wise managers learn to reconcile the inevitable conflicts between values. There are innumerable practical manifestations of one simple value. Practices that are congruent with one value may be incongruent with another one. The challenge for the manager is to communicate what are seemingly conflicting messages. Managers must seek a balance between the values. They must be sensitive to specific practices that emphasize one value at the expense of another. Taken to the extreme, an employee might believe that customer service means providing an excessively costly service to clients. Of course, such practices need to be balanced with the reasonable profit motive. The employee might retort, "I was only trying to serve the customer's needs. After all, that is what our company stands for. Is it wrong to serve the customer?" The effective manager then has a unique opportunity to guide the employee into an understanding of how the corporate values balance one another. Indeed, values that seem to be at odds philosophically may, in practice, actually augment and strengthen one another. The wise manager toils and searches for this synergistic effect, and encourages employees to do likewise. This discussion may sound something like the incantations of a Zen master, and in many ways that is precisely the role of the manager.

9. Routinely Evaluate Progress on the Core Values

This is relatively easy to do with employee focus groups and surveys. One medical clinic uses this process to reinvigorate a commitment to the core values, clarify the meaning of the core values, and develop specific action plans. Once a year, they close the clinic for an afternoon to ponder the clinic value statements. The procedure is simple: all the employees and physicians rate the clinic on its seven core values using a 0 (*low*) to 10 (*high*) scale. After the ratings are compiled, everyone starts to discuss the reasons for their ratings. Sometimes the physicians' ratings differ greatly from the staff's. Sharing perceptions, for instance, on what *convenient patient care* actually means often proves revealing. In one instance, a physician who was notoriously late in completing follow-up reports, learned that his patients often complained about not getting back test results in a timely manner. One month later, after getting rid of the backlog, the problem was resolved. The collective scrutiny of the group was just the right prescription. The meeting ends with a decision about the projects most likely to improve the ratings for the following year. This organizational ritual not only provides a safe haven for conflict resolution, but also symbolizes the importance of the value system. After all, the clinic never closes for any other reason. In short, a routine checkup on the culture provides an assessment of the organization as well as a source of renewal.

10. *Assist in the Evolution of the Meaning of the Values*

One of the signs of change can be the temporary clash between the stated values and the practiced ones. The conflict can be healthy. Not practicing what one preaches becomes unhealthy if there is not some movement toward greater congruity. Many corporations espouse the "wellness" value, which embraces advice like "eat right, exercise, etc." The *et cetera* is the tough part. How far should a company go? How fast? For example, in the late 1970s, Johnson & Johnson initiated the "Live for Life" program, in which employees completed a comprehensive questionnaire about health risks. Based on the results, each employee was counseled by a nurse practitioner about appropriate lifestyle changes. Employees were encouraged to eat right, quit smoking, and exercise in the company-provided gym. But it was only in 1990 that the corporate headquarters became totally smoke-free. In other words, it took almost fifteen years to create and integrate policies compatible with the wellness values. The wise manager recognizes the inevitability of the clash between word and deed while searching for specific ways to bridge the chasm.

Anticipating and shaping cultural changes can be beneficial in building employee commitment to the values. One wonders if a smoke-free environment could have been implemented in the late 1970s. Typically, the corporate culture changes slowly, taking time to embrace the values fully. But there are benefits in incrementally increasing employee commitment to corporate values. For Johnson & Johnson, the result was a savings of $378 per employee in reduced health care costs. They also formed a new company, Johnson & Johnson Health Management, Inc., to market their program (Templin 1990). Indeed, a culture that does not change and continually renew its values can become stagnant and unhealthy.

Conclusion

As a youngster I remember watching an old black and white movie about a World War II naval battle. An American ship was dropping depth charges on a German submarine. Inside the submarine, the results were devastating. Water was flooding one chamber after another, equipment was failing, and the crew faced what they thought was certain death. To make matters worse, the crew had been instructed to maintain strict silence so that the American ships could not pinpoint their location. Morale was steadily eroding, which prohibited the necessary repairs from being made and the appropriate offensive tactics from being engaged. The crew was demoralized, exhausted, and terrified. Then, in a flash of brilliant insight and in direct violation of military procedure, the Captain ordered that the German national anthem be played over the speaker system. Because of the silence code, the Captain's officers were stunned. At first, they refused. Then, with some gentle urging, one weary sailor placed the old scratch-laden record on the record player. At first, one by one, then two by two, and finally the whole crew joined in the singing. With each measure, the strength, the determination, and even the courage of the crew returned as if it were a corpse being resurrected. They still faced the grim task at hand, but they were emboldened by their anthem, their music. In the end, they triumphed over their peril. Likewise, many managers need to know when morale is more important than procedure, how values can provide meaning and purpose, and why courage triumphs over all. They need to know when to play the music.[1]

Notes

1.   An interesting sidelight to this story is that the U.S. Army had, for years, lost international military contests that simulated small scale skirmishes. In 1987, they won two of the most prestigious contests, and, in part, they cited the use of rock and roll music in the training sessions as the reason. The songs played included the theme music for the movie *Top Gun* and Bruce Springsteen's "Born in the USA" (Fialka 1987).

FOUR

Managing Data, Information, Knowledge, and Action

Information is not a neutral product of organizational activity, but is a result of an inherently political activity—a political activity often hidden from those engaging in it largely due to presumed neutrality.

Stanley Deetz and Dennis Mumby

Business isn't complicated. The complications arise when people are cut off from information they need.

John F. Welch, Jr., CEO of General Electric

If information had nutritional labels, it would be intriguing to study a manager's dietary habits. The typical manager encounters a virtual smorgasbord of information. In fact, one commentator noted that "a weekday edition of the *New York Times* contains more information than the average person was likely to come across in a lifetime in seventeenth-century England" (Wurman 1989, p. 32). How do managers cope with this bountiful harvest? Some gorge themselves and face the inevitable consequences. Many subsist on informational McNuggets that are easily consumed but of little nutritional value. There are far too many managers who have grown fat on information, but are starved for knowledge. This chapter discusses how to manage data, information, and knowledge effectively to produce appropriate actions. Properly nourished organizations learn to shun bad habits and establish healthy ones. As surely as wise nutritional habits cultivate healthy bodies, wise data, information, and knowledge management practices cultivate healthy organizations.

Myths

Three commonly believed myths contribute to the difficulties in effectively managing data, information and knowledge.

Myth 1: More Data Is Better

Some managers, especially Circuit ones, tend to wait until "all" the data have been gathered and processed before making a decision. Such a posture can lead to unnecessary delays, unwarranted uncertainty, and missed opportunities (O'Reilly, Chatman, and Anderson 1987). Furthermore, there is a fundamental error in this kind of thinking: data can never provide a 100% guarantee of what the future holds; the picture is never complete. President Kennedy's father, Joe Kennedy, commented about Wall Street, "I always said that with enough inside information and unlimited credit, you are sure to go broke" (Martin 1983, p. 24). Indeed, data can provide only the mere illusion of certainty. At some point, leaps of faith, inferences, and even hunches must be used.

Sending a proposal to committee for further study or requesting more detailed analysis are often ways to delay decision making rather than to gather more accurate data. Walter B. Wriston (1986), former chief executive officer of Citicorp, has said, "Our ability to discern what is important and what is not may be impaired if we are inundated by a sea of numbers. Too many numbers may make the decision making process harder, not easier" (p. 65). Laboratory studies echo the theme by revealing that decision makers seek more data and information than they can possibly use, even to the point of hindering performance. The extra data, however, serve to "increase the decision maker's confidence. The net result may be that decision-makers arrive at poorer decisions but are more confident in their choices" (O'Reilly, Chatman, and Anderson 1987, p. 617).

Myth 2: Information Is a Commodity

Information can be bought and sold in the marketplace. In this sense information resembles a commodity. The similarity ends there, however. Information changes form when transmitted; commodities rarely do. Information is filtered when transmitted; commodities are not. Once sold, the seller no longer possesses the commodity. Not so with information: both the sender and receiver possess that "commodity." In short, information operates on the cognitive plane whereas commodities operate on the physical plane.

So what? Quite simply, problems occur when managers treat information as a commodity. Automobiles can be transferred from the manufacturer to the distributor, to the dealer, and finally to the customer without materially changing the car. Information "transferred" through a similar series of linkages would change dramatically. The automobile could even be given back to the manufacturer and still remain in basically the same condition. However, if information goes through a similar process, it is likely the original sender of the message would not even recognize the message. The transferal process does not change the essence of a commodity, but it does change the essence of information. In sum, information cannot be "transferred," only transmitted.

Myth 3: Information Is Knowledge

Information does not always translate into understanding. Knowledge goes beyond the facts; it connects and explains them. The "facts" often contradict one another; knowledge seeks to reconcile seemingly disparate findings. Consider the case of Rosalind Franklin, who studied the DNA molecule at Kings College in London during the 1950s. She was the first person to take clear X-ray–diffraction photographs of the B form of DNA. Yet she was not the one who won the Nobel Prize. That was Crick and Watson. The photograph was the final piece of the DNA puzzle, and Crick and Watson put it all together to form a working model of the DNA molecule (Watson 1968). Franklin had information, exceedingly important information, but Crick and Watson went further. They transformed information into knowledge. The elegant simplicity of the DNA structure, with all its implications for explaining sexual reproduction and controlling disease, unfolded because Watson and Crick knew how to use information. Crick reflected on why others did not discover the DNA structure:

> They missed the alpha helix because of that reflection! You see. And the fact that they didn't put the peptide bond in right. The point is that evidence can be unreliable, and therefore you should use as little of it as you can. And when we confront problems today, we're in exactly the same situation. We have three or four bits of data, we don't know which one is reliable, so we say, now if we discard that one and assume it's wrong—even though we have no evidence that it's wrong—then we can look at the rest of the data and see if we can make sense of that. And that's what we do all the time. I mean, people don't realize that not only can data be wrong in science, it can be misleading. There isn't such a thing as a hard fact when you're trying to discover something. It's only afterwards that the facts become hard. (Judson 1979, pp. 113–114)

In a similar vein, part of the task of a manager is to weigh the evidence, to evaluate the information, and sometimes to disregard it. All information is not equally relevant. Some crucial data may even be missing or unattainable. Assembling a lot of information is not enough. Plans, theories and models need to be set forth to organize the information. Hence the data begin to "make sense," to have meaning. Tests can be conducted, projections made. The wise manager seeks a more encompassing perspective by linking fact to fact, like some kind of conceptual scaffolding. Those who produce information are important, but the prizes usually go to those who can produce knowledge.

The D-I-K-A Model

Intuitively the relationship between data, information, knowledge, and action seems fairly clear. The detective solving the murder mystery provides a familiar template. The detective starts by examining the crime scene, interviewing potential witnesses, and researching various documents. These facts become the detective's database. Most of the data, such as the color of the victim's watch, prove irrelevant. But a few facts emerge that are particularly informative; they tell the detective something useful, such as the time of death. The plot thickens, and the detective starts thinking, ruminating, and theorizing. Columbo or Miss Marple puts all these tidbits together to form a theory of the crime, which they test out in wonderfully clever ways. Once confirmed, we know "whodunit." The final action sequence awaits. Then, the detective makes the theatrical arrest. In a nutshell, here is what happens: the detective gathers lots of data, some proves informative, which leads to an understanding or knowledge of what happened, and ultimately culminates in some sort of action.

This time-honored plot provides several useful insights. First, note the skills needed by the detective: data gathering, assessing data relevance, transforming data into information, managing information, transforming information into knowledge, creating knowledge out of limited facts, managing knowledge, transforming knowledge into action, and taking the right action. Effective managers need all these skills. Second, note that the detective uses a winnowing process, starting with a lot of data and ending with a single action. Likewise, effective managers must use a similar process in deciding how to respond wisely to organizational events. Finally, note the implicit definitions of the key concepts. Effective managers instinctively know the differences between data, information, and knowledge. More importantly, they know the limitations of data, information, and knowledge. The following section explores these implications in more depth.

Concepts

Figure 4.1 provides a model of the veteran detective or manager's view of the situation. Scholars debate the definitions of these terms, but for our purposes the concepts can be described as follows:

Data = Representations of reality.

The detective who observes that the victim wore a Citizen watch chooses to depict or represent the situation in a particular way. This representation, like all

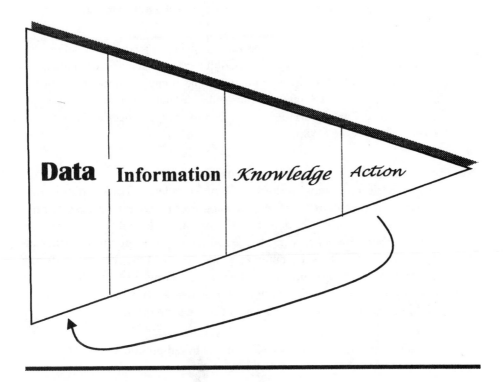

Figure 4.1. The D-I-K-A Model

others, may be flawed; the watch could be a fake. For a manager, data might be the results of a particular customer survey, which might be flawed as well.

Information = Data that provides relevant clues or news.

The detective needs to know the time of death because that provides relevant clues about who could have possibly committed the murder. The manager scanning the customer survey usually ignores most of the data, focusing instead on the key piece of news. Perhaps the manager is monitoring a particular issue about customer service. The manager, like the detective, focuses on data relevant to the problem at hand. But distinguishing the relevant from the irrelevant often presents some unique challenges. What might appear relevant at one time may or may not be relevant at another time. The color of the victim's watch may at some point provide the crucial piece of evidence to solve the mystery. Likewise, the manager may look back on the survey results and spot an important trend.

Knowledge = The framework or schema for organizing the relationships between pieces of information.

Two well-respected authors define knowledge in the following way:

> Knowledge is a fluid mix of framed experience, values, contextual information, and expert insight that provides a framework for evaluating and incorporating new experiences and information. It originates and is applied in the minds of knowers. In organizations, it often becomes embedded not only in documents or repositories but also in organizational routines, processes, practices, and norms. (Davenport and Prusak 1998, p. 5)

Note how they define knowledge in a personal and subjective way. There is something elusive, subtle, or perhaps mysterious about knowledge. The key may be that the knowledgeable person or organization recognizes patterns that are often too difficult to capture in words. The detective, for instance, takes all the relevant facts and pieces together a theory of what happened the night of the murder (they always happen at night). Likewise, a manager might connect the survey results to a particular management decision made months ago. How does the detective or manager learn to make the right connections? Scholars, consultants, and executives still do not have a satisfactory answer. But we keep on trying.

Action = The deeds or decisions made based on knowledge.

Easy enough—for the detective. Once she figures out who committed the murder, she arrests the culprit. It is not so easy for the manager. Figuring out what went wrong may be only half the battle. Correcting the problem in the proper way through a new policy, procedure, or perhaps a personnel change requires special insight.

Relationships

These definitions are necessarily a bit fuzzy. That should not be a surprise. After all, philosophers have debated about the true nature of knowledge for eons. Nevertheless these distinctions can provide insight into the pragmatic problems facing managers. In particular, learning how to effectively manage the relationships between the variables proves useful.

Managers, like detectives, can discover how to analyze critically the whirlwind of reports, opinions, rumors, and numbers spinning around them by making conceptual distinctions between data, information, and knowledge. Some data will be assimilated, some discarded. Some information will be integrated into the manager's thinking, some filed away for another day. And knowledge of a situation may or may not be acted on. The D-I-K-A model assumes fluid feedback between the various phases. For instance, the detective may arrest a person, only to discover that after this action a similar crime is committed. This situation creates new data and information that needs to be assimilated into the detective's mental model. Likewise, a manager may try to control customer complaints by a policy change, only to create even more customer dissatisfaction. In essence the action sets in motion a whole new D-I-K-A cycle.

Skills

Effective managers master the special skills associated with each phase of the D-I-K-A model. The skills of data management rest on understanding the nature of data. The notion of "representation of reality" provides the key to understanding the inherent characteristics of data. Representations are partial and based on human perceptions.

Even the scientist must recognize the inherent limits of quantitative data. One thoughtful scientist, Abraham Kaplan (1963), made the following observation:

> The fact is that no human perception is immaculate, certainly no perception of any significance for science. Even if perception itself were immaculate, the perceptual report exposes us to sin, as a necessary consequence of the way in which language works. (pp. 131–132)

Managers who believe in "immaculate perception" in essence assert their own divinity and are destined to an unenviable fate. Such a belief leads to a false sense of security and certainty that precludes looking at a situation from various perspectives. A mousetrap works because the mouse believes that cheese is cheese. Of course, data, like cheese, is not just data. Data are always gathered for certain reasons, from different perspectives, and reported in particular contexts, which alters their nature and meaning. Failing to recognize this can lead to making uninformed decisions, prematurely ending discussions, stifling innovative ideas, and even falling into seductive political traps. In short, data are not divinely conceived; they have all the stains and scars of distinctively human hands.

Likewise, the skills of information management rest on understanding the true nature of information. Reporters often pride themselves on their objectivity, but their assertion lacks credibility upon closer examination. Reporters, like managers, have to determine what constitutes the news, the story. The choice itself reflects the values of the reporter. Why does the fiery crash of an automobile get reported on the evening news, but not the successful blood drive at a local business? The choices are guided by the values of the reporter, which are usually not readily apparent. The values, in turn, influence what is seen, heard, and reported—what constitutes information. So, too, with managers. Assumptions underlie all observations. These assumptions or values determine "what counts" and "what does not count" as information. Choices are made about what is important and what is not. In short, all information is value-laden.

Data and information can be more easily stored, processed, and shared than knowledge. The skills of knowledge management rest in finding ways to transform implicit schemas and frameworks into something explicit. Rules of thumb can capture a portion of an expert's knowledge base, but skilled teachers and coaches provide the most effective way to transmit knowledge.

The skills of "action" are closely related to knowledge management skills, because they evolve out of knowing "how to get things done." Traditional management functions, such as planning, organizing, leading, controlling, and motivating, also play a central role in the final stage.

Table 4.1 summarizes the D-I-K-A model, addressing the special combination of people, research, and intellectual skills managers need to acquire, along with requirements for producing, transmitting, and storing data, information, knowledge, and action.

Variations on the Model

I would love to say that the D-I-K-A model actually describes what happens in most organizations. Unfortunately, it does not. Organizations do not typically process data and information like the detective or scientist. Why? There are a number of reasons, including office politics, time pressures, and uneducated workers. Another way to look at these issues is to think about data, information, knowledge, and action as blocks that can be arranged in any order, disregarding some when it is appropriate. Some pretty interesting relationships emerge. A few of the more typical ones are discussed below:

The D-I-K Loop

Academic and government organizations demonstrate a peculiar fondness for this arrangement. Here is how it works: The chancellor of a university, for example, commissions a study on faculty productivity. A committee dutifully develops a survey and generates data, which yields some interesting information. The committee reports that some departments produce a lot more than do others. The interpretation of the information becomes pivotal. How does this finding fit into existing frameworks and prejudices? Well, it does not fit in. The low producers do not like the results, so they want a new study conducted. The process starts over again, looping back to the data-gathering stage. Notice that action *per se* never occurs—only the appearance of it. To summarize: lots of activity, but no action. And that is why some organizations appear to be very busy, but never accomplish anything.

The K-A Loop

Will Rogers once said, "It ain't the things that people don't know that's the problem. It's the things they do know that just ain't so." He perfectly described the mindset of those stuck in a K-A loop. They are not open to new information or interpretations. They are so stuck on what they know or what they think they know that nothing changes the way they respond to particular situations. Sometime this

TABLE 4.1 Summary of the D-I-K-A Model

	Data	Information	Knowledge	Action
What is an example?	▷ Victim's time of death	▷ Timeline of victim's activities	▷ Theory of the crime	▷ Arrest of the murder suspect
	▷ Stock price	▷ Stock performance update	▷ Advice from stockbrokers (Hopefully, they have a good theory!)	▷ Stock purchase
What form does it typically take?	▷ Numbers ▷ Impressions	▷ Facts ▷ Tables ▷ Charts	▷ Stories ▷ Rules of thumb ▷ Theories ▷ Models	▷ Action plans ▷ Procedures ▷ Recipes
How do you measure if it is effective?	▷ Timely ▷ Accurate	▷ Relevant ▷ Timely ▷ Accessible	▷ Applicable ▷ Synthesized ▷ Explanatory ▷ Predictive	▷ Resolving
What skills do you need?	▷ Generate ▷ Gather ▷ Research ▷ Store	▷ Filter ▷ Organize ▷ Analyze ▷ Distribute ▷ Interpret	▷ Think critically ▷ Communicate ▷ Analyze ▷ Synthesize	▷ Plan ▷ Motivate ▷ Lead ▷ Communicate
What is required to produce it?	▷ Some expertise	▷ Some expertise	▷ Much experience and expertise	▷ Some experience and expertise
How difficult is it to transmit?	▷ Easy	▷ Moderately easy	▷ Difficult	▷ Moderately difficult
What is the best way to store it?	▷ Computers ▷ Web pages	▷ Computers ▷ Databases ▷ Books, journals, etc.	▷ Experts	▷ Employees
What are typical organizational problems?	▷ Poor research skills ▷ Information overload	Lack of: ▷ Timeliness ▷ Access ▷ Distribution networks ▷ Organization	▷ Few venues for sharing ▷ Inadequate storage	▷ Resistance to change ▷ Uneven follow-through ▷ Ineffective communication

works; more often it does not. Consider, for instance, the stereotypical iconoclastic inventor who refuses to give up on an idea, even in the face of contradictory evidence. He insists that if he tinkers a little longer it will work. On occasion, his determination leads to some stunning achievement. More often, it leads nowhere. All the tinkering in the world cannot transform a fundamentally unsound idea into a smart one. Zealots caught in the K-A loop believe they possess "the truth," and nothing can dissuade them. This, of course, generates both their appeal and threat.

The I-A Loop

Managers caught up in the "program of the month" cycle unwittingly create an I-A loop. Here is how it works:

Step 1: They read about the latest management fad.
Step 2: They seize on a compelling fact about how the fad improves productivity, morale, commitment, and so forth.
Step 3: They implement the program.
Step 4: They return to step one.

The result is a workplace that spawns an endless supply of story lines for the Dilbert cartoon strip. Employees in these organizations become frustrated and respond cynically to the latest initiative. No one clearly thinks about how the new program fits with existing strategy and organizational culture. Information (the fad) leads to action, not knowledge of *how* the fad fits in with the big picture. Consequently, the managers look exactly like the dolts parodied in the Dilbert strip: they do stupid things because they do not think about the meaning of the information.

Clearly, we could discuss more patterns that might emerge, but I will leave those exciting discoveries to the inquisitive reader. The larger lesson is simple. Perceptive managers learn first to recognize the emergent organizational pattern and then determine the strengths and weaknesses of the pattern. Finally, the manager needs to decide whether or not the pattern produces the desired outcomes. Some patterns clearly breed frustration, like the I-A loop. Ideally, wise managers use the D-I-K-A loop or some related variant. Therefore, the remaining sections of the chapter discuss how to strategically manage the key relationships implied in the model.

Managing the Data-Information Relationship

Effectively managing the data-information relationship requires the generation of timely and accurate data that can be transformed into relevant information. A wristwatch meets all three criteria.

Timely: When you want the information you simply turn your wrist.
Accurate: Most watches provide enough precision to be useful.
Relevant: Knowing the time allows you to plan, organize and
           accomplish tasks.

A wristwatch does not overwhelm us with irrelevant data; most are not synchro-nized with the atomic clock. It is also easy to maintain, access, and purchase. It is not expensive. Almost everyone has one, styled according to their wants and syn-chronized to their time zone. In short, the wristwatch provides the ideal template for the characteristics of an effective data-information management system.

Sounds great. But how do managers put together such a system? After all, be-fore the wristwatch was the sundial, the town crier, and the clock tower. The lesson is that effective data-information systems evolve over time. The following strate-gies may not make managers digital watchmakers, but they may, at least, allow them to move the evolutionary clock forward.

Determine What Employees Really Need to Know

Employees seem to have an insatiable desire for information (Goldhaber et al. 1978). In communication assessments, we asked employees to indicate how much information they currently received on a wide range of subjects versus the amount of information they wanted to receive. Remarkably, employees wanted more in-formation in *every* topic area. Employees are naturally curious about their organi-zation. Part of the problem is that employees assume that those in management know about changes far in advance, which is not always the case. Effective manag-ers learn to distinguish between desires and needs. Providing all the informa-tion employees desire may prove to be costly and ultimately debilitating to the or-ganization; therefore, priority must be given to certain types of information. Our research has shown that employees most frequently complain about not being in-formed of changes, decisions, and future plans. Another survey found that em-ployees are highly interested in the organization's future plans, productivity im-provements, and personnel policies (Foehrenbach and Rosenberg 1982).[1] These findings, presented in Table 4.2, provide some target areas. Expert data-information managers must become sensitive to the particular needs of their col-leagues, and not burden them with unnecessary data and information.

Find Ways to Increase the Efficiency of
Data and Information Transmission

Some relatively simple measures can improve employees' ability to process data and information efficiently. Consider the following questions:

TABLE 4.2 Subjects of Most and Least Interest to Employees

Rank	Subject	% Very Interested or Interested
1	Organizational plans for the future	95.3
2	Productivity improvements	90.3
3	Personnel policies and practices	89.8
4	Job-related information	89.2
5	Job advancement opportunities	87.9
6	Effect of external events on my job	87.8
7	How my job fits into the organization	85.4
8	Operations outside of my department or division	85.1
9	How we're doing vs. the competition	83.0
10	Personnel changes and promotions	81.4
11	Organizational community involvement	81.3
12	Organizational stand on current issues	79.5
13	How the organization uses its profits	78.4
14	Advertising/promotional plans	77.2
15	Financial results	76.4
16	Human interest stories about other employees	70.4
17	Personal news (birthdays, anniversaries, etc.)	57.0

▷ Can the physical setting be changed to improve information-processing capabilities? For example, ergonomically designed chairs have been shown to increase productivity.

▷ Can office noise and distractions be decreased?

▷ Can the physical layout of the office be changed to increase or decrease certain types of information flow?

▷ Can audiotapes be used to brief employees while they drive?

▷ Can the phone system be made more efficient with new features?

▷ Can regularly requested information be put into a handy Q/A form or brochure?

Managers also may want to look at improving efficiency from another angle as well. A number of consumer products have started to harness the power of what might be called Product Embedded Information (PEI) and Just-in-Time Information (JITI). Consider these minor wonders:

▷ A washing machine that rings a bell upon completion of the cycle.

▷ A toothbrush that lets the user know when it's time for a replacement.

▷ A word-processing package that provides a timely tip during a critical operation.

In each case, relevant information arrives at just the right time for the user. The information also is embedded right in the product, so that the users do not have to locate the relevant fact in some long-ago misplaced manual or flyer. Likewise, managers can harness the power of JITI and PEI by reviewing current data and information practices.

One university heeded this advice. They published a weekly one-page flyer detailing the campus events, and distributed it in boxes located throughout the campus. The staff, however, was not satisfied with the readership level. Two simple changes almost doubled readership. First, some of the distribution boxes were strategically relocated in higher traffic zones. Second, every week the color of the publication was changed. Previously, the information sheet was printed on plain white paper and students rushing through the halls could not be sure if it was new information or just last week's news. The color change from week-to-week provided that information at a glance; the product became embedded with critical information.

Technology can also help. Cisco Systems saves millions of dollars every year by handling a remarkable 80% of customer service issues through its web site (Reinhardt 1999). Customers receive information just in time and do not have to wait for a customer service representative to answer the phone. Personnel are freed to handle more complex matters, rather than merely routine information requests.

Table 4.3 provides some questions that managers can pose to help them implement JITI and PEI practices. Other methods may prove equally useful. But be cautious; improving efficiency often involves some unpleasant tradeoffs. Web sites, for instance, can be confining and frustrating for customers or employees with unique needs.

Pay Attention to the Form of Information

Form may be as important as substance. Images are powerful communication vehicles. They can summarize or capture a great deal of information easily and quickly. The complex can be made simple. Some information simply cannot be made meaningful without the use of imagery. There are two principle uses of imagery: to personalize information and to summarize quantitative information.

The Tropicana ad in Figure 4.2 is an excellent example of how imagery can be used to personalize information. There are many ways to state the ad's essential message that "Tropicana orange juice is fresh." Tropicana, for instance, could explain the juice abstraction process. Although such an approach may prove enlightening, it fails to arouse the senses. Perhaps various consumers could testify as to the freshness of Tropicana. Yet the emotions are still not aroused by this approach. The beauty of the straw-and-orange imagery is that everyone can relate to it. Clearly, no one can use a straw to extract juice from an orange. No one, that is, ex-

TABLE 4.3 Efficient Information Management Practices

Creating JITI Management Practices	Creating PEI Management Practices
Can a web site be structured to provide employees with relevant information to meet their needs?	Can machinery instructions be located on the equipment rather than in a manual?
Can reports (e.g., benefits information, customer complaints, etc.) be generated when employees desire them?	Can forms include instructions on the document instead of on a separate enclosure?
Can employees have more direct access to their personnel records?	Can different types of written messages be color coded by priority or urgency level?
Can tracking systems be developed to more accurately monitor the progress of a project or purchase order? (Think about a system like the UPS tracking system.)	Can simple screening devices be used to eliminate "junk mail?"
Can reliance on interoffice mail systems be reduced in favor of e-mail attachments?	Can "help screens" be incorporated into a computer program or web site?
Can those who desire information serve their own needs, like in a supermarket?	Can products be designed to recognize and adjust to different users?

cept Tropicana. Through the imagery, consumers can see, feel, and taste the freshness of Tropicana juice.[2] The image is vivid.

Images can be created verbally as well. For example, President Theodore Roosevelt's response to his critics, "I have about as much desire to annex more islands as a boa constrictor has to swallow a porcupine," conveys something more than a simple denial (Morris 1979, p. 13). It has power and verve. There is no doubt where he stands on this issue. In short, the well-conceived image can often be more captivating than reams of statistical data or a finely honed argument.

The graphs that effectively capture quantitative data provide another powerful communication tool. In his marvelous treatise *The Visual Display of Quantitative Data* (1983), Edward R. Tufte notes,

> Modern data graphics can do much more than simply substitute for small statistical tables. At their best, graphics are instruments for reasoning about quantitative information. Often the most effective way to describe, explore, and summarize a set of numbers—even a very large set—is to look at pictures of those numbers. Furthermore, of all methods for analyzing and communicating statistical information, well-designed data graphics are usually the simplest and at the same time the most powerful. (p. 1)

For instance, three scientists developed one graphic, Figure 4.3, depicting the results of over 200 experiments assessing the thermal conductivity of copper (Ho, Powell, and Liley 1974). There is probably no better way to summarize the results of that much research.

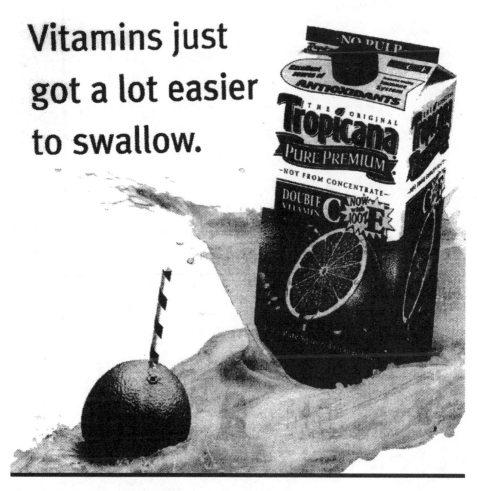

Vitamins just got a lot easier to swallow.

Figure 4.2. Tropicana Diagram

Graphics software makes creating visual images of data relatively easy. Yet, as with any powerful tool, graphics as well as imagery can be misused. There is some evidence to show that using graphics that are not accompanied by precise figures can actually undermine managerial confidence in decision making (Sullivan 1988). The sword cuts both ways. Information of import can be overlooked, and the trivial can appear important. The wise manager recognizes this while still knowing that the form of the information may be as important as the substance. Or, as Isadora Duncan, the famous ballerina, once said, "If I could tell you what it meant there would be no point in dancing it" (Comstock 1974, p. 226).

Be Wary of Data or Information Filtered
Through a Chain of Communicators

The more links in the communication chain, the greater the likelihood that information passed along the chain will be distorted and context stripped away. The

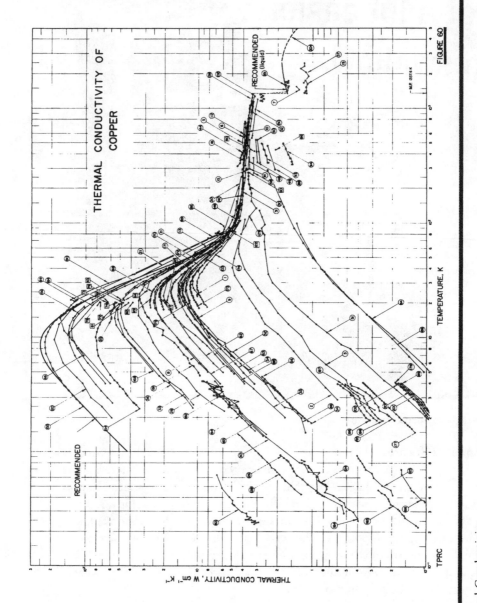

Figure 4.3. Thermal Conductivity
Reprinted by permission from Ho, Powell, and Liley (1974).

86

child at the end of the line in the game of telephone receives the least accurate and usually briefest message. Organizations are no different, except the results can be more tragic. Indeed, on a cold January morning, the civilized world was shocked by the fiery disaster that befell the Space Shuttle Challenger. The television pictures recorded in gruesome detail what the mind could not comprehend. In due course, the sorrow and grief gave way to inquiry and investigation. There was really one central but tough question: Was the disaster the price of innovation or carelessness?

There may never be a definitive answer. Perhaps carelessness, as defined in hindsight, is always part of the innovative process. Yet the commission did find flaws—fatal ones. One of the critical findings was that messages sent up the chain of command became severely distorted. In particular, engineers from both Rockwell and Thiokol were deeply alarmed about the impact of ice on the shuttle launch. Consider the following sequence of exchanges:

1. Rockwell engineers reported to their superiors that they did not have a proper database on how the shuttle would perform at temperatures below freezing. They concluded that the situation created an "unquantifiable hazard."
2. Two Rockwell vice presidents reported to NASA that "Rockwell cannot be 100% sure that it is safe to fly."
3. The Director of the National Space Transportation System reported to his team that "Rockwell did not ask or insist that we not launch." He "felt reasonably confident that the launch should proceed."
4. NASA's associate administrator, who was in charge of the final decision, stated, "I never thought the ice presented a serious safety problem." (McConnell 1987, p. 229)

This sad tale vividly illustrates the fundamental communication principle about what happens to a message as it is passed from person to person. The distortion occurs quite naturally, because people have different responsibilities, beliefs, and concerns. Details are omitted. Some are highlighted. Inferences become facts. Even something as permanent as a written memo can be interpreted differently at various levels of an organization. Priorities can shift. Nuances are lost. Indeed, NASA felt so much pressure for a launch that they actively discouraged any messages that might call for a delay. Two scholars summed up the situation aptly: "Messages in serial reproduction, like water in a great river, change through losses, gains, absorptions, and combinations along the route from the headwaters to their final destination" (Pace and Boren 1973, p. 137).

Generate Both Hard and Soft Data

Data comes in a variety of forms. Corporate decisions are increasingly based on "hard data," or quantitative output. Statistical decision making has become the vogue. Although a useful tool, the hard approach has its limitations. Music cannot really be understood or appreciated through statistical analyses. Likewise, a problem cannot be fully understood or an opportunity realized with information gleaned from a spiritless set of statistics. Few people appreciate the rich wealth of information that lies silently at their fingertips, like some obscure composer's score waiting to be discovered. In sum, the wise manager listens to the right brain as well as the left.

One of the most potent ways to understand any phenomenon is to examine the metaphors used to describe it. Jonathan Miller notes that great strides were made in understanding how the human heart works when the dominant metaphor changed from a furnace to a pump (Miller 1978). This switch in perspective opened a new realm of explanations, theories, and treatments. Metaphors make reasonable what was heretofore unreasonable. They simplify the complex. They provide a structure for the experience of phenomena. And they highlight key attributes and obscure others. After all, the human heart looks no more like a pump than a furnace. But there is a price; different conceptions go unseen and old visions are eclipsed by the new. Unmasking the dominant metaphor reveals the way it implicitly structures information and knowledge. Thus, we can more fully understand the strengths and weaknesses of any particular conception.

The organizational environment offers a cornucopia of captivating metaphors (see, for example, Morgan 1986). The military metaphor is one of the more predominant. "Orders" are given and "carried out." If not, the "troops are reprimanded" for "insubordination." This metaphor, a favorite of Arrow managers, naturally underscores the importance of the "chain of command" and stresses hierarchical relationships between the "ranks." Consequently, messages are transferred like supplies, and information is treated like a commodity. The favorite organizational metaphor of the Circuit manager is the family. Difficulties arise when the "lines" of communication are not "open." Families resolve conflicts by "talking through their differences." After all, one cannot be "discharged" from the family like they can in the army.

The same type of metaphoric analysis can be applied to a whole range of other organizational practices. One telemarketing company had a room in which sales calls were regularly monitored by management. Employees referred to it as the "spy room." The image was completed with certain "spies" on the staff and a "need-to-know" communication policy. Amazingly, when the corporate executives were told about the metaphor, they simply laughed and dismissed it as trivial. But such characterizations revealed both the intensity and depth of employees' feelings; they felt deeply mistrusted by management. If taken seriously, this captivating metaphor could have been more useful to management than any detailed analysis of an employee survey.

Every organization has operative metaphors. Managers should be concerned about the unforeseen consequences of an undetected metaphor. Why? Because particular metaphors may narrow employees' vision, cutting off potentially rich sources of information and possibilities. We shape our metaphors and, after that, they shape us. Although most managers pay little or no attention to the subtle workings of the imagery, the wise manager recognizes the need for both "hard" and "soft" information.

Recognize and Manage All
the Information Networks

Every organization has two basic information networks: formal and informal. These networks may complement, conflict with, or work independently of one another. Ideally the most important information comes through formal channels. Sadly, this is rarely the case. Employees often express dissatisfaction with receiving news from the grapevine, and in some organizations even report that this is the major communication channel. One survey of employees in nearly 300 organizations found the grapevine to be the second most frequent source of information. But the grapevine was ranked last in terms of the methods preferred (Foehrenbach and Goldfarb 1990, p. 7). Supervisors were the most preferred source. Moreover, numerous communication assessments have shown that the grapevine is the only information channel from which employees desire to receive *less* instead of *more* information.

Why, then, is the grapevine used so frequently? First, it is amazingly fast. One employee said news "spreads like wildfire" in her organization. This is not uncommon. Second, informal channels provide outlets when formal channels are clogged. There are rarely information vacuums in organizations. When crises occur or changes are pending, employees usually seek out any information that helps reduce their uncertainty. Moreover, the grapevine may satisfy affiliation needs not met through formal channels. Third, the grapevine carries a great deal of information. In one organization, employees reported hearing about "everything" through the grapevine, including promotions, salary adjustments, layoffs, and merit raises. This smorgasbord of information provides a virtual feast for the curious employee. Finally, despite the fact that most employees distrust the grapevine, it tends to be fairly accurate. A number of researchers have shown that information gleaned from the grapevine is 80% to 90% accurate (Davis 1972). The problem, of course, is that even a small error can have dramatic consequences.

When informal channels are overused, poor quality information can circulate throughout the organization. When this occurs, all the inevitable consequences spring forth: unwarranted anxiety, poor decisions, low morale, perceptions of favoritism, and lower productivity. Moreover, the overuse of informal channels by management may send powerful secondary, albeit unintended, messages to employees—messages such as "We don't have time to communicate with you," translate into, "We don't respect you enough to provide you with formal information." Although employees tend to understand management time constraints, they may still have a feeling of discontent. Parents will sometimes withhold information from their children, but employees expect to be treated respectfully like adults. There is no more effective way to send this message than through honest, official, and formal communication.

Managing the Information-Knowledge Relationship

Managing the information-knowledge relationship requires the ability to judge, analyze, evaluate, and synthesize. Two scholars, with backgrounds in accounting, discovered that

> successful managers develop the ability to collect and use diverse, ambiguous, and sometimes contradictory information effectively and efficiently. They develop the capacity to evaluate the reliability of information by considering its source and their experience with that source. More frequently than not, that source is not the accounting systems in place in the firm. They develop the ability to know where to go to ask crucial questions about information that intrigues or troubles them. (McKinnon and Bruns 1992, p. 15)

In other words, successful managers learn how to transform information into knowledge. How do they do it? To some extent this remains a mystery, but we know that these managers use rules of thumb such as the ones described below.

Consider the Source's Credibility

Like it or not, every message has a kind of credibility tag attached to it that determines, to a large extent, how that message will be treated. Because there are more messages than people, credibility provides an efficient screening mechanism. All messages emanating from a single source can be lumped together for assessment. In essence, credibility acts as a labeling system, tagging messages with "Pay Attention to Me," "Ignore Me," or "I May Be True."

For example, Albert Einstein, at the urgings of his colleagues, wrote his famous letter to President Roosevelt encouraging the development of the atomic bomb. Einstein's prestige as a scientist assured that the letter would be considered at the highest levels of government. Others might have presented the same message, but the President might not have read it or treated it seriously. The "Einstein tag" on the message signalled, "Highly Important Information. Read Me!" Students will dutifully listen as the teacher reflects on the importance of having a professional-looking resume, but when a personnel director for Microsoft relates the same message the students do more than nod their heads. Messages cannot be separated from people, because the source forms part of the context.

Who creates the data and sends the information also may provide an important insight into its reliability, validity, and utility. Some messages never get transmitted because of who gathers the information. One of the top salespersons of a large pharmaceutical corporation quit her job in disgust over the practices of her immediate supervisor's boss. During the exit interview, when she was asked why she quit the job, she forthrightly told of her legitimate grievances about the situation. Yet the information never reached the personnel office or the people who could do something about the problem. The reason was that the immediate supervisor conducted the interview, and he had to forward the report to this very person. On the exit interview form, under the question about why the employee was leaving, the supervisor wrote, "Personal reasons."

Be Aware of How the Hierarchy Affects the
Flow and Availability of Information

The law of gravity does not apply to information flow in organizations. Information held at the top of the organizational hierarchy (e.g., financial results, pending mergers, etc.) does not always filter down. And some information, such as major success stories, held in the lower echelons shows exceptional buoyancy in reaching the top, almost as if defying the laws of gravity. Effective managers know that the hierarchy inherently filters information.

Researchers have recently confirmed what Sir Winston Churchill (1931) noted long ago:

> The temptation to tell a Chief in a great position the things he most likes to hear is one of the commonest explanations of mistaken policy. Thus the outlook of the leader on whose decision fateful events depend is usually far more sanguine than the brutal facts admit. (p. 673)

Sending the good news up is only natural for those who wish to get ahead in the organization. "This tendency is so strong," write O'Reilly, Chatman, and Anderson (1987), "that subordinates who do not trust their superior are willing to suppress unfavorable information even if they know that such information is useful for decision making." (p. 612). Therefore, managers should be wary of excessively glowing reports.

Acknowledge What You Do Not Know

Why acknowledge what you do not know? This creates the proper climate for a dialogue in which knowledge can be shared and created. Managers who know a lot of facts might be considered intelligent, but those who also know what they *do not* know are considered wise. We could call this kind of insight "knowledgeable ignorance," representing the known unknowns. The manager or the organization realizes that something is missing. Knowing the right questions, even if the answers are elusive, blazes the trail to enlightenment. Saul Wurman (1989), who "reinvented the guidebook" and restructured the Pacific Bell SMART Yellow Pages, said, "My expertise is my ignorance. I ask the obvious questions, the ones everyone else is embarrassed to ask because they are so obvious" (p. 45). As a youngster,

Albert Einstein asked, "What would it be like to ride on a beam of light?" Later in life, he provided the answer—the theory of relativity. Jacob Bronowski said, "The hardest part is not to answer, but to conceive the question. The genius of men like Newton and Einstein lies in that they ask transparent, innocent questions which turn out to have catastrophic answers" (Bronowski 1973, p. 247). Asking penetrating questions provides the scientist as well as the manager with the ultimate tool for creating knowledge.

Managers often unwittingly fall into an information trap. By devoting so much of their time to processing information already generated, they often fail to devote time to asking the insightful questions. An illusion can emerge that they already have all the necessary information. Walter Wriston (1986) put it this way: "Since we are the prisoners of what we know, often we are unable to even imagine what we don't know" (p. 66). Wise managers do not let the existing information obscure their vision of the more fundamental issues. They acknowledge their ignorance. Although the answers may not be easily unveiled, at least a more sober view of a situation or decision may be taken. And perhaps a brilliant insight or theory may even emerge.

Reconcile the Tension Between Facts and Theory

The quintessential detective, Sherlock Holmes, said in his first adventure, "A scandal in Bohemia," "I have no data yet. It is a capital mistake to theorize before one has data. Insensibly one begins to twist facts to suit theories, instead of theories to suit facts" (Doyle 1978, p. 1). In contrast, the quintessential physicist, Albert Einstein, felt that if the evidence did not agree with the theory, then the evidence must be faulty. Such a perspective might explain why Einstein slept in peace and confidence the night his general theory of relativity was being experimentally tested (Clark 1971). But what does a physicist's ruminations or Sherlock Holmes's imagination have to do with the world of management? In a word, much.

Managers often face the unavoidable tension between the "facts" and the "theory." The facts can contradict the strategic plan (the theory) and vice versa. For example, the market surveys (the facts) showed there was no market for the Xerox machine. Yet the marketing model suggested that the device seemed like a sure winner. The model was clearly right; The "facts" were incorrect.

But sometimes the model or theory is faulty. A tenacious belief in the theory despite evidence to the contrary can be disastrous. In theory, the Sargent York tank should have been a good weapon. Even after repeated evidence of holes in the theory, more money was spent on the project. In the end, the tank design was abandoned, having accrued a net loss of $1.8 billion. The facts were right, the theory faulty (Biddle 1986).

One of the great ironies is that often, the more money spent on a project, the more credible the idea becomes, regardless of the "evidence." The battle cry becomes, "It must be good; we paid a lot for it" or "We can't be wrong; after all, we spent so much time on it." **The implicit but incorrect assumption is that money or**

time spent translates into theory confirmed. The actual reason money and time are spent is because no one wants to admit that a mistake has been made. The same faulty reasoning can explain an overdependence on the evidence. Not only are money, time, and effort tied up with our theories, but also our passions, values, and reputations.

Which should the manager trust—the theory or the facts? There are no easy answers to that question. As a starting point, managers need to keep an objective distance from both the evidence and theories. But that is difficult. Perhaps the only safe course is to have a clear sense of the nature of theory and proof. Two important notions should be mentioned.

First, evidence inherently reflects a bias. There are always more questions than answers. Consequently, we make choices about what information *is* and *is not* important to generate. But what is reported both blinds and enlightens. Sometimes the difficulty is not that the wrong answers have been found, but that the wrong questions have been asked. Perhaps the marketing analysts for Xerox asked the wrong questions, the wrong people, or both.

Second, a good model has a simplicity, an elegance, and even a beauty about it. Scientists have long marveled at the simple elegance of the DNA molecule or even the theory of relativity. Einstein even dismissed certain ideas because they were not "beautiful enough." Likewise, business plans, strategies, and designs that are theoretically sound have a certain elegance and simplicity about them. Steven Jobs commented about the design plan for the MacIntosh computer:

> If you read Apple's first brochure, the headline was, "Simplicity is the Ultimate Sophistication." What we meant by that was that when you first attack a problem it seems really simple because you do not understand it. Then when you start to really understand it, you come up with these very complicated solutions because it's really hairy. Most people stop there. But a few people keep burning the midnight oil and finally understand the underlying principles of the problem and come up with an elegantly simple solution for it. But very few people go the distance to get there.[4]

The wise manager, of course, goes that distance.

Organize the Same Information in Different Ways to Extract the Underlying Meaning

The organization of information significantly alters the meaning gleaned from it. Different relationships can be highlighted; different meanings discovered. For example, Figure 4.4a provides the raw data for five employee performance ratings. Figure 4.4b underscores the differences between them, by ranking them from highest to lowest. Yet, using the same data, when the employees are individually plotted, they all appear above-average, as seen in Figure 4.4c. In Figure 4.4d, no real pattern seems to emerge from the same data. But displaying the average ratings by

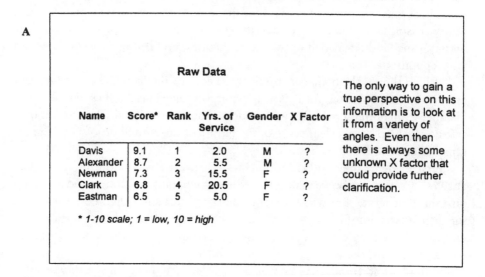

Figure 4.4a–e. Different Ways to Organize the Same Information

gender, as seen in Figure 4.4e, almost begs the viewer to draw a conclusion. The structure of the information acts like the mirrors at carnivals; one stretches the reflection up and down, the other side to side. It is the same image, but different parts are accentuated causing the spectator to have dramatically different perceptions.

Managing the Knowledge-Action Relationship

Knowing what to do and doing it are two very different things. In one study of over 350 organizational decisions, only 50% of the decisions made were ever fully implemented and sustained (Nutt 1999, p. 75). Why? One commentator explained, "Managers know what to do to improve performance, but actually ignore or act in

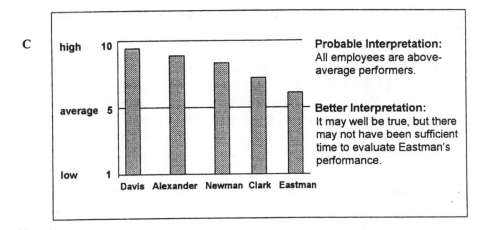

C

Probable Interpretation:
All employees are above-average performers.

Better Interpretation:
It may well be true, but there may not have been sufficient time to evaluate Eastman's performance.

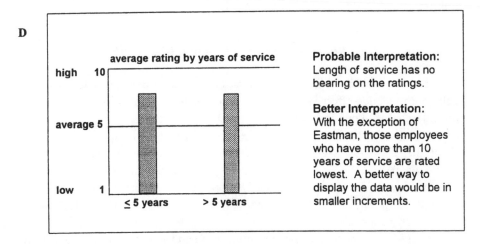

D

Probable Interpretation:
Length of service has no bearing on the ratings.

Better Interpretation:
With the exception of Eastman, those employees who have more than 10 years of service are rated lowest. A better way to display the data would be in smaller increments.

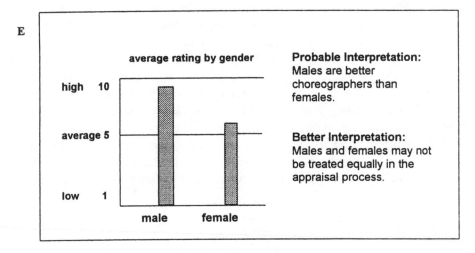

E

Probable Interpretation:
Males are better choreographers than females.

Better Interpretation:
Males and females may not be treated equally in the appraisal process.

Figure 4.4a–e. Continued

contradiction to either their strongest instincts or the data available to them" (Cohen 1998, p. 30). Consider the case of Southwest Airlines, as described by one scholar:

> Southwest Airlines is a firm that uses fairly simple business practices that are widely known, but it continues to have the best financial performance in the airline industry. Numerous books, case studies, and television shows have described Southwest's management approach, but the firm's competitors have either not tried to imitate what it does or, when they have, like the United Shuttle did, they have not been nearly as successful as Southwest. (Pfeffer and Sutton 1999a, p. 87)

Clearly, bridging the chasm between knowledge and action requires special skills. Effective managers learn to transform knowledge into action through a combination of experience and critical thinking. Experience comes with time, but critical thinking can be more finely honed by heeding the notions discussed below.

Create Strategic Knowledge-Sharing Communities

For years, scholars, commentators, and consultants have grappled with how to share knowledge effectively. Some have advocated establishing vast organizational databases. They did not work out. Others have suggested that corporate intranets provided the answer. They failed, as well. As one thoughtful scholar and consultant, Thomas Davenport (1997), concluded, "Knowledge is often sprawling and messy, and the ways in which knowledge workers use it are manifold and unpredictable. More to the point, early attempts to 'engineer' knowledge have often failed" (p. 18). To sum up, knowing how to share knowledge effectively remains a fairly elusive goal.

Strategic knowledge-sharing communities seem to unravel at least part of the mystery. These communities are created in organizations as a strategic asset to facilitate knowledge-sharing. They are strategic, because they focus on broader goals than a task force. The agendas, procedures, and direction tend to be rather fluid and dynamic (Wenger and Snyder 2000). One such community allows supervisors to get together every two weeks for an hour to discuss major issues, share "war stories," and discuss problem-solving tactics. Other organizations, such as Xerox, bring together groups of greater diversity, but the goal remains the same. Two commentators who made an extensive study of such communities note that "a strategic community forms and shares knowledge by 'pulling' individual members into an environment in which they learn from each other" (Storck and Hill 2000, p. 73). They also found that these communities often yield benefits, such as

▷ Higher quality knowledge creation
▷ Fewer surprises and revisions in plans
▷ Greater capacity to deal with uncertainty

▷ Increased likelihood that decisions will be implemented

▷ Further employee development

Of course, reaping these benefits requires a major organizational investment: employee time. But the organization profits immensely by effectively transforming knowledge into action. The CEO of British Petroleum, John Browne, observed, "In order to generate extraordinary value for shareholders, a company has to learn better than its competitors and apply that knowledge throughout its businesses faster and more widely than they do" (Prokesch 1997, p. 168). The bottom line is strategic knowledge-sharing communities can create value for the organization and shareholders.

Reevaluate the Role of Organizational Reports

Routinely circulated information has a way of shaping the beliefs, thoughts, and actions of organizational members by directing attention to certain issues and deflecting it from others. Reports can hinder performance in two general ways. First, the report may contain too much information. In this case, employees either ignore it or pay attention to only those items that serve *their*—not necessarily the organization's—needs. Second, the report may contain too little actionable information. In this case, employees learn to disregard it because they feel they cannot affect the results in any meaningful way. Between these two extremes lies the sweet spot where reports allow employees to learn how they directly impact critical organizational results.

Developing reports with this kind of dynamic requires considerable effort. But asking the following questions can put managers on the right track:[3]

▷ Are reports directly related to actionable tasks?

▷ Does information in the reports match the scope of responsibility and concerns of the employees?

▷ Do the reports present information in a simple, straightforward, and concise manner?

▷ Are the reports timely?

▷ Is the content in the reports presented in a familiar and well-organized format?

▷ Do the reports allow readers to easily understand critical organizational relationships?

▷ Does the report have a reputation for reliability?

Some organizations use these questions as criteria to grade the quality of their reports. They usually discover that the vast majority of their organizational reports fail to receive a passing grade. No wonder most companies experience difficulties moving from knowledge to action.

Applying the D-I-K-A Model

Constructing a map or drawing a schematic of how the organization manages the D-I-K-A relationships can prove revealing. Maps help managers identify gaps, shortfalls, and obstacles. For example, after discussing the D-I-K-A model with one executive, he realized his organization created a lot of data and information, but did very little with it. His schematic was a big *D* and *I* followed by a little *k* and *a* (see Figure 4.5). Another executive found a key insight by looking at the distance between D-I-K-A in his organization (see Figure 4.6). He realized the problem was not one of *generation,* but of *speed:* how quickly data and information were transformed into knowledge and action. By the time the solution was agreed on and implemented, the problems had changed. One thoughtful scholar explains the challenge this way: "The manager really needs a research process that yields results faster than the time taken for the problem to change"(Mackenzie 1994, p. 113). Thus, by examining the size of the letters in the map or the distances between them, managers can gain valuable insights into how to more effectively manage these critical relationships. Sometimes, the schematic even reveals dysfunctional practices such as the K-A-K-A pattern discussed above.

These dysfunctional patterns have a way of weaving their way into every organizational level, often with some seemingly bizarre twists. Many overload and underload problems continue to occur because of patterns that feed on each other. Employees point to management as the culprit and vice versa. Managers, like employees, see only one part of the cycle, and they propose solutions that perpetuate the difficulty. Only through a broader, more encompassing view can this destructive cycle be halted. Most of the time the participants are too close and entwined in the situation to see it clearly. Perceptive outside consultants can often provide just the needed insight.

Consider the following situation: At one branch of a bank, the frontline employees complained about not getting enough information about new procedures. As one teller put it, "I feel this particular office is sort of left out in the cold on many things." At another branch office some 40 miles away, employees did not complain of underload but of *overload.* They felt they received too much information, and it tended to be confusing. In all, six branches complained of overload and four of underload. Thus, the managers of these various branches were doing an uneven job of informing their employees. Or so it seemed. Interestingly, information overload was the most significant complaint of every branch manager. Upon deeper examination, the source of the difficulty became clear.

The real source of the problem was at the administrative level. Branch managers were receiving memos from one administrator saying one thing and from another saying something else. Sometimes two administrators would ask for the same information in slightly different forms. This trickled down to branch managers in the form of information overload. When confronted with this, some branch managers heavily screened this information, particularly ambiguous directives,

$$\text{D} - \text{I}_{\text{-k-a}}$$

The company generates a lot of data and information but does very little with it.

Figure 4.5. An Executive's Schematic

$$\text{D} - \text{I} \overset{\text{9-12 months}}{\text{---------K---A}}$$

The company generates useful data and information but takes a long time to act on it.

Figure 4.6. Another Executive's Schematic

before passing it on to the frontline employees. Four branch managers did this, creating an A-I loop in which actions were taken and information provided only after the fact. As a result, employees failed to grasp the big picture. Other branch managers provided all the information to the employees and hoped they would understand it. Six managers chose this strategy, unwittingly creating a D-I loop in which more data and information led to greater confusion and little action. Yet both approaches were inadequate; neither loop allowed employees to create useful knowledge. When the administrators were confronted with the situation, they reported that they had never talked to one another about the messages they sent to their managers. They did not know it was a problem despite the fact that they saw each other every day.

These problems are all too common. The principle is basic: difficulties at one level of the organization frequently get amplified in a variety of ways at other levels of the organization. At this savings bank, once the messages were coordinated at the administrative level, both managers and employees had more acceptable communication loads. A broader perspective allowed executives to determine how the situations related. Armed with this knowledge, they easily broke the dysfunctional pattern. To sum up, the power to break problematic organization cycles often lies in clearly mapping out critical relationships.

Conclusion

In the past, business schools taught that organizational excellence basically consisted of effective people and task management. Today, a third dimension has emerged: managing data, information, and knowledge. This makes the traditional managerial functions of planning, organizing, leading, and controlling all the more complex and difficult. Yet this may well be the single greatest challenge facing the modern organization. Data and information may not be tagged with nutritional labels, but wise managers learn to wisely monitor their diets.

Notes

1. The findings of Foehrebach and Rosenberg (1982) parallel a follow-up study by Foehrebach and Goldfarb (1990). Unfortunately, the 1990 study did not include the complete results from 1982.

2. Grinder and Bandler (1976) have suggested that people process information in one of three primary modes: (1) visual, (2) auditory, and (3) kinesthetic. This advertisement appeals to all three modes.

3. These questions are adapted from a study by McKinnon and Bruns (1992), pp. 132–133.

4. 1984. *Byte.* Interview: The Macintosh design team. February: 52-80, p. 60.

FIVE

Communication Channels

The medium is the message.

Marshall McLuhan

Media choice is not the simple, intuitively obvious process it may appear to be at first glance. Appropriate media choice can make the difference between effective and ineffective communication. And media choice mistakes can seriously impede successful communication—in some cases with disastrous consequences.

Trevino, Daft, and Lengel

Who has most influenced the course of history? An unanswerable question? Perhaps. Of course, the names Jesus, Muhammad, Buddha, Newton, and Einstein readily come to mind. Even if it were possible to construct such a list, what criteria should be used? And who would be qualified to construct such a list? Michael H. Hart (1978), a physicist and astronomer, took a stab at these intriguing questions. He reveals his answer in a fascinating book titled, *The 100: A Ranking of the Most Influential Persons in History*. Disclosing who was ranked first would be like revealing the ending of an Agatha Christie mystery, so I will resist that temptation. Nevertheless, the person ranked seventh on the list would raise some eyebrows. He is a man so unfamiliar to most Westerners that few have even heard the name before. Ranked ahead of Aristotle, Marx, Einstein, Moses, Luther, Hitler, and da Vinci is the inventor of paper, Ts'ai Lun. He was an official in the

Chinese imperial court around 105 A.D., and he developed the basic process for creating paper that we still use today.

Before paper, communication was constrained by space and time. Generally, communication could only occur when two individuals occupied the same physical space and interacted in synchronous time periods. Paper changed all that, and along with Gutenberg's press (ranked eighth by Hart), profoundly altered the course of history.

Few scholars have thought deeply about the impact of paper on society. In fact, many encyclopedias (ironically a paper product), fail to mention Ts'ai Lun. Paper was the first in a long line of communication channels that could readily be used by the masses. Telephones, bulletin boards, interoffice mail systems, employee publications, and personal computers are integral parts of the modern business. Yet, just as many Westerners overlook Ts'ai Lun's influence, most managers often overlook how communication technologies influence their communication.

Messages must pass through some kind of channel. And the channel necessarily alters the messages, just as the composition of an electrical wire affects the flow of electricity. In fact, Internet service is slowed down because traditional copper wire cannot transmit the bandwidth of fiber optic cable. Consequently, the physical limitations influence what we communicate on the Internet. Likewise, some channels accentuate certain attributes of the message, while de-emphasizing others. For example, written messages typically imbue in communications a sense of finality and formality that may not be intended by the sender.

Communication channels can also radically alter the organization's social structure. Certain channels restrict access to key individuals, whereas others encourage interactions. For instance, some executives require that all communications be put into writing. Others are more freewheeling, and encourage active verbal interchanges in group meetings. In addition, the communication channels have an impact on organizational efficiency and effectiveness. Telephone tag wastes employee time, whereas electronic mail has the potential to eliminate this futile game. Other new technologies will no doubt radically change the office environment in ways yet to be discovered.

Learning to manage these communication channels effectively presents a major challenge. In what way does the communication channel affect a message? How should a manager decide on what channel to use in communicating with employees? These are the types of questions considered in this chapter.

A Model for Selecting Appropriate Channels

Consider all the ways by which a typical employee can communicate these days: memo, phone call, e-mail, bulletin board, electronic bulletin board, voice mail, fax, pager, and audiotape, to name the most familiar. With this bewildering array of options, many are tempted just to spin the wheel and select a channel. In fact, this is exactly what many do. **Personal convenience guides most channel selec-**

Sender	**Message**	**Channel**	**Receiver**
Objectives	*Choices*	*Options*	*Characteristics*
▷ Educate	▷ Terminology	▷ Fax	▷ Channel access
▷ Get Attention	▷ Theme	▷ E-mail	▷ Personality profile
▷ Motivate	▷ Metaphor	▷ Phone	▷ Beliefs
▷ Flatter	▷ Nonverbals	▷ Face-to-face	▷ Values
▷ Persuade	▷ Stories	▷ Computer conference	▷ Age
▷ Compliment	▷ Facts and figures	▷ Bulletin boards	▷ Gender
▷ Confuse	▷ Arguments	▷ Group meetings	▷ Education level
▷ Equivocate	▷ Evidence	▷ Formal presentations	▷ Socioeconomic background
▷ Ridicule	▷ Tone	▷ Web page	▷ Occupation
▷ Deceive	▷ Emotionality	▷ Hotlines	▷ Religious orientation
▷ Inform	▷ Length	▷ Audio and videotapes	▷ Interest level
▷ Express empathy	▷ Complexity	▷ Voice mail	▷ Location
▷ Deny	▷ Professionalism	▷ Videoconference	▷ Race
▷ Impress	▷ Formality	▷ Pager	
▷ Ingratiate	▷ Timing		
▷ Honor	▷ Sequencing		
▷ Entertain			
▷ Shift focus			

Figure 5.1. SMCR Model

tions. As a channel's ease of use increases, so does the likelihood of use. Few employees consider how the channel filters the message. Yet scholars have discovered that *effective* executives are sensitive to the impact of the medium and select the appropriate channel for their messages (Lengel and Daft 1988). How do they do it?

A simple model of communication might intuitively guide the successful executive (see Figure 5.1). Selecting the appropriate channel resembles hitting a row of cherries on a Las Vegas slot machine. The objective should be to align four elements:

1. The objectives of the sender
2. The attributes of the message
3. The attributes of the channel
4. The characteristics of the receivers

Unlike a one-armed bandit, however, the alignment of these four communication variables should be a product of skill and insight rather than chance. The odds of "winning" can be markedly increased by carefully considering five fundamental questions.

1. Are the Sender's Objectives Compatible With the Attributes of the Intended Message? (The S-M Test)

All messages have attributes that characterize their content. Messages can vary along numerous dimensions, including level of complexity, length, personal warmth, formality, and degree of ambiguity. Senders of messages also have a wide variety of intentions in communicating messages, including motivating, informing, persuading, and soliciting ideas or opinions.

Ideally, the needs of the sender should harmonize with the characteristics of the message. That does not, however, always happen. A manager seeking to motivate employees should not communicate an overly complex message. But some do. Or consider the case of a manager who desired to "establish goodwill" with the executive team, and proceeded to relay a sexist joke. Not very smart, or very effective. Communication efforts often fail because of incongruities between the senders' objectives and their choices about message content and style.

2. Are the Messages Sent Compatible With the Channels Utilized? (The M-C Test)

William F. Buckley, Jr., when running for mayor of New York City, was asked to explain his economic plan for the city on a television talk show. He refused. He believed his plan was too complex to be explained in a cursory fashion within the time constraints of that television show. Some might call this arrogance. Yet his position makes perfect sense when viewed from the perspective of the channel limitations. Simply put, the message he had to convey could not effectively be communicated via this channel.

Likewise, managers must realize that every channel has limitations that filter out parts of the message. Channels that are nondynamic, such as memos or bulletin boards, are not effective in communicating extremely complex messages. On the other hand, bulletin boards can be useful and efficient when communicating a fairly simple message, like the company softball schedule. Hence, to effectively communicate, managers must be alert to the dynamic interplay of the message and channel attributes.

3. Are the Sender's Objectives Compatible With the Type of Channels Utilized? (The S-C Test)

Suggestion boxes have been used for years in countless organizations. Yet most businesses have found them of limited utility. Why? First, many new ideas or suggestions are not readily captured on paper. Second, the suggestion box does not provide the personal recognition than many innovators desire. Indeed, employees are often told that suggestions should be made anonymously, which even further removes the incentive. One employee artfully described his feelings in a picture that nicely captures the essence of the problems with suggestion boxes (see Figure 5.2). This employee's motivations are not really compatible with the channel. Ideas are personal, warm, and alive. They are a source of joy for employees. Impersonal media strip away these very elements from the message. The result is inevitable: innovative ideas never surface in such channels.

The fundamental lesson is that because communication channels have certain attributes, senders must be sure that their intentions are congruent with the dynamics of the channel. One young entrepreneur who owned a limousine company with revenues in excess of $350,000 a year, took this principle to heart in an unusual way. He used the telephone almost exclusively as his communication tool. Why? Many of his clients and even employees did not take him seriously because of his obvious youth. With the telephone, the problems disappeared (Robichaux 1989). The lack of visual cues worked to his advantage; the channel was congruent with his purpose.

Likewise, if the sender seeks to imbue the message with a sense of formality, then more formal channels, like written memos, should be used. If the sender seeks to relay a confidential message, then a face-to-face meeting beats the fax machine. If an executive wants to stimulate creativity but fears that status differences inhibit a free exchange of ideas, then computer conferencing would be best. If the CEO wants to instill an emotional commitment to corporate values, then a visual channel, such as a formal presentation, videoconference, or videotape, would be the channel of choice. In sum, formal intentions require formal mediums, dynamic intentions require dynamic mediums, and so on.

4. Are the Messages Compatible With the Receivers' Characteristics? (The M-R Test)

Effective communicators learn to craft their message in ways that are compatible with their receivers' characteristics. Consider this unfortunate incident: A college freshman with little computer expertise asked his professor for some help on a paper. The professor responded, "Just make a copy of your disk, and I'll make comments on it." The student complied by taking his disk to a photocopy machine, making a "copy," and dutifully slipping it into the professor's mailbox. Crazy things like this happen all the time. Why? The message characteristics did not match the receiver's abilities. Had the professor recognized how little the student knew about computer disks, he could have changed the message. As a rule of thumb, a message's level of specificity should be adjusted to the receiver's knowledge base.

Likewise, the choice of metaphors in a message should be adjusted to the occupational background of employees. A paper company executive was more successful in getting employee participation in a survey assessing organizational commu-

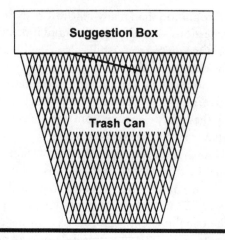

Figure 5.2. The "Suggestion Box"

nication effectiveness when he changed his message from "It's like going to the dentist for a checkup" to "It's just like doing a routine inspection on your machine." Both metaphors "work," but employees can more readily identify with the machine assessment, because it is an activity they do regularly to catch any mechanical glitches before they cause harm. Besides, how many people really like going to the dentist?

Take your pick of items in the second and fourth columns of Figure 5.1. Any of these combinations could yield useful rules of thumb for crafting messages. By thinking about these kinds of questions, managers increase the probability that their communication will be effective.

5. Are the Channels Utilized Compatible With the Receivers' Characteristics? (The C-R Test)

Several years ago, we conducted an analysis of how information was distributed at a Midwestern university. Most of the students were commuters, and a high percentage held outside jobs. Most students (i.e., receivers) experienced heavy time constraints. The research showed that message senders relied heavily on communicating via bulletin boards. The data also revealed that many students felt inadequately informed about campus events.

When we investigated this issue, it was apparent why students felt uninformed. Students needed channels that presented information in an easily consumable format. Bulletin boards could not do the job, because the students did not have time to read them, given the unique dynamics of the campus. Students were typically on campus for their classes, then left shortly after to pursue their work responsibilities. Ironically, the fact that the boards were located in high traffic areas actually inhibited effective communication. Why? Because at high traffic times, the crowd pushed students by the boards too quickly. The solution was to widely distribute information through a transportable channel so that students could easily read at their leisure. Hence boxes containing a one-page weekly schedule of activities were placed at the entrances and exits of the campus. A new campus Internet system also helped. The results were quite positive.

Thus, the channels used must be uniquely suited to the receiver. For instance, sometimes managers assume that written communication is compatible with their receivers. It may not be. After all, one agency estimates that over 60 million American adults are functionally illiterate (Casse 1986). In one case, a man recently promoted to a job as shipping and receiving foreman had to shelve special orders until he could discretely ask for help reading the instructions (Mikulecky 1990). The social stigma attached to the problem often makes it difficult to discuss.

Receivers may not even be aware of their underlying needs. For example, voice mail or e-mail would be particularly useful for employees who need to communicate across time zones. A fax machine would best serve an employee who needs to see a diagram as soon as possible. In fact, the ability to transmit handwritten messages is particularly important to the Japanese, because the written form of their language contains over 1,000 ideographic characters. The traditional Japanese typewriter was extraordinarily cumbersome to use, and keyboard-based communication devices proved equally problematic (Pierce and Noll 1990). In sum, effective communicators adapt both their messages and channels to their audience.[1]

The five questions reviewed above provide a glimpse into the complexities involved in effectively communicating. Fundamentally, communicators need to find a fit between their objectives, messages, channel choices, and receivers' attributes (see Table 5.1). Suppose that for each of these four variables there were five possible alternatives, much like a column of a slot machine. Senders could have one of five possible purposes for communicating a message. Likewise one could chose among five possible channels: bulletin boards, memos, group meeting, telephone calls, or face-to-face meetings. There are many more, but if we limited each variable to only five, then there would be 625 different combinations! This illustrates the range of choices facing communicators. The odds of correctly aligning each variable are exceedingly small. Yet a prudent manager can effectively manage this complexity, unlike that of a slot machine, by pondering the questions reviewed above.

Lessons Learned

Models like the one discussed above and other research findings have revealed some important lessons about channel choices. These are reviewed in this section.

TABLE 5.1 Sample Situations of Media Choice

Situation 1	**Poor Choice**	**Better Choice**
A midsize construction firm wants to announce a new employee benefit program.	Memo	Small group meetings

Rationale

The memo does not offer the feedback potential necessary to explain what may be seen as arcane information. Moreover, some employees might have a literacy problem. A group meeting will provide an oral explanation and will allow participants to easily ask questions about any of the complex material.

Situation 2	**Poor Choice**	**Better Choice**
A manager wishes to confirm a meeting time with ten employees.	Phone	E-mail or voice mail

Rationale

For a simple message like this, there is no need to use a rich and synchronous media, where sender and receiver simultaneously communicate, when a lean and asynchronous one will do the job.

Situation 3	**Poor Choice**	**Better Choice**
A midsize insurance company wants to garner support for a program that encourages employees from different departments to work on the same project teams.	E-mail, voice mail	Face-to-face meeting, telephone

Rationale

Persuasive situations demand that the sender be able to quickly adapt the message to the receiver in order to counter objections. This is not a feature of either e-mail or voice mail. Face-to-face communication offers the sender the greatest flexibility. The phone is the next best alternative.

Situation 4	**Poor Choice**	**Better Choice**
A group of geographically dispersed engineers wants to exchange design ideas with one another.	Teleconference	Fax, computer conference

Rationale

A teleconference may overly accentuate the status and personality differences between the engineers. Fax or computer conferencing would allow the quality of the ideas to be the central focus of interaction. Moreover, quick feedback is still possible in these media.

Situation 5	**Poor Choice**	**Better Choice**
A company needs to describe a straightforward but somewhat detailed updated version of the voice mail system to 1,000 geographically dispersed employees.	Newsletter	Videotape

Rationale

As long as employees are already persuaded of the system's merit, the sender can use asynchronous media, where senders and receivers do not have to communicate simultaneously. Also, videotape more easily conveys messages that require demonstrations.

Most Effective Knowledge-Sharing Occurs Face-to-Face

In the last chapter, I discussed the differences between managing information and managing knowledge. E-mails and web pages may be effective tools for sharing information, but they are poorly suited for sharing knowledge. Why? Knowledge is more complex and subtle than information. A more appropriate channel provides for the inherent complexity and nuance of knowledge, creating an S-C compatibility. Face-to-face communication nicely fits the bill.

Communicating face-to-face provides us with a wide variety of cues, such as visual images, vocal tone, body movements, office decor, language, and even smell. Almost unrestricted access to these signals allows us to sense subtle distinctions necessary to understand complex issues. Moreover, the communicators, not a cameraperson, determine what cues to attend to. A manager can "get the feel" for the person. Three preeminent scholars made this argument:

> Face-to-face [communication] conveys emotion and strength of feeling through facial expressions, gestures, and eye contact. It is as important for a manager to know that participants are satisfied, angry, cooperative, or resistant, as it is to have accurate production data. . . . Memos and other written directives convey a predefined, literal description that can hide important issues and convey a false sense that everyone understands and agrees. (Trevino, Daft, and Lengel 1990, p. 88)

That is why teaching, training, and analyzing difficult problems are best handled in a face-to-face channel. It is the most dynamic medium available to the manager. No other channel permits communicators to send and receive messages of such an interpersonal nature, on the one hand, and cognitive complexity, on the other. Both of these are necessary for effective knowledge-sharing.

Even a teleconference does not effectively simulate a face-to-face meeting. Small or large groups can simultaneously communicate in a single conversation via the phone line. One company holds a teleconference every Friday morning with up to 100 employees in five different locations to keep everyone informed of upcoming events. Although this provides a useful tool for information-sharing, it limits knowledge-sharing. Why? Teleconferences discourage secondary conversations that are often vital to learning (see Figure 5.3). During face-to-face group meetings involving more than four or five people, other conversations often occur simultaneously in smaller groups of two or three. Because a single phone line transmits the communication in a teleconference, employees tend to avoid secondary conversations (Williams 1987). Moreover, the lack of visual communication filters out many subtle cues necessary for knowledge sharing. In short, a teleconference offers an efficient alternative to many face-to-face group conferences, but it cannot completely simulate one.

Some Channels Focus More Attention on the Message, Others on the Communicators

We might label channels that focus attention on messages and communicators *what* and *who* channels, respectively. *What* channels, such as e-mail, web pages, and computer conferencing (the formal counterpart of a chat room), tend to emphasize information and idea sharing. *Who* says it fades into the background. These channels muffle many cues, such as frowns, verbal hesitations, and seating arrangements, that signal status and role differences. For example, one study of computer conference participants indicated that 40% of the users did not know the gender of the senders and 32% had no idea of the sender's position in the hierarchy (Sproull and Kiesler 1986). Because of the channel characteristics, the group processes less person-centered information. In fact, a few studies revealed that a computer conference was up to 55% faster than a typical meeting. When Phelps Dodge Mining Co. conducted its first planning meeting electronically, the process took twelve hours instead of the normal couple of days. One of the reasons was that a lot of people could "talk" at once without being considered rude (Bartimo 1990). Additionally, some employees who feel physically unattractive report being more confident and participative in a computer conference than they are face-to-face. The playing field is different in a chat room or computer conference; employees engage in a battle of wits, not of power.

But being message-centered instead of person-centered in an organization can become problematic. Why? Organizations are social entities. Status and power differences not only exist, but also often play a major role in decision making. Those who fail to take this organizational fact of life into account will experience significant implementation problems, even with a brilliant insight or idea.

Who channels underscore the relational elements inherent in any communicative event, often accentuating status and hierarchical differences. Group meetings, formal presentations, and many teleconferences highlight person-centered messages. A videoconference may provide the purest form of *who* channel. One expert counsels,

> Video teleconferencing is a . . . medium where, in a sense, you become the visual aid. And just as you are not born with the ability to communicate brilliantly, so you are not born knowing how best to utilize video communicating. You must learn to make the medium work for you rather than the other way around. (Frank 1989, p. 142)

The expert's liberal use of the "you" pronoun signals the importance of personality over content.

Television often tests one's ability at verbal ping-pong and imagery rather than the mental rigor of deep thought. On the plus side, *who* channels clarify any relational ambiguities. On the negative side, these channels might actually inhibit certain employees from voicing concerns or even sharing better ideas.

Face - To - Face Meeting

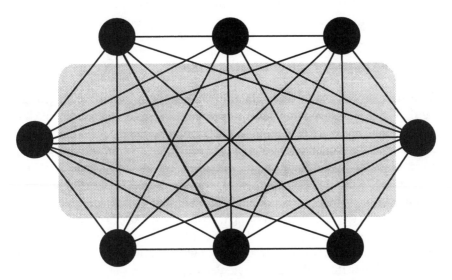

In the typical face-to-face meeting, participants can break into smaller groups for discussion without interrupting the primary conversation because all the communication lines are available.

Teleconference Meeting

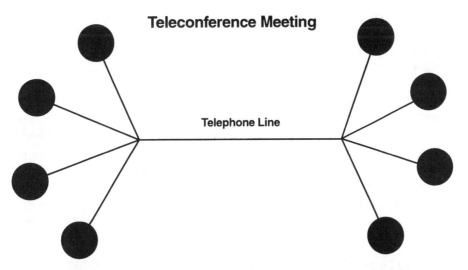

Telephone Line

In a teleconference meeting, any person can talk to any other person - but the conversation occurs on a common communication line, unlike a typical face-to-face meeting.

Figure 5.3. Comparison of Teleconference and Face-to-Face Meetings

What to do? Both kinds of channels have strengths and weaknesses. Wise managers recognize this and choose the appropriate channels for the situation. They often use different combinations of channels to maximize their effectiveness. In other words, they routinely think about the implications of the S-C test.

Different Channels Require Different Skills

Effective communicators learn not only the generic speaking, writing, and listening skills, but they also know how to maximize the utility of each channel. For instance, composing successful e-mails and memos requires somewhat different talents. An effective e-mail need not contain finely honed prose. Memo writers, in contrast, ought to make the attempt. Although brevity and clarity are highly prized business writing skills, they are even more critical in e-mails, where the readability on the computer screen is more difficult than on a printed page. Writers who lack necessary skills, such as writing with clarity and brevity, plague many organizations. For example, Figures 5.4 and 5.5 show two different versions of the same memo. Figure 5.5, however, was drafted with almost half the verbiage. One study revealed that the high impact style demonstrated in Figure 5.5 took about 20% less time to read, was more effectively comprehended, and did not need to be reread as often as the bureaucratic style of Figure 5.4 (Suchan and Colucci 1989).[2]

Likewise, holding a successful meeting requires more than merely knowing how to carry on a good conversation. Effective meeting management occurs when facilitators know what to focus on, what to ignore, how to build consensus, how to encourage discussion, and how to stick to an agenda.[3] Facilitators also must guard against "groupthink," in which employees fear sharing opinions contrary to the group norms (Janis 1982).

Making a formal presentation requires special skills as well. In one poll, people ranked public speaking as their number one fear, even over death and going to the dentist. Overcoming this anxiety in order to motivate or persuade employees often requires special training. Pick any channel, and you can probably find a special skill associated with it. Even something as simple as using voice mail may require some modest training. We have all probably had the frustrating experience of asking someone a simple question via voice mail, only to receive a "please call me back" return voice mail. Not a very efficient way to communicate. To sum up, managers cannot assume employees will be equally skillful in using every channel.

Writing Fosters Critical Thinking

George F. Kennan (1993), a recipient of the Presidential Medal of Freedom and former U.S. Ambassador to the Soviet Union, warned about the danger of a society dominated by television by noting that "a mental world dominated by fragmentary images . . . can hardly be a thoughtful one" (p. 177). The eloquent author Annie Dillard (1989) elaborated on the special quality of the written word:

To: All employees of Pas de Deux, International
From: Human Resources
Representatives from Pirouette Financial Group will be available on Tuesday, April 24, to acquaint you with ways that can help you build a secure, comfortable retirement. They will be discussing investment alternatives, and will be happy to sit down with you for a few minutes to answer any questions you may have about your retirement and financial planning program.
There is no cost for this service and no appointment is necessary. Feel free to stop in any time between 10:30 a.m. and 1:30 p.m. in the alcove area for this review.

Total Word Count = 102

Figure 5.4. Traditional, Bureaucratic Memo.

To: All employees
From: Human Resources
Find out how Pirouette Financial Group can help you build a secure, comfortable retirement.
Date: Tuesday, April 24
Place: Alcove
Time: 10:30 a.m. to 1:30 p.m.
Representatives will discuss your personal financial concerns about your retirement planning.
No appointment necessary.

Total Word Count = 46

Figure 5.5. Short, "High Impact" Memo

> When you write, you lay out a line of words. The line of words is a miner's pick, a woodcarver's gouge, a surgeon's probe. You wield it, and it digs a path you follow. Soon you find yourself deep in new territory. . . . The writing has changed in your hands, and in a twinkling, from an expression of your notions to an epistemological tool. (p. 3)

Writing facilitates clear thinking. Sometimes, ideas that make perfect sense in conversation turn to mush when you try to write them down. Why? Writing forces us to think in a more linear style. For instance, one computer science professor requires that all his students submit their class questions to him on e-mail. He claims that 90% of the time, the very act of writing down the question solves the problem. The rigors of writing demand a greater precision of thought than speech.

But written communication has noticeable drawbacks. Letters, memos, and employee publications by design do not encourage clear and timely feedback. The difficulty occurs when readers fail to understand the memo or, more seriously, fail to recognize that they do not understand. Thus, the major responsibility for communication effectiveness lies with the writers, forcing them to simplify, clarify, and specify ideas. Consequently, successful publication editors learn how to be liaisons with core audiences, essentially conducting the M-R test (Mirel 1990).

Citibank, for example, addressed this problem head-on by establishing a committee to examine consumer-related problems. One difficulty they discovered dealt with the complexity of promissory notes issued to consumers. Without any pressure from the government, they radically revised the written document. Their challenge was to ensure that the information was legally binding, while being understandable to the public at large. The committee had to act as a liaison between the legal department and the general public in order to create a document that would not suffer from readership drop-off. In one instance, an immensely detailed paragraph filled with legalese was reduced to one sentence. The results were overwhelmingly positive, and resulted in increased market share, a dramatic reduction in the number of lawsuits against consumers for default, and even praise from one of the biggest critics of financial institutions, Senator William Proxmire. He said, "Mr. President, as one who has never been shy of criticizing financial institutions when criticism is deserved, I am just as liberal with praise when I hear of a big bank with a progressive idea" (U.S. Department of Commerce 1984, pp. 6–7). Therefore, when used properly, written channels can be effective as well as lucrative.

Speed Often Trumps Completeness

Many formal communication systems make extensive use of channels designed more for thoroughness rather than speed. Some companies, for example, make extensive use of quarterly employee meetings designed to provide thorough briefings on the "big picture" items. Unfortunately, in our era, the big picture often changes more quickly than every quarter. Other organizations rely on regular newsletters to keep employees informed. But, again, the news may change more quickly than the beleaguered editorial staff can handle. In short, the responsiveness of the communication system often does not match the pace of organizational events.

Lingering in the background lies an improper assumption: executives can control the flow of information. They reason, "Why not wait until all our 'ducks are in a row' before informing employees?" But the Internet, along with corporate intranets, change the dynamic. The "ducks" start quacking long before executives can line them up. An employee may hear something from a vendor or a competitor and pass it along. So employees' misconceptions, apprehensions, and resistance points often surface prior to any formal announcement. Consequently, building support and consensus proves more difficult. Executives often resist sharing "partial information," because it undermines their credibility. Yet we do not expect the meteorologist to predict what will happen next month except in the most general of terms. We do, however, watch the daily forecast. It provides timely, but necessarily partial information. Meteorologists allow the big picture to emerge over time. Their credibility emerges from their speed more than from long-range accuracy. The environment imposes this constraint on both meteorologists and organizational communicators. The CEO of Novell, Eric Schmidt (2000), put it this way, "The fastest learner always wins." Effective managers learn to shape employees' understanding by using more timely channels designed for speed rather than for thorough, long-range planning. In days past, a communication system based on the quarterly newsletter may have met the C-R test. But no longer.

Channel Choices Affect Power Relationships

The former chairman of Citicorp, Walter Wriston (1990), once commented, "The most basic fact about the world we live and work in is this: information is a virus that carries freedom" (p. 83). He might have added that communication technologies provide the delivery system. The CEO of Hewlett Packard, Carly Fiorina (2000), argues that because of the Internet, information no longer constitutes power because everyone has it. For example, administrators of one Fortune 500 company reported that 60% of the messages they received from e-mail would not have been sent via other channels (Kiesler 1986). This fundamentally changes the job of leadership. Leaders can no longer control the flow of information through their organizations, so they must learn to shape the employees' interpretations of news, rumors, and opinions.

Executives and managers often find this state of affairs frightening. Why? First, their traditional levers of power no longer exist. Second, they do not know how to exert influence under the new rules of the game. In one organization, the computer conferencing system led to such internal revolts and lack of concern with traditional power/status issues that top management felt threatened, and dismantled the entire system (Zuboff 1984). That is an extreme example, but instructive. Employees' (i.e., receivers') capabilities have changed. Consequently, executives (i.e., senders) must alter their messages in order to wield influence. When communication technologies began to emerge, some commentators forcefully argued that the technology would "democratize the workplace" (Brown and Duguid 2000). Maybe they took the argument too far. Power and status differences still prevail, but they can be tempered by information technologies. As two scholars observed,

> In FTF [face-to-face] groups, higher-status people talk more than lower-status people, men talk more than women, and managers talk more than subordinates. Those who participate have more opportunities to influence decisions. Because e-mail reduces status cues, status-induced imbalances also are weaker. E-mail can encourage more open and equal discussion, leading to decisions based on knowledge rather than on the influence of high-status members. (Garton and Wellman 1995, pp. 440–441)

No wonder many executives feel threatened by new technology. To sum up, the relationship between managers and employees has been forever transformed by the channels widely used in today's organizations.

Different Channels Fill Particular Niches in the Organization

Adam Gopnik (1999) provided the following wonderful observation about e-mail in the *New Yorker*:

> The reason this medium has blossomed is not that it gives you *more* immediacy; blessedly, it gives you *less*. The new appeal of E-mail is the old appeal of print. It isn't instant; it isn't immediate; it isn't in your face. Written language gives you a hat and a Groucho nose and glasses; it's you there, but not quite you. E-mail has succeeded brilliantly for the same reason that the videophone failed miserably: what we actually want from our exchanges is the minimum human contact commensurate with the need to connect with people. "Only connect." Yes, but *only* connect. (p. 49)

Other channels, such as a phone call, take us beyond a mere connection. In other words, e-mail fulfills a particular role. As channels compete for employees' attention, they take on specific functions. Generally, old channels do not die; they find a new niche. AM radio did not die when FM came along, although many predicted it would. Talk radio thrives on AM stations.

In a similar way, different media in organizations evolve and secure a particular niche in the communication system. For instance, commentators have long complained about the quality of employee newsletters (D'Aprix 1982). The dreaded "three Bs"—birthdays, baby pictures, and bowling scores—dominate most newsletters. Indeed, our research, as shown in Table 5.2, confirmed that most articles revolved around employee recognition (Clampitt, Crevcoure, and Hartel 1986).

At one time, I thought this was an inappropriate use of this often costly communication tool. Now, I believe that newsletters with this orientation may satisfy a particular employee need. After all, Abraham Maslow taught us about the fundamental need for recognition and esteem. The newsletter may provide a tangible and permanent communication designed to meet this need. This may not be the *best* channel, but it may be an *adequate* one, given other competing demands on the communication system.

Channels fill niches as they dynamically interact in the communicative marketplace of organizations. In the communication system of a paper mill, top management primarily used a bimonthly newsletter and quarterly meeting to keep employees informed. Despite the editorial staff's best effort, over time the newsletter evolved into the typical three-B type of publication. Any attempt to provide more company-oriented news was resisted by employees. Why? Because they heard

TABLE 5.2 Most Commonly Published Articles In Employee Publications

Rank	Type of Article	Percentage[a]
1	Employee recognition	93
2	Company awards	86
3	Personnel changes/promotions	78
4	Benefit programs	76
5	Recognition of departments/divisions	74
6	Company policies	70
7	Organization's community involvement	68
8	Company social functions	66
9	Company sponsored sports activities	65
10	Organization's future plans	64
11	Safety	64
12	Promoting goodwill between management & employees	63
13	Effect of external events on company	58
14	Motivational	55
15	Financial results	51
16	Personal news (birthdays, anniversaries, etc.)	51
17	Questions & answers	42

a. Percentage reflects the number of editors that perceived a type of article was "most frequently published." The sample consisted of 135 editors.

more timely news elsewhere. As good editors, the top management listened to their readers, applying the M-R test. But this did not mean that employees' other needs were being adequately met by other channels. In fact, employees often complained about not getting accurate and timely information. A newsletter did not, and indeed *could* not, meet the need. So they created a new communication channel, a bi-weekly supervisor meeting centered around several "talking points." The supervisors, in turn, communicated this information to their employees in crew meetings. The new channel satisfied the particular communicative need. The lesson is that managers need to think about the right niche for each communication channel. Often, existing channels fail to meet fully the needs of communicators. New channels may need to be created, while old ones may need to be renovated.

Channel Choices Send Symbolic Messages

Several years ago, a tale circulated around the Internet about a "techie" who broke up with his girlfriend. He decided to e-mail her the news because he thought faxing her was too impersonal. Ugh. Well, at least he had the right sentiments. The moral of the story: one's choice of channels also sends a message, shaping its tone and character. For example, an employee handbook makes explicit the mutual responsibilities of employees and employers. Likewise, memos and letters imbue a message with a sense of formality and credibility, allowing recipients a document as a reference point. In general, written communication signifies authority, legitimacy, and responsibility. After all, judges issue a *written* rather than *oral* court summons. Face-to-face conversations often lack these qualities. Several researchers found that managers use face-to-face communication "to signal a desire for teamwork, to build trust, goodwill, or to convey informality" (Trevino, Daft, and Lengel 1990, p. 86).

These symbolic messages link to the underlying constraints of the particular medium. E-mail, for example, crudely communicates emotional messages. Consider the thoughts of two scholars:

> Attempts to introduce typographic cues become thin substitutes for nonverbal cues: There is no way to distinguish mild amusement from hilarity with a "smiley,":-). There are few reminders in e-mail of others or of the social context. When cues and controls are weak, people may pay less attention to the presence and opinions of others. (Garton and Wellman 1995, p. 442)

Paying "attention to the presence" of others is often the point of communication— a point that our techie friend failed to understand. Miss Manners, no doubt, intuitively knew what the scholars discovered when she wrote this useful rule of thumb:

> The more emotional the content, the more cumbersome should be the means of conveying it. Highly emotional communications are best made in person, where the effect can be assessed and the message tempered to the reaction. (Martin 1997, p. 22)

In sum, paying attention to the symbolic overtone of channel choice means applying the C-R test.

Senders and Receivers Often Evaluate the Effectiveness of a Channel Choice in Different Ways

What channel should managers use to discuss an employee's performance problem? That depends on whose perspective you adopt and how you evaluate effectiveness. Usually, employees (i.e., receivers) prefer face-to-face meetings, allowing them to ask timely questions, discuss details, and more accurately judge the severity of the issue. They want a dynamic and rich channel. Managers may not, for the very same reasons. They do not want to answer questions, provide further details, or create a potentially emotional scene. In fact, I have interviewed several managers about this issue. One manager, known by his employees as "Stealth," never left his office all day. He bombarded his employees with e-mails. I asked him, face-to-face, about his peculiar interface with his employees. He responded, candidly but anxiously, "They get too emotional and I can't handle it. I get my point across another way." His employees got *a* point all right—"He doesn't care about us." They rarely got the point he intended. Stealth would have never communicated his concerns without e-mail. In fact, these less dynamic channels may be the *only* way some managers feel comfortable confronting conflict. Understandable? Perhaps. Justifiable? Probably not.

What to do? There may be no perfect answer. Stealth will never be an effective manager (although he thinks he is), but at least his channel choice allows issues to surface that he would normally avoid. In a sense, this conundrum brings us right back to the five congruency tests. It may not always be possible to line up the channel with the needs of senders and receivers. Ideally, managers would use the guidelines outlined in Table 5.3. But this is not always possible. As a sender, we should recognize when our personal needs may compromise the efficacy of our communication. And as receivers, we should be aware of how our colleagues' limitations alter their communications.

Conclusion

John R. Pierce (1983), who had a distinguished career at Bell Laboratories, said of musical composition,

> Indeed, the kind of sound that is available influences the kind of music that peoples and composers produce. Piano music is different from harpsichord music in more than the sound of the individual notes. The music of Liszt, Chopin, and Debussy exploits the unique capabilities of the piano. So do Beethoven's and Mozart's piano sonatas and concertos. But Mozart's piano was different from ours, less loud and with less dynamic range. Later music would suffer if played on it. (p. 2)

Likewise, the point of this chapter has been that the communication channel alters the message, sometimes overtly, but more often subtly. There is no one best communication medium, as there is no one best musical instrument. Rather, a communicator, like a composer, seeks to choose the proper instrument to precisely communicate a particular theme. To select the proper instrument wisely requires a complete knowledge of the possibilities and the complexities of the entire process. Then the message becomes something more than mere notes on a piece of Ts'ai Lun's paper.

TABLE 5.3 Effective Use of Channels

Channel	Most Effective Use	Examples
Telephone	▷ Sending short, simple messages ▷ Sending confidential messages ▷ Providing feedback ▷ Providing quick turn-around time	▷ Negotiating a meeting time and place ▷ Discussing work problem
Fax	▷ Sending informal messages ▷ Seeing visual display of information ▷ Providing hard copy	▷ Viewing a copy of brochure ▷ Providing directions to a meeting
E-mail	▷ Sending impersonal, brief messages ▷ Keeping employees updated on routine matters ▷ Efficiently gathering routine information	▷ Conducting in-house survey ▷ Confirming meeting time
Voice mail	▷ Sending short, simple messages ▷ Sharing routine information ▷ Informing others when feedback isn't needed	▷ Responding to an information request
One-on-one (face-to-face)	▷ Sharing potentially emotional, complex information ▷ Communicating confidential material ▷ Persuading and negotiating ▷ Providing feedback ▷ Communicating personal warmth ▷ Reading nonverbals ▷ Sharing knowledge	▷ Holding a performance appraisal ▷ Promoting/firing an employee
Memo	▷ Sending short, simple message ▷ Distributing to numerous receivers ▷ Informing others when feedback isn't needed ▷ Providing information that can be scanned quickly	▷ Communicating a routine update ▷ Confirming a policy change
Letter	▷ Sending message needing personal touch ▷ Conveying formality ▷ Providing detailed information ▷ Providing written record	▷ Expressing thanks, condolences ▷ Writing complaint letter
Web page	▷ Communicating noncontroversial, nonconfidential, general information ▷ Efficiently sharing routine information with large audiences	▷ Summarizing company's expertise, career opportunities ▷ Responding to frequently asked questions
Video conference	▷ Connecting emotionally with large audiences ▷ Sending noncomplex, unambiguous messages	▷ Updating company performance ▷ Outlining a major corporate initiative

1. Of course, axiomatically, if the sender's needs were compatible with the message attributes and the message attributes were compatible with the channel attributes, then the sender's needs would match up with the channel attributes. But that is in an ideal world. More realistically, a sender has to make trade-offs. Hence the question must be raised about the degree of congruency between the sender and the channel. Then the sender can decide on the appropriate message and channel, as the attributes of each variable modify one another in a dynamic, interactive kind of dance.

2. Surprisingly, Suchan and Colucci (1989) also found that "bureaucratic" writing was seen as more "dynamic and forceful." A bureaucratic style included abstract language, passive verbs, no personal pronouns, and the purpose statement in the last paragraph. One explanation offered was that the bureaucratic style fits more closely with the organization's culture by allowing the writer coverage of his "vital assets." Perhaps this is to be expected from a study conducted with U.S. Naval officers. Sometimes the culture demands a cluttered writing style.

3. For an excellent and short primer on how to hold effective meetings, see Tropman (1996).

SIX

Performance Feedback

Feedback is one of the fundamental facts of life and ideas of science, yet only in the last fifty years have we recognized its all-pervasive presence. The idea is simple: a feedback mechanism registers the actual state of a system, compares it to the desired state, then uses the comparison to correct the state of the system. Feedback is goal-oriented. . . . Movement is the essence of feedback. It implies purpose and progress. Like a walker on a high wire, it continually achieves balance in order to achieve something beyond balance. It can never rest.

Horace Freeland Judson

What if there were no feedback? What if feedback not only rested, but also took a Rip Van Winkle sojourn? Cells would not know when to stop multiplying. The economy would fly out of kilter. Democracy would collapse. Without feedback, the world as we know it would not exist; the high wire walker would fall. No system can survive without feedback.

Yet employees in organizations throughout the world feel that is just what they are expected to do. In every organization in which my colleagues and I at MetaComm have conducted an analysis of the communication system, feedback about performance has surfaced as a problem area (see Appendix B). Over 53% of the employees expressed below-average satisfaction with feedback. An astonishing 12% of the employees surveyed indicated they had little or no satisfaction with the feedback system. In countless interviews, employees have made such comments as, "Performance evaluations don't really exist here. If they do, I don't know what they look like. It's like pulling teeth." In short, there is probably no more pervasive and perplexing difficulty in the modern organization than how effectively to give feedback to employees about their performance.

The cynic might ask: So what? Does performance feedback actually make any difference? Indeed, I mentioned to one vice president that employees felt they did not get adequate feedback. He responded, "They get their paychecks every two weeks, don't they?" Researchers have a more critical view. Performance feedback has a high correlation with job satisfaction (Downs and Hazen 1977). In another study, employees indicated that performance feedback had a greater impact on their performance than every other communication variable, including the communication climate, coworker communication, and even supervisor-subordinate relationships (Clampitt and Downs 1993). In sum, employees like to know how they are doing.

Why? There is no one simple reason. For some, feedback serves as a reward or motivation, whereas for others, it provides useful information to correct behavior or a way to build self-esteem. Employees do not want information only; they want recognition, as well. At Oxford Industries, a nonunion clothing manufacturer, modern computer technology can monitor how long it takes an employee to sew a pocket on a pair of pants. The company bases pay on how closely employees match standards (Miller 1985). Although this system provides accurate and timely feedback, it still may not satisfy other noninformational desires for feedback. In fact, many employees who are at the mercy of these so-called "electronic watchdogs" complain of stress and report numerous health problems. Although feedback about performance is clearly one of the most important communication tasks of the manager, it is equally clear that the design and implementation of the feedback system has a major impact on its effectiveness.

The Fundamentals

Effectiveness in football, dance, or management ultimately comes down to a complete mastery of the fundamentals. For the design of an effective feedback system, the following seven principles provide a solid basis.

1. Everyone, Whether They Acknowledge It or Not, Has Standards of Performance

In every task, duty, and decision, employees assess their own level of effectiveness. If deemed satisfactory, they seek to maintain it. If they fall short, they make changes. Mike Schmidt, the Philadelphia Phillies's perennial all-star third baseman, retired in the middle of the 1989 baseball season without any pressure from the owners. He felt he was not living up to his personal performance standards. He could have continued earning millions for several more years. In contrast, employees who send memos chock full of spelling errors have implicitly communicated what is acceptable to them. Performance standards are a nonoptional part of the human experience; they guide our behavior, determine our aspirations, and ultimately define our essence.

2. *The Ideal Feedback System Drives Employees to Identify, Perform, and Commit to the Performance Standards*

Employees and managers do not always share the same standards. In particular, new employees, because of their different backgrounds, training, and experiences, often have quite different standards than their managers. Indeed, researchers have shown that the initial employee training period is the single most critical time in which managers can impart their standards, values, and expectations (Clampitt and Downs 1993). After that period of time, employees tend to be more influenced by their coworkers and other organizational factors. As seen in Figure 6.1, if proper selection procedures have been utilized, employees will share, to some extent, the performance standards of their managers. The training process should result in a more complete sharing of expectations, therefore increasing the degree of overlap. The standards may be altered as situations change, the manager matures, and the employee develops. Yet the objective endures: to close the gap between the standards of the employee and the manager.

The employee must not only know the standards, but must also perform as expected and be committed to them. The effective feedback system involves the mind, the will, and the heart. A teacher, for instance, may set a standard of professionalism in writing, which includes not having any spelling errors on reports. The teacher may announce this at the beginning of the term, but such exhortations are useless unless the students actually turn in papers of this quality. Clearly, the teacher can encourage proper writing by actually grading down students who fail to meet the standards. The long-term goal, however, is for the students to recognize the importance of correct spelling and be committed to this level of professionalism. The aim is not merely knowledge, but performance and commitment. It is one step to know what is right, it is another to turn knowledge into action, and it is yet another to transform action into resolve.

3. *Performance Standards Foster Employee Development While Promoting Corporate Integrity*

Ultimately the integrity of a company's products or services is bound inextricably to the organization's viability. One of the reasons for the preponderance of Japanese products in the United States is that their performance standards have, in the recent past, been more rigorous than their American counterparts. Lee Iacocca admitted as much in rallying Chrysler to its incredible turnaround. When organizations have lower standards of reliability, performance, and service than their

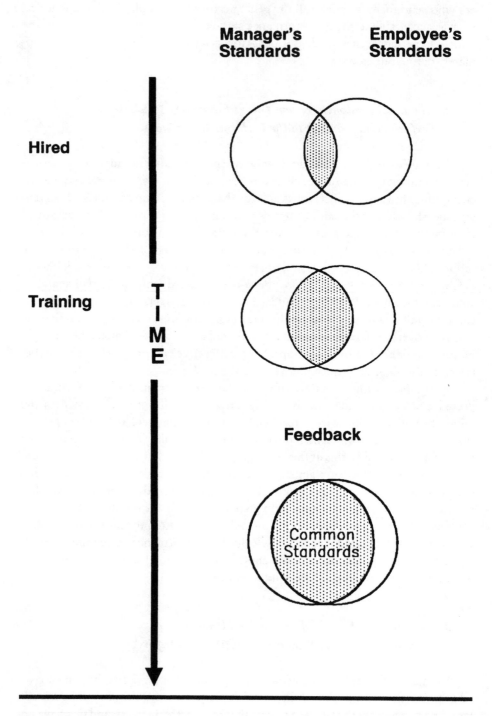

Figure 6.1. Feedback Process

competition, the final result is as inevitable as it is fatal. Companies and managers need have no apologies for high performance standards.

Moreover, employees also benefit from high performance standards. Those who are challenged to achieve their potential are more satisfied and productive. "Self actualization," the term Abraham Maslow made famous in his theory of the hierarchy of human needs, places this assertion on firm theoretical grounds.[1] The famous philosopher and poet Jacob Bronowski (1973) beautifully expressed it:

> The most powerful drive in the ascent of man is his pleasure in his own skill. He loves to do what he does well, and having done it well, he loves to do it better. You see it in his science. You see it in the magnificence with which he carves and builds, the loving care, the gaiety, the effrontery. The monuments are supposed to commemorate kings and religions, heroes, dogmas, but in the end the man they commemorate is the builder. (p. 116)

Most people would like to fulfill their potential. Companies should not frustrate this desire, but should rather seek to utilize it by offering challenging tasks and high standards. To sustain performance in this demanding atmosphere, employees' efforts and accomplishments must be acknowledged, supported, and rewarded. When standards are low in one department, productivity in other divisions suffers and may eventually threaten the job security of all employees.

4. All Employees "Receive" Feedback About Their Performance

Frequently, employees complain that they "don't get any feedback." But this is a misnomer of sorts, because even if employees do not receive explicit feedback, they will make inferences about the acceptability of their work. From the organizational context, employees extract messages and come to conclusions like "No news is good news," or, "I must be doing OK; I haven't heard any complaints." When employees receive no explicit feedback, they infer it and continue to perform at levels they deem acceptable to themselves. To put it another way, a manager cannot *not* "give" performance feedback. Of course, to use words like *receive* and *give* is somewhat misleading, because no one explicitly sends or receives a message. But context and inference are powerful instruments of communication. Indeed, in many cases this is the only method used to "communicate" about performance.

5. Few Employees Receive Useful Feedback About Their Performance

Unfortunately, this inferential method of feedback encourages employees to make inaccurate speculations. For example, one insurance claims adjuster had never received any explicit feedback in his short, nine-month tenure. He had an exceedingly pleasant manner, but was disturbingly sloppy in his work habits. The manager had already decided to fire him after the mandatory nine-month trial period. Top management knew of the decision. The other employees knew. Everybody knew but the employee. And he quite literally went on his merry way, doing his job in perfect peace and in complete ignorance of his impending fate. In due course, when the man was fired, he justifiably expressed complete bewilderment. Predictably, he filed a lawsuit, which was later settled out of court for a considerable sum of money. This is a case where an employee made a terribly inaccurate inference based on an information vacuum. The manager's lack of courage in confronting the situation was regrettable, but all too typical.

A less dramatic though more frequent situation occurs when managers sugarcoat their feedback (see, for example, Cusella 1987). They overemphasize the positive and downplay the negative. On the one hand, employees may assume the best, in which case true problems go undetected and uncorrected. On the other hand, employees may assume the worse, in which case anxiety and undue stress are the likely results. Either way, employee performance suffers. In the end, both the employee and the company lose.

6. Effective Managers Should Specifically Note Both Positive and Negative Deviations From the Standards

Although the precise techniques that should be employed are discussed in detail later, the fundamental process is really quite simple. Managers who have, as a first step, informed employees of the standards, should use the standards as a springboard for both praise and criticism. If the employees exceed the standards, they should be praised. If their performance dips, they should likewise be informed. Initially, even if they just meet the standards, they should be told.

The benefits are many. First, employees will realize that management takes the standards seriously. This is why it is particularly important to mention specifically when new employees achieve even the minimal standards. Also, some standards are, by necessity, ambiguous, and employees may not even be aware of what they are doing right. Second, precise feedback acts as a motivator. In one study, employees were asked to recall a specific incident that caused their productivity to increase. Over 65% of the employees mentioned some kind of feedback from management—a written note of praise from the company president or an extra bonus for effectively completing a challenging task (Clampitt and Downs 1993). Finally, employees are more likely to develop a commitment to the standards if they are given feedback. Ultimately, the goal of any feedback system is to have employees internalize the standards instead of depending on external commentary by others. After repeated performance at a certain level and aided by appropriate feedback, employees begin to develop a set of personal expectations. Actions then spring from a well of resolve and determination. This is why true professionals in any field, whether sports, dance, or management, consistently strive for excellence. To paraphrase an old jingle, "They expect more of themselves and they get it."

7. *Organizations Should Regularly and Systematically Reevaluate Standards of Performance*

The competitive environment changes, technology changes, and consequently expectations change. Thus, managers naturally need to reconsider the usefulness of the current performance standards. Are the present standards sufficient to meet corporate goals? To be competitive? Have the employees suggested any new standards? These are the kinds of questions that must regularly be asked to ensure the viability of the standards. For instance, only a few years ago it took up to two months to process an insurance claim. Now some companies can do it in several hours. A new standard has been forced on the industry because of both competitive pressures and technical improvements. Firms that cannot meet those industry standards will eventually perish. This is not to say that standards are always in a state of flux. Somewhere between frozen rigidity and chaos lies a semipermanent middle ground that provides both flexibility and reasonable certainty.

Implementing a Successful Feedback System

The principles previously discussed provide a useful background, but they cannot ensure a successful feedback system. Success is a product of both sound principles and effective actions. There are countless systems and methods for providing employees with feedback. No doubt more will be developed in the future. Yet, ultimately, the success of any system hinges on four basic questions:

1. Do employees know their job responsibilities?
2. Do employees know the standards of evaluation?
3. Is the informal feedback system effective?
4. Is the formal feedback system effective?

There cannot be a weak link in the chain. The answer to each of these questions must be affirmative for the feedback system to work. If there is weakness at any point, the entire system collapses.

Do Employees Know Their Job Responsibilities?

Dynamic and ever-changing organizations tend to experience the most difficulties in the area of ensuring that employees know their job responsibilities. For instance, an employee at a large newspaper said, "I would like my position more defined. Where exactly do I fit in this organization? What is my importance?" These are the kinds of comments that indicate problems with the job description link in the feedback system. Our research in over thirty companies revealed that almost 20% of the employees felt unsatisfied with information about their job requirements (see Appendix B). Clearly, if employees do not know their job responsibilities, they are probably not doing their job. The reasons for this are many. A manager may have assumed the employee already know. Employees may not have read their job descriptions. Situations may have changed so much that the written job descriptions are outdated. The employee may get conflicting messages about the actual job duties from coworkers and the supervisor.

A variety of tactics have been used to inform employees of their job duties. For instance, managers often use the appraisal interview to "compare notes" with their employees on job duties. Another highly touted suggestion is to have written job descriptions for every employee. But, because job duties are always evolving, this approach often falls into disfavor. Here is a classic example of confusing the end-product with purpose: the list of job duties (i.e., the end-product) is less important that the *process* of writing out the duties. Writing out job descriptions forces managers and employees to think and communicate about job duties.

Do Employees Know the Standards by Which They Are Being Evaluated?

The evidence indicates that evaluation standards is an area of great concern for employees. Research suggests that 43% of the employees are unsatisfied with information about how they are being judged. For example, one manager at a bank said, "I know my job, my manager knows I know my job, but I haven't a clue in this world how he evaluates me." More specifically, an employee may know her job is to troubleshoot for an engineering division, but may be completely unaware of how her performance will be judged. Is it the number of problems she solves that counts? Does the complexity of the problem matter? What about the elegance of the solution? These are questions about standards of evaluation, not about job duties. Employees need to see the yardstick.

Why such problems exist is less easily determined. Sometimes managers never sit down to discuss, even in general terms, how employees will be evaluated. Managers may even feel some comfort in the ambiguity, which allows them greater flexibility in evaluating. Or, they may think that it is too difficult to specify criteria.

Some criteria can be easily quantified. A bank teller can be told that one performance criterion is the number of IRA accounts sold. In almost every job, there are at least a few quantifiable criteria. Surely managers should discuss these with employees. But there are also qualitative aspects of every job that are equally important. Bank tellers must be concerned with effective customer relations. Some overly enthusiastic behavioral psychologist might argue that even this can be quantified. A few businesses, for instance, insist that the employee smile at the customer at least six times while conducting a transaction and conclude with a canned, "Have a nice day." These dictates may work for robots, but they quickly wear thin with employees and clients. Thus, I do not share in the behaviorist's mad rush to quantify everything that can be counted. Harry Levinson (1970) has perceptively commented, "The greater the emphasis on measurement and quantification, the more likely the subtle, non-measurable elements of the task will be sacrificed. Quality of performance frequently, therefore, loses out to quantification" (p. 127).

How then can these qualitative criteria be communicated while maintaining employee accountability? There is no easy answer. Discussions need to take place with employees so that they can begin to get the feel for the more subtle criteria. Sometimes it is only through daily feedback and coaching that an employee develops an understanding of the more qualitative criteria. It happens over time. There is an added benefit of using some qualitative criteria. Employees will often think of novel ways to fulfill the criteria. There are countless ways to maintain effective customer relations, and as employees learn what the criteria mean, they may discover new approaches. Moreover, employees will develop greater commitment to their own novel ideas as opposed to a manager's edicts. In the end, these employees are far more effective than the six-smiles-a-client automaton.

Is the Informal Feedback System Effective?

In the long run, the day-to-day "pat on the back" or reprimand may have a greater impact on employee performance than any other communication event. Regrettably, most employees are not satisfied with the daily feedback they receive, as the following comments demonstrate:

> ▷ "Specific positive reinforcement is [management's] worst problem. They can't seem to praise anyone. You'd think it was costing them money. "(Airline reservation clerk)
> ▷ "You feel good when someone says you've done good, but thanks are not given around here." (Newspaper employee)
> ▷ "[I need] more feedback on how well I'm performing at other times besides the annual job development review." (TV station employee)

The problem pervades organizations across the spectrum, from service-oriented companies to manufacturing firms. Indeed, over 40% of the employees in our databank were dissatisfied with the extent to which their efforts were recognized by the organization (see Appendix B).

There are two primary reasons for this problem. First, many managers do not take the time to give regular feedback. The inherently different perspectives of employees and managers compound the difficulty. For example, assume that a manager of a twenty-person department decides to spend three minutes every week giving honest feedback to each employee. From the manager's viewpoint, a substantial commitment is being made: an hour a week. On the other hand, three minutes a week is a mere commercial break to the employee. Thus, managers almost always overestimate, at least from the employees' perspective, the amount of daily feedback they communicate.

Second, many managers simply do not notice employee performance unless there are difficulties. Managers get more credit for problems solved than problems avoided. No wonder they are quick to comment when employees fail, but are slow to praise a job well done. Employees want to be recognized, and they bemoan the "No news is good news" managerial philosophy.

Executives at Preston Trucking found this out the hard way. The relations between management and labor became so unsettling at the company that they instituted the "Four-to-One Rule." Managers were required to give four messages of praise for every message of criticism. One can imagine the truckers' initial reaction. Over time, not only did tensions ease, but relations even became collegial. In fact, in one year alone, employees submitted over 4000 ideas to the suggestion program with an average value to the company of $300 each (Farnham 1989).

Is the Formal Feedback System Effective?

Much ink has been spilled over the issue of performance appraisals. Business journals, periodicals, and books are filled with discussions on how to conduct the performance review more effectively. And with good reason; there is probably no greater area of employee dissatisfaction. In fact, in a survey of 300 public and private agencies, Lopez (1968) found that 75% maintained performance evaluation plans but less that half said that the plans were achieving their stated objectives. This disgruntled employee expresses the sentiments of many:

> My immediate supervisor felt it was her duty to give me my evaluation as required once a year. It was handed to me with, "I'll discuss it later." When I asked her, "Why not now?" she said, "I don't have time." This was my year's work and it was no big deal! *It was to me.*

Other complaints abound. Unfair rating scales, lack of objectivity, and lack of specific examples are just a few of the ones frequently mentioned (Laird and Clampitt 1985). But this is not to say employees want to avoid the formal appraisal. Employees want this kind of feedback. In spite of problems, one survey found that 90% of the employees reacted favorably to the idea of a formal evaluation (Mayfield 1960). In short, the manager who wants to develop an effective feedback system faces a formidable challenge.

There are a variety of reasons for the problem, but three are particularly noteworthy. First, **many managers react negatively to the feedback process because it is used to accomplish multiple goals that are sometimes incompatible** (see Table 6.1). One airline we investigated used the appraisal process to provide individual feedback to employees, as well as to determine promotion potential and make salary adjustments. Many of the managers felt the variety of goals encouraged distortions, such as inflated ratings and a lack of negative comments. Some managers did not want to hurt employees' long-term promotion opportunities, so they made vague general comments. Others were less virtuous. One manager took a Machiavellian approach. He gave a troublesome employee high marks so as to promote

TABLE 6.1 Potential Objectives of Appraisal Systems

Objective	Concern
Make salary adjustments	Salary decisions are rarely based solely on performance. Factors like market conditions, length of service, and corporate economic outlook affect the decision.
Determine promotion potential	An employee may perform one job with a high degree of competence, but be unsuitable for greater responsibility.
"Grade" past performance	At times, a "grade" may not motivate employees. It may also fail to uncover important reasons for performance levels.
Motivate	Many managers leave out the "bad news" when trying to motivate employees.
Improve performance	Sometimes, managers are so problem-oriented they fail to praise employees effectively and specifically.

him out of his department. That is, of course, one way to get rid of a problem—give it to someone else.

The following manager speaks for many regarding the lack of clarity in his appraisal system's objectives:

> The uses are very nebulous. I don't know who sees the form or what is done with it. We are told one thing and another happens. The first year, they told us our workbooks were for our private use, so everyone was very candid. Then the department head collected them and put them in his files. It leaves great uncertainty as to how it is to be used.

This is the price of imprudence: the entire system falls into disrepute. And the basic purpose, indeed the entire rationale, for the feedback process falls by the wayside.

Second, many managers feel compelled to inflate ratings. It might be called the *Lake Wobegon Phenomenon,* where everyone is good looking and all the employees are above-average. Part of the problem lies in the natural competition between different departments. Many managers feel that other department managers rate their employees highly, and if they do not do the same, then their employees will be penalized in the long run. Another part of the problem lies in the meanings attached to the numbers or categories typically used in appraisal forms. In one study, we asked a group of managers from the same company to respond to a series of precise questions about what they meant when they used terms *above-average, average,* and *below-average* on their appraisal form. Many discrepancies were found. One of the more striking was the meaning of the word *average.* Over 60% of the managers believed it meant "the employee completed all jobs satisfactorily," while 37% felt it meant that "performance was uneven, some above-average and some below" (Laird and Clampitt 1985). Clearly, such discrepancies can lead to uneven evaluations.

Third, many managers resist the appraisal process because they feel that they are "playing God." Douglas McGregor (1972) expressed it eloquently:

> Managers are uncomfortable when they are put in the position of "playing God." The respect we hold for the inherent value of the individual leaves us distressed when we must take responsibility for judging the personal worth of a fellow man. Yet the conventional approach to performance appraisal forces us not only to make such judgments and to see them acted upon but also to communicate them to those we have judged. Small wonder we resist! (p. 134)

Understandably, managers try to avoid situations involving the deity-to-sinner kind of relationship. Yet, in many cases, this fear of "playing God" masks the deeper problem of an inability or unwillingness to face conflict.

Regardless of the actual reason for the reticence, managers are destined to "provide" some kind of feedback. The key, then, is to provide useful information. Furthermore, providing objectively based judgments need not imply a divine verdict on a person's worth. The alternatives are worse. Harold Mayfield (1960) put the matter in perspective:

> Is there one of us who has not kicked himself for some inglorious episode in our human relationships? This risk I believe to be one of the prices we must pay for any attempt at serious communications. Against it, we must weigh the cost of silence. It, too, leaves scars. (p. 83)

Summary

The four questions reviewed in this section provide a report card on the feedback system. A failing grade in any area undermines the entire system. Few managerial tasks are more important than properly training employees. Reviewing job duties, discussing evaluation criteria, providing daily feedback, and conducting formal reviews educate employees in a variety of ways. This kind of schooling helps employees learn the performance standards, especially the qualitative ones, as well as reinforces the importance of the standards. It also fosters commitment to the standards while encouraging productive behavior. The result: straight A employees capable of instructing new "students."

Communicating Performance Feedback

Providing effective informal and formal performance feedback may well be the singular characteristic distinguishing the merely adequate manager from the superior one. The skillful manager recognizes three essential aspects of this vital communicative task: the message, manner, and method.

The Message

Given the imperative to provide feedback, it is important to consider precisely what should be communicated. What should appraisers appraise? What should they talk about? These issues are discussed in this section.

First, provide feedback about performance directly related to agreed-upon standards. Therefore, both positive and negative deviations from the standards should be specifically noted. If a teller is required to sell twelve IRA accounts over the year, and after three months has not sold one, then this should be brought to the employee's attention. Likewise, if the teller has already sold six, then the employee should be praised.

Second, discuss uncommunicated performance standards. Some standards, by their nature, are difficult to articulate ahead of time. It is impossible to specify every standard. Who could anticipate, for instance, that an employee needs to be told about some specific grooming habits or proper modes of address? There are countless other examples, all of which can be dealt with only on a case-by-case basis, ever widening the circle of congruence.

Third, focus on the employee's unique abilities. Traditionally, managers "motivated" employees by rewarding or punishing specific performance behaviors. But people are more than rats. These behavioral techniques encourage the repetition of the same behavior. However, repeating the same behaviors may actually become dysfunctional, because situations change and novel contingencies arise. There is a better, more strategic approach. Character qualities such as thoughtfulness, attentiveness, flexibility, discretion, sensitivity, thoroughness, and diligence profoundly affect the quality of organizational life. Any opportunity to reinforce these values should be seized by the manager.

Specifically, the manager should praise both the behavior and the implicit character quality. The employee who submits an insightful proposal that has anticipated numerous potential objections could be praised for an "excellent report." Such a comment might encourage future reports of this type. But more could be said: "Your report is remarkable. It shows a quality of thoroughness and insightfulness that we value in this organization." The manager reinforces a specific behavior (i.e., report writing) but more importantly highlights the quality of thoroughness and insightfulness. Linking the specific behavior to the character qualities encourages employees not only to continue writing quality reports, but also to find other novel situations in which to exhibit these qualities. The charm of a character quality such as "thoroughness" or "insightfulness" lies in its ambiguity. It can be applied in so many different situations that even the wisest manager could not anticipate (see Figure 6.2). Such an approach brings to bear the naturally motivating creative instincts in people. It has the indelible mark of the human touch.

Focusing on the employee's unique capabilities motivates employees in special ways. Great statesmen, like great managers, seem to have special insights into the unique characteristics of those with whom they work closely. They have an extraordinary grasp of the essential and fundamental qualities of the person. One of the greatest leaders of all time, Winston Churchill (1931), wrote of Lloyd George:

> The new Prime Minister possessed two characteristics that were in harmony with this period of convulsion. First, a power of living in the present, without taking short views. Every day for him was filled with the hope and the impulse of a fresh beginning. He surveyed the problems of each morning with an eye unobstructed by preconceived opinions, past utterances, or previous disappointment and defeats. In times of peace such a mood is not always admirable, nor often successful for long. But in the intense crisis when the world was a kaleidoscope, when every month all the values and relations were changed by some prodigious event and its measureless reactions, this inexhaustible mental agility, guided by the main purpose of Victory, was a rare advantage. His intuition fitted the crisis better than the logical reasoning of more rigid minds. (pp. 688–689)

This is the kind of praise the wise manager gives. It is based on keen observation and shows deep thought into the person's uniqueness. Employees will perceive this type of praise as sincere and be motivated by the manager's thoughtfulness. It is not some blanket "warm fuzzy" cast on any passerby. In short, it demonstrates insight into an individual's character.

This is not enough, however. Otherwise, all biographers would be great statesmen. There must also be the knowledge and willingness to transform insight into action. In addition to Churchill's extraordinary discernment into Lloyd George's qualities, he also demonstrated an amazing perceptiveness into situations in which the Prime Minister would be most effective. Herein lies the essence of world-class management.

The Manner

How performance discussions are handled may be as important as the message itself. Many people react more to style than substance. The wise manager is attentive to both.

First, be specific and descriptive when making evaluations. The most frequent problem with management's effort to praise employees lies in the level of specificity (Larson 1986). Typically, praise runs along these lines: "Good job," "Way to go," or "Atta-boy." Although abstractness is useful in some circumstances, it is not in this case. Moreover, this kind of praise tends to be more evaluative than descriptive.

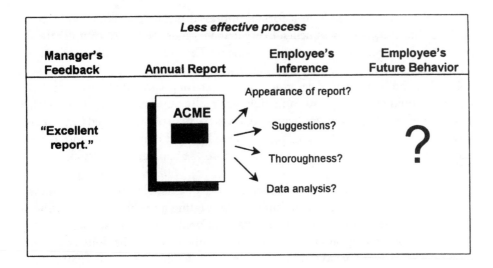

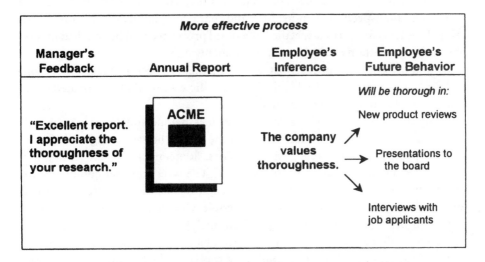

Figure 6.2. Linking Praise to Attributes

Researchers have found that descriptive praise is more effective (Downs, Johnson, and Barge 1984). For example, the typical manager tends to say, "You really are effective with customers." A more useful and descriptive comment might be, "You really have an ability to communicate effectively with customers. The way you smile and ask pertinent questions shows your sensitivity to their needs." These remarks show that the manager pays precise attention to the employee's performance. Moreover, the manager links the behaviors to the character quality of "sensitivity," while personally recognizing the employee—one life touching another.

Applying this principle in a formal appraisal means providing evidence to back up the ratings or assessments. Every manager must be able to confidently answer this question: can I prove my assessment? The problem usually does not occur on the negative items, but surprisingly with the positive issues. Instead of saying, "You did a great job designing the advertising campaign this year," the manager could say, " Your ad campaign was really quite successful. Our market share increased after it was implemented. I was particularly impressed by your creative use of dialogue in the campaign." These kinds of remarks are more readily accepted by employees and provide insight into the manager's yardstick.

Second, criticize tactfully. Criticism needs to be handled with equal finesse. "Giving criticism must satisfy multiple goals—stating a problem clearly while at the same time remaining attentive to the relational implications," write Tracy, VanDusen, and Robinson (1987, p. 46). Certainly, it should be done in private, with an emphasis on behavioral corrections (Arvey and Ivancevich 1980). Managers should distinguish between personality traits, which are most often treated as nonchangeable aspects of an individual, and character qualities that anyone can develop. Indeed, criticism of a specific behavioral problem could be couched in terms of acquiring a certain character quality. Students may be encouraged to spell correctly and use grammar properly by exhorting them to become more professional and show an attentiveness to detail. Thus, specific writing skills are related to two qualities useful in a wide variety of settings.

Employees are naturally defensive if they feel their personality is what is really being evaluated. If managers deeply ponder the matter, however, they will often see that the problems lie in some basic behaviors. Someone, for instance, might remark, "You are a very stubborn individual." The wise manager comments on a specific behavior: "During meetings, you need to listen more carefully to others' ideas and suggestions. You could look at people while they talk and even try to restate their opinion rather than your objections." Even linking the behaviors to a character quality might prove useful: "I personally appreciate the way you stand by your convictions. This is admirable, but this could be balanced with a greater sensitivity to others. It is important to be a person of conviction, but it is equally important to know when to use this quality." The employee still might bristle at those comments, but, in the long run, change is more likely.

There is probably a no more delicate situation than when criticizing someone. Buck Rogers (1986), who served as vice president of marketing at IBM for ten years, remarked:

> I think that at one time I was perceived as an easygoing type of manager with a superior staff of people. That's because I always praised in public and criticized in private. I never thought it necessary to let others know that someone in my department didn't do his job properly. . . . I entered each of these private conversations with the assumption that both of us wanted to accomplish the same thing: perform our job with the highest degree of excellence possible. And, with a minimum of bruised feelings, correct our mistakes and get on with the job. (pp. 40–41)

Clearly, the proper motivation and setting is the place to start. Note that Rogers links his criticism to a larger positive context. This is one of the keys to effective criticism. Another is that the feedback should be maximally informative and minimally evaluative (Downs, Smeyak, and Martin 1980). People react differently to criticism. Employees who are confident and have a high need for achievement react more positively. They may even actively seek negative feedback in order to improve their performance. Employees with lower self-esteem and achievement needs may become disheartened and discouraged (McFarlin and Blascovich 1981). Clearly, the wise manager adapts to these different contingencies.

Third, capitalize on employee motivations. Effective managers not only are sensitive to the natural motivators of their employees, but also know how to link the motivators to critical objectives. Indeed, there is abundant evidence from scholars that feedback without employee commitment to improve does not increase performance (see, for example, Pinder 1984). In Figure 6.3, the manager fails to pick up on the fact that the employee is highly motivated to provide quality service to the customer. The manager could have linked customer service to the problem areas of organization and selling NOW accounts. For example, the manager might have said, "I'm impressed by your commitment to quality customer service. By being organized you can better service the customer. For instance, you will be able to find vital information more quickly, which will translate into speedier service for the customers." Such linkages may be difficult to execute, but they reap great dividends.

While at a conference in Philadelphia, I noticed a building a few blocks from my hotel that was being torn down to make way for a new structure. A massive crane with a huge wrecking ball pounded into the building and slowly ripped apart the structure. For five days this enormous crush of iron on brick went on, and still, the small ten-story structure was only partially demolished. What a contrast to the instantaneous destruction of much larger buildings by the careful placement of dynamite charges at strategic points. In a matter of seconds, even a fifty-story building can be toppled. Unfortunately many managers thrash into their employees with salvo after salvo of criticism like this massive wrecking ball. They ignore employee motivations, focus on personality characteristics, refuse to specify their concerns, and fail to notice employees' unique abilities. The result—the source of irritation is never really removed, thus a new structure cannot be built. A wise manager, like demolition expert, discerns those strategic points and quickly removes the offending behaviors so as to erect in the same spot a new and gleaming building of character.

The Methods

One critical issue remains: the manager needs the proper message and manner, but without the right methods, all is for naught. This section outlines guidelines for managing the feedback processes.

Speaker	Dialogue	Commentary
Manager:	Hi Chris. Welcome. Please sit down.	
Employee:	Thank you.	
Manager:	As you know, this is the regularly scheduled performance appraisal that I conduct with each employee. The purpose of this talk is to review your performance during the past year. Actually, there should be few surprises, because I've tried to keep you informed throughout the year. You've read over my report, I assume, so I want to spend our time discussing some critical areas and answer any of your questions.	*The manager does an effective job of orienting the employee. Could discuss how the information in the interview will be used.*
Employee:	Fine. That sounds good, because I do have some questions.	
Manager:	I'd like to start with the positive areas. Let me just list your greatest strengths:	*The manager has clearly thought about the strengths of the employee.*
	1. You seem to be able to handle the cash drawer without assistance or errors.	*The manager could discuss specific communication abilities that are valued by a company that stresses customer service.*
	2. You have the ability to explain savings products effectively to customers.	
	3. Your general attitude toward the job is quite positive.	*The manager could isolate a quality, like enthusiasm, that is essential for the job, and provide examples of how Chris exhibited this quality.*
	In general, I'm impressed by your abilities after being here only nine months.	
Employee:	Well, thanks—I've really tried hard. I enjoy working here, and that really helps. My coworkers are really a joy to work with—they make it easy.	*The employee reveals that coworkers are a source of motivation.*
Manager:	Now, I'd like to explore with you three areas of improvement. First, I've rated you average in organizational abilities. At times, you seem unorganized.	*The manager does not bring up specific evidence or the harm done by poor organization.*
Employee:	Well, I just try to do so much—sometimes I don't take time to keep things organized. I mean, I try to keep my papers straight and stuff, but my priority is on customer service.	*The employee sees no relationship between organization and customer service.*
Manager:	Oh, but I still think some improvement is needed here.	*The manager should show some link between organization, working well with coworkers, and effective customer service.*

Figure 6.3. Sample Appraisal Interview

Employee: I've always had this problem and, frankly, it seems more important to serve customer needs.	*The employee fails to take responsibility for the problem.*
Manager: The second area that I'd like to see improvement in is cross-selling. We set a goal of cross-selling seven NOW accounts. You actually sold five NOW accounts. I'd like to see that up to par next year. You know this is a priority in the business.	*The manager ignores the employee's denial and fails to offer useful suggestions. The manager does provide specific evidence to back up the second evaluation.*
Employee: I know I've kind of failed in that area, but sometimes it's so hard. I feel kind of awkward mentioning it—I just try to be friendly. I don't want to offend the customer. I feel like I really do service the customer effectively.	
Manager: Well, you do, but I'd still like to see more cross-selling. The third area is bringing in new customers. We set a goal of ten new customers—I have only five new customers credited to your efforts this year.	*The manager misses the opportunity to link the sale of NOW accounts to customer service.*
Employee: You know that goal is practically impossible. All my friends are already customers, and I just don't know what to do.	*The employee attributes the problem to the goal, not to self.*
Manager: I understand. This isn't really criticism. Overall, you're doing a fine job—I want to emphasize that! For only being here nine months, I'm impressed. Really!	*The manager soft-pedals the criticism.*
Employee: So you think I'm doing a good job!	*The employee seeks out a positive evaluation.*
Manager: Yes, basically, yes. You are making progress—I'm pleased. Do you have any questions?	*The manager obliges.*
Employee: No, it's basically what I expected. I mean, you always tell me I'm doing a good job. Thanks.	
Manager: Well, there are some areas of improvement.	*The manager is halfheartedly fulfilling an obligation, but is not trying to change Chris's behavior.*
Employee: Yes, I know, but basically I'm doing a good job. I mean, I like my job and the people I work with. Is that all?	*The employee feels good and sees no need to change.*
Manager: Yes, I guess so, except I need you to sign this form.	*The manager feels relieved, because the review is over.*

Figure 6.3. Continued

First, utilize "task-inherent" feedback. Sometimes, the most useful feedback comes from the task itself, not the supervisor. For example, commissioned sales-people are inherently aware of their level of sales. In this case, a supervisor may not need to comment on the discrepancy between goal and performance level. Rather, the supervisor's role becomes more of a coach and counselor. Indeed, when an employee has developed a commitment to certain standards, task-inherent feedback may be more important to the employee than feedback from a supervisor. Employees are more likely to accept feedback from those who have directly experienced their work and who they deem credible. This may include clients, coworkers, and even top management (Cusella 1987). The wise course for a supervisor might be to create mechanisms for employees so that they receive feedback about their performance from the task itself. For example, a group of tellers could observe a videotaped focus group about the bank's service reputation. Such methods are a subtle way to augment the appraisal process. For many managers, conducting a performance appraisal is a perfunctory and sometimes dreaded task. Indeed, Figure 6.3 provides an example of the all too common approach to this critical communication event. Part of the problem is that training is either nonexistent or lax (Moscinski 1979). Yet the wise manager makes virtue out of necessity by effectively managing the message as well as the process.

Second, seize every opportunity to provide employee feedback. The *One-Minute Manager* has dominated the best-seller lists much longer than the title might suggest. The premise is simple: "Catch" employees doing the right things and tell them. Admonish them on the spot when you find them doing the wrong things. The timing and informality are critical, because these one-minute discussions provide helpful feedback in a nonthreatening environment. Corrections can be made quickly, and core company values can be reinforced specifically. In fact, several one-minute chats may do more good than the most carefully planned appraisal interview. Perhaps this is why the one-minute manager's advice endures over time.

Third, decide on a useful technique to assess employee performance formally. Essay evaluations, rating scales, observation periods, ranking methods, and critical incident techniques are just a few of the options (Oberg 1972). The specific objectives of the system should dictate the type of approach (see Table 6.2). If the purpose is basically to encourage employee growth, then written essays about employee performance would prove useful. If there is a highly competitive situation within the unit (i.e., a sales force) then maybe ranking employees is the best approach. Rating scales are the most widely used approach. Those consisting of five to nine categories tend to produce the most consistent ratings. Regardless of the method used, training is the key to ensure that practice harmonizes with purpose.

In some cases, managers do not have a say in the evaluation methods. They are told by the company what forms to use. This makes it all the more important to know the limitations and advantages of the various options. The wise manager can then supplement the mandatory system with other "homegrown" measures.

TABLE 6.2 Appraisal Techniques

Method	Strengths	Weaknesses
Rating scale	Allows comparison between employees without forcing distinctions	Might be disagreement over meanings of the numbers
	Easy to use	
Essay	Allows appraiser flexibility to uniquely characterize each employee	Is difficult to compare employees
		Might have variances between raters in level of specificity
Rank order	Creates clear distinctions between employees (Often used for salary purposes)	Forces unfair or artificial comparisons between employees
Critical incidents	Focuses on employee behavior	Takes time to record every incident
	Avoids appraisals of employee personality	May cause manager to delay daily feedback
	Provides specific evidence	May encourage an overemphasis on the peaks and valleys of performance, rather than typical performance
Management by objectives	Increases employee motivation and understanding of standards	Takes significant time and effort
		May be difficult to compare employees

Fourth, discuss with employees the exact purpose of appraisal interviews. As has been well documented previously, numerous problems arise when employees and management do not precisely understand the purpose of the interview. It can become a sham. A written policy that is widely available throughout the organization detailing the purposes of the process is a useful starting point. All managers in the organization should have a similar view of the purpose of the formal feedback system. At the outset of the interview, every employee should be reminded of the appraisal's purpose as well as of how the information will be used. This helps new employees determine what type of information is appropriate to share. Even though this may become a bit repetitive over the years, it helps ensure that employees are continually focused on one objective. Setting a specific time and place for the interview sends a powerful secondary message that the interaction has great significance. Interruptions and phone calls should be avoided. Even the written documentation used can communicate the serious nature of the encounter.

Fifth, assign employees specific preparations for the appraisal process. Many organizations provide appraisal forms for both the manager and the subordinate that are parallel in format. The manager rates the employee's performance in designated areas, and the employee rates his or her own performance on a similar form. These documents are to be completed before the actual appraisal interview, and may even include task-inherent measures. This step reinforces the importance of the process, while ensuring that employees come to the meeting fully prepared. The two documents can also serve as a stimulus for focused discussion on the employee's performance. No topics are skirted out of fear or anxiety. All issues are more objectively addressed. Using these forms, the interview can proceed after a thorough discussion of the employee's job responsibilities.

Sixth, carefully consider how interpersonal needs influence the feedback process. Generally, managers try to avoid giving negative feedback unless severe problems have been recognized. Moreover, because managers do not wish to appear judgmental, they frequently distort their feedback in a positive direction (Fischer 1979). For example, note how the manager in Figure 6.3 says, "This isn't really criticism . . . Overall you are doing a fine job." On the other hand, employees seek to maintain a positive self-esteem and typically see negative information as more positive than it actually is (Ilgen, Fischer, and Taylor 1979). They often attribute problems to factors beyond their control. Compounding the matter is that poor performers actively try to short-circuit criticism by seeking out positive comments (Larson 1989). Note, for example, how in Figure 6.3 the employee implies that there is simply not enough time to be organized. In other words, it is not Chris's fault.

Poor performers may even build the excuses into their inquiries or ask leading questions about their performance (Larson 1989). Notice that Chris's final remarks end with a question that almost begs the manager for confirmation of an overly glowing assessment. Therefore, the manager and employee, by virtue of their predispositions, co-create a process in which each party inevitably draws seemingly reasonable but decidedly warped impressions. Employees "may hold positively inflated views of their organizational performance" (Cusella 1987), but managers frequently have an equally skewed view, and feel that employees have a clear understanding of the areas of improvement, when in fact, they do not. Certainly, this is what happened in Figure 6.3, and the end result was that the employee's performance never improved. Wise managers are aware of these powerful forces at work in the appraisal interview. They seek to control the process so employees have an unclouded view of their performance, while carefully avoiding needless damage to self-esteem. Charles Ames (1989), the former CEO of three companies including Uniroyal Goodrich Tire Company, summarized the manager's responsibility best:

> There is nothing kind about glossing over weaknesses that could be corrected if the individual were aware of them. Nor is there anything kind about deluding someone into thinking that he or she is doing well or has greater opportunities than is actually the case. Failure to be completely honest can easily hurt someone's chances of becoming an effective contributor. And it may even jeopardize the person's career. No manager has the right to do that. And if the manager can't get up

the nerve or confidence to talk straight about this, that manager shouldn't remain a manager—because that person isn't. (p. 138)

Finally, use past performance as a bridge to the future. Although part of the feedback process should be dedicated to an evaluation of the past, there is also a need to seek change for the future. New contingencies brought on by the inevitable changes in the organization and the competitive environment can be discussed as a focal point for new standards and goals. After all, the focus of the entire feedback process is the relationship between actions and goals—in a word, performance. Goal setting can be addressed at the latter part of the interview. In the end, the employee, regardless of the course of the appraisal, should be offered the most basic of all human needs: hope.

Conclusion

In the long run, the effective feedback system seeks to improve employee performance so as to increase organizational performance. Whatever method is chosen to accomplish this end, this goal must be central in the manager's mind. As Harold Mayfield (1960) put it, "Stripped of all jargon, it is simply an attempt to think clearly about each person's performance and future prospects against a background of this total work situation" (p. 27). It takes effort, thought, and dedication to accomplish, but the rewards to managers, employees, and the organization alike are manyfold.

At MetaComm we conducted one communication assessment in which the company scored considerably below-average on every feedback question. Upon arriving at the company to present the results, we walked past an isolated cluster of brown, brittle, and dying shrubbery in front of the company's office. At the time, I thought this was a perfect symbol for this company's management philosophy! The company watered and cared for those bushes about as well as they gave feedback to their employees. The employees had no job descriptions, they had no idea how they were being evaluated, they were never praised, and appraisal reviews had not been conducted in years. The end results were predictable: low job satisfaction, poor motivation, uneven performance, and a host of other communication difficulties. Most companies are not in such severe shape. Nevertheless, every company could pay much closer attention to its feedback system. As any horticulturist knows, this can be done only day-by-day and with the utmost of care.

Note

1. For an insightful review of Maslow's contributions, see Gabor (2000), pp. 153–186.

SEVEN

Communicating Change

> There is nothing more difficult to carry out, nor more doubtful of success, nor more dangerous to handle, than to initiate a new order of things. For the reformer has enemies in all those who profit from the old order, and only lukewarm defenders in all those who would profit from the new order, this lukewarmness arising partly from the incredibility of anything new until they have had actual experience of it.
>
> *Machiavelli*

> Failure is never fatal, but failure to change might be.
>
> *John Wooden*

An organization's long-term survival may be best judged by its ability to manage change rather than by its current balance sheet. Yet most organizations are far more adept at evaluating budgets and rates of return than they are at measuring the effectiveness of their change efforts. Perhaps it is easier to judge financial results than it is to evaluate the rate and degree of acceptance of an effort to change. To be sure, some changes, such as downsizing, result in short-term economic gains. But the long-term financial results are often questionable. James Champy (1995), one of the founding fathers of reengineering, acknowledged quite candidly, "On the whole, however, even substantial reengineering payoffs appear to have fallen well short of their potential" (p. 3). One reason for an organization's spotty record on change management is that the methods used to introduce change are poorly understood.

Take your pick of recent managerial buzzwords: empowerment, lean manufacturing, reengineering, quality, or e-commerce. Implicit in each of the ideas is change. More precisely, each of these notions requires major communicative efforts. Employees do not just accept an idea because it sounds progressive. For example, an underlying assumption of empowerment is that employees want to be empowered. Yet we have interviewed numerous employees who freely admit that they would prefer to be told exactly what to do. Thinking is hard work, or least a kind of work that the many employees are not used to doing. Often, major organizational changes require employees to take on new or different duties. How are they convinced to do so? In short, regardless of the organization's motivation for implementing change, there is a need to properly communicate it. Ironically, almost all the fathers of these movements recognize the importance of communication, but few develop systematic communication plans.

Approaches to Change

All organizations either explicitly or implicitly have an orientation to change that defines for employees who can suggest, institute, and act on a new idea. Three typical patterns emerge: management orientation, employee orientation, and integrative orientation.

Management Orientation

Traditionally, top management assesses the need for change and dictates that the change be carried out through the chain of command. This is the approach taken by the Arrow manager. The assumption is that those in leadership positions are in a better position to recognize the need for change, to know what needs to be changed, and even to know how the change should be implemented. There are variations on this general theme, but such is the archetype.

Some corporations, out of necessity, adopt this approach because of a turbulent business environment or rapidly changing conditions. The court-ordered reorganization of AT & T and Bell telephone companies is certainly one such example. Mr. Zane Barnes, the CEO of Southwestern-Bell, remarked that after deregulation, top management identified 2000 different major changes that were needed to comply with the court order. Not only was rapid change needed, but phone service, telephone hookups, and other services had to continue to be maintained at the high level of service that customers had come to expect. According to Barnes, "It was like trying to take apart and reassemble a 747 while in flight." If leadership from the top was not exerted, then chaos would have been the likely result. In this case, as in many others, the top-down strategy was the only reasonable alternative.

Change may also be instigated at the top when a CEO or a manger has a bright, new vision of where the organization can be in the future. Former Secretary of State, Henry Kissinger (1982), has perceptively written on statesmanship:

> A nation and its leaders must choose between moral certainty coupled with exorbitant risk, and the willingness to act on unprovable assumptions to deal with challenges when they are manageable. I favor the latter course. . . . The statesman's duty is to bridge the gap between his nation's experience and his vision. If he gets too far ahead of his people, he will lose his mandate; if he confines himself to the conventional he will lose control over events. The qualities that distinguish a great statesman are prescience and courage, not analytical intelligence. He must have a conception of the future and the courage to move toward it while it is still shrouded to most of his compatriots. (p. 169)

Likewise, some prescient managers see beyond the sights of the colleagues and predict with astonishing regularity the future trends while leading the company in that direction. A. P. Giannini of Bank of America was such a man. As the corporate founder, he was one of the first to introduce advertising by banks, bankcards, and a host of other ideas. By leading the way, visionaries ensure the organization has a stake in the future. Without courageous leadership, a company can only adopt the innovations of others, when it usually proves more costly and difficult to capture the market share. Or the opportunity is simply lost. There is a price for complacency.

An overly zealous management orientation, however, can be problematic. Stifling the innovative spirit of employees is one possible result. If the operating principle appears to be, "The only good ideas come from the top," then opportunities can be squandered with amazing ease. Moreover, employee satisfaction and productivity may decline. And even "visionary leadership" can go awry. Coca-Cola is not the only company to have had a new product, New Coke, hailed as a bold new innovative change, that subsequently had difficulties in the marketplace. Visions do not always translate into reality; they may be mere delusions.

Employee Orientation

The heart of this approach is *intrapreneurship*; ideas for changes and innovations percolate up through the organizational hierarchy (Pinchot 1985). Employees are encouraged to have input into changes and methods of implementation. The underlying premise of this approach is that employees are in the best position to suggest changes. The basic operating principle is that those who participate in making the decisions for a change are more likely to wholeheartedly accept and implement the change. Circuit managers favor this approach.

Lucrative opportunities may be lost when employee ideas are ignored. A kind of collective blindness can occur in which management views a situation in a similar way. Ralph Lauren tried for years to sell his superiors and colleagues on his unique fashion concept. He failed. But he struck out on his own, becoming one of the most successful retailers in the world. Not only did he create the distinctive "Polo look" in clothing, but he has also branched out into home furnishings (Trachtenberg 1988). The voice of a solitary prophet in the wilderness may be more trustworthy than the chants and choruses of the multitudes.

Integrative Orientation

The critiques of the two previous approaches suggest a third and more appropriate choice for managing change. The central focus is not on *who* champions the change, but on the *who, what, when,* and *where:* the situation. In the integrative approach the manager has to determine if the situation warrants the management orientation, employee orientation, or some combination of the two. There is no one best strategy for coping with change, just as there is not one best form of transportation. It all depends on who is traveling with you, what you intend to do, when you plan to leave, and where you intend to go. A car is best for a trip to the grocery store, but the plane would surely prove more useful on a transatlantic journey. Likewise, the wise manager needs to choose the appropriate vehicle for change.

Many effective and useful changes can be initiated at the grassroots of the organization. Benefits such as greater understanding and commitment to change naturally flow from this approach. However, all changes cannot be initiated at this level of the organization. The very element that makes grassroots innovation so uniquely enlightening also acts as a conceptual blinder. Employees with the grassroots vantage point usually focus on grassroots problems, which often preclude a clear understanding of changes needed at other levels of the organization. For example, the supervisor of the printing shop may have excellent suggestions about how to improve the efficiency and effectiveness of that department. However, the supervisor's boss, who manages the printing, purchasing, and maintenance departments may need to ask a more fundamental question: Can the corporation as a whole function more effectively by having material printed by an outside vendor? Almost by definition, this is a change that the print shop supervisor cannot recommend. On the other hand, the manager has a broader companywide perspective from which to view the situation. Indeed, a study by Paul, Robertson, and Herzberg (1969) makes precisely this point. They found that when personnel specialists were asked to suggest changes in their own jobs, the specialists typically came up with fewer than thirty minor changes. Yet their managers came up with a list of over 100 ideas involving substantial change to enhance the personnel job.

Labeling this approach *integrative* is not incidental. Management and employee orientations are needed in an organization. The successful business uses a strategy in which the natural strengths of each approach are realized, while the unique weaknesses of each are masked. I am not implying that in some haphazard way employees should be given orders one moment and asked for participation the next. Rather, the point is to integrate the two approaches in a logical and meaningful way, just as our left eye compensates for the distortions of the right eye. Employees need to understand why certain changes are appropriately and necessarily made at different levels of the organization. There is an added bonus: binocular vision, which produces depth perception. And almost every organization could benefit from a deeper and clearer vision.

Types of Change

All changes are not of equal magnitude. Effective managers create unique communication strategies based on the degree of change. Changes can be described on a continuum from routine to nonroutine. On the routine extreme would be changes that occur on a regular basis. For instance, financial institutions frequently change interest rates and airlines typically have a variety of different promotions. On the other end of the continuum are such changes as major reorganizations, new product lines, or a redeployment of resources, such as Microsoft deciding to embrace the Internet.

But everyone does not share the same perspective about the magnitude of change. Figure 7.1 illustrates how the perspectives of the initiator's and receiver's of change interact to create different communication scenarios. Ideally, managers view changes from the perspective of the receivers, and communicate accordingly. They avoid over- or undercommunicating.

Frequently, those instituting changes underestimate the impact that the change will have. For instance, upgrades in software may cause organizational havoc because the programmers see the changes as relatively minor, but users have a decidedly different view. This is illustrated in quadrant D of Figure 7.1. The key in situations such as this is to get the initiators of change to understand the situation as receivers do (i.e., to move from quadrant D to quadrant B). This is often not an easy task. A committee may devote weeks studying a new office procedure. Committee members become familiar with all the arguments and counterarguments for various perspectives through an almost countless number of iterations of talk back and forth. Unconsciously, they transition through various difficult reaction stages leading to the proposal's acceptance. Yet they will devote little time communicating about those matters, and instead communicate only the final proposal. The end result is undercommunication.

Occasionally, employees will overcommunicate, and provide their colleagues with more information than they desire (a tendency in quadrant A). Unfortunately, the ease of forwarding e-mail encourages those who fail to understand others' priorities and information needs. More information does not necessarily equal better communication. Ideally, change initiators would understand the perspectives of their intended audiences. Routine changes would be treated as simple information-sharing situations and conform to the principles discussed in the chapter on information management (Chapter 4). Nonroutine changes would be seen as a time for strategic communication and conform to the principles discussed in the remainder of the chapter.

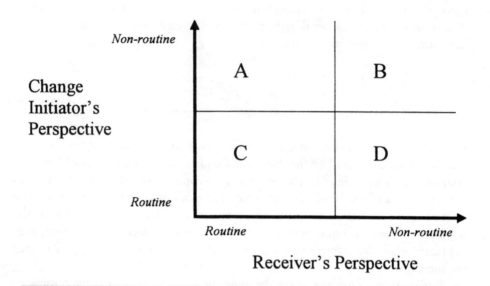

Figure 7.1. Perspectives on Change

Reactions to Change

Major changes almost always involve at least a temporary loss of employee productivity. As seen in Figure 7.2, there are two dimensions of the drop: the depth of the drop (A) and the duration of the drop (B). An effective communication strategy seeks to minimize both the depth and duration of the loss.

In fact, employees also often experience a loss of a different sort, more akin to bereavement. Few scholars know more about this process than Elisabeth Kubler-Ross. Her keenly perceptive work, *On death and dying* (1969), presents a theory about the psychological stages that terminally ill patients go through in learning to cope with their impending death:

▷ Stage 1—Denial and Isolation
▷ Stage 2—Anger
▷ Stage 3—Bargaining
▷ Stage 4—Depression
▷ Stage 5—Acceptance

Her approach focuses on easing the natural pain, stress, and trauma of the situation by using communication strategies that are compatible with the patient's stage in the coping process. Such efforts require a deep sensitivity to the patient's unique psychological makeup. There are no pat answers, only some general princi-

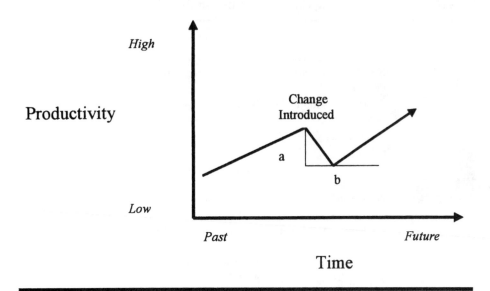

High

Productivity

Change
Introduced

a

b

Low

Past   Future

Time

Figure 7.2. The Effect of Change on Productivity

ples to follow (see Table 7.1). Moreover, Kubler-Ross makes the important point that how well a patient handles the situation depends, to a great extent, on how effectively the doctors, nurses, and family members communicate.

When faced with major changes, many employees will go through similar, though less severe, stages of reactions. The manager's skill in guiding employees through this process greatly affects the smoothness of the transition. If a manager can be sensitive enough to the verbal and nonverbal cues so as to discern the stage of employee reaction, then communicative adaptations can be made in order to enhance the acceptance of the change.

In Stage 1, *Denial and Isolation,* employees often react with comments like these: "Oh, no, not here" or "It can't happen like that, not with my job." In the denial stage, it is important for the manager to communicate clearly and calmly the particulars of the change while providing as much factual material as necessary. An employee may react emotionally, but the manager should realize that it is a normal reaction and should allow the denial to take its natural course. An unduly negative reaction may indicate that the announcement of the change did not take place at the right time and place, or that it was done in an insensitive fashion. A common problem at this stage is that, upon encountering initial emotional reactions, managers may back off or sugarcoat the change, thus not fully informing the employees. The other tendency is to try to browbeat or ridicule employees into acceptance. This does not demonstrate much sensitivity, and may lead to resentment. Moreover, it rarely helps managers achieve their objective. If these tendencies are avoided, then employees, in due course, experience a partial acceptance.

TABLE 7.1 Communicating Change at Different Reaction Stages

Stage	Identifying Actions	Appropriate Actions	Inappropriate Responses
Denial	Not showing up for meetings	Discern actual points of resistance	Ignore the resistance
	Overly busy with routine tasks	Discuss positives and negatives of change	Ridicule the person's denial
	Less socializing	Legitimize concerns	
	Procrastinating	Discuss rationale of the change	
Anger	Being irritable	Stay calm and professional	Escalate into a relationship conflict
	Contemplating sabotage	Clarify the details of the change	Threaten
	Being confrontational	Show understanding of the anger while firmly emphasizing need for change	Blame others for the change
	Appearing "short-fused"		Take anger personally
		Allow some ventilation	Ignore anger
Bargaining	Trying to make deals	Be flexible with regard to inconsequential items	Reject suggestions briskly
	Trading favors	Be firm with regard to the basic position	Give in to employee demands
	Making promises	Focus on long-term benefits	Give the impression of agreement
Depression	Being untalkative	Show concern	Pressure for full acceptance
	Appearing apathetic	Provide "space"	Jest about feelings
	Missing work	Encourage discussions with others who have fully accepted change	Be overly happy or giddy
	Appearing listless		
	Looking somber		
Acceptance	Fully implementing change	Encourage auxiliary suggestions	Say, "I told you so"
	Returning to normal atmosphere	Resume "normal" communication	Joke about previous reactions
		Praise	

Stage 2 involves a kind of anger over the "whys" of the change: "Why did this happen to me?" "Why is this happening at this time?" Little incidents can set off major emotional outbursts. Employee behavior may seem inexplicable. The worst response is for the manager to take the anger personally, thus exacerbating the difficulties. A pattern of "mutual pretense" might emerge in which the manager and employee play a game: "I know that you know, but I won't talk about it because it might upset you. And you won't talk about it because it will upset me." The net result is an implicit conspiracy of silence, with resentment simmering underneath the veneer of civility. Then the problem is compounded by interpersonal conflicts. The best response is for the manager to acknowledge the anger while gently guiding the employees' attention to the real source of anger and helping them work through it. Then the anger should subside.

Bargaining, the third stage, occurs when employees attempt to make various exchanges to forestall the impending change. Creativity abounds when faced with an unpleasant alternative. Deal-making with various people is attempted as employees seek to alter the course of events. Many times, deals are attempted outside the normal chain-of-command structure; in essence behind the manager's back. But making deals at this stage only prolongs the matter and puts off the inevitable. Resolve and perseverance are the manager's tools at this point.

In Stage 4, employees display signs of listlessness and depression. It is the phase in which employees begin to accept the inevitable. Just allowing the employees to voice their concerns or feelings at this point can be helpful. At other times, sensitive silence or a gentle touch may be most effective. Sharing sadness with someone who can empathize can be amazingly therapeutic. An insensitive, "Hey, it's not that bad," can have the opposite effect.

In the final stage, employees accept the situation by honestly and wholeheartedly endorsing the change. It is important for the manager to show respect for the employees and not chide them for their initial reactions. They are still a bit fragile at this point. Even seemingly innocent verbal jousting may be deeply and secretly wounding. The critical point is to preserve employee dignity.

This may sound like a fairly drawn out process, but these reactions can take place in the span of hours or extend over several months, as in the case reviewed in Table 7.2. Doubters, like the Arrow manager, may even question if an employee really goes through those reactions. Circuit managers may become overly sympathetic and actually delay acceptance. Effective managers learn to communicate strategically about major changes in order to hasten employee acceptance and boost productivity. Doing so requires a thoughtful analysis of the situation as suggested by the model reviewed in the next section.

The Iceberg Model

Most of an iceberg's bulk lies below the surface. Ships that ignore the ice below the water are in mortal danger. Likewise, organizational change efforts may flounder because of a lack of strategic communication planning—the "below the waterline" issues. The Iceberg model in Figure 7.3 outlines a strategic approach to communicating change based on four levels of planning:

TABLE 7.2 Case Study: Reaction Stages to a Change

Situation: Smith's Solid Waste, a small family-owned disposal company, is being bought out by B. L. Disposal, a larger disposal company. Smith's owner and two managers are aware of the pending sale. They are preparing to tell the employees about this change in ownership. The owner and two managers plan to stay on as supervisors, but there will be some changes in the operations. More office staff will be hired, and the way records are kept will change. Drivers will be required to keep more accurate records and submit more reports to the office staff. In the past, very few records were kept and drivers had a lot of freedom about how they ran their routes.

Chronology of events		*Analysis*
Day 1:	Mr. Smith calls a meeting for all drivers and announces the sale of Smith's Solid Waste to B. L. Disposal. All drivers will be required to reapply for their jobs with B. L. Disposal. He distributes the applications, and tells the drivers to turn them in within one week so he can send them to B. L. Disposal.	
Days 2–10:	No activity.	
Day 11:	Mr. Smith notices that no one has turned in an application. He asks all the drivers why he has not received any of their applications. They respond, "We were unsure if we had to. We didn't think you were really going to sell." Mr. Smith replies, "B. L. Disposal is buying this company. I will still be your direct supervisor. However, you must reapply for your jobs in the next week; B. L. will not wait for these applications forever. I will be handing over whatever applications I have in one week."	*Employees are clearly denying that the company is going to be bought out, and avoiding anything that would dispel the myth. It is the game of "mutual pretense." Mr. Smith's response might seem appropriate, because it gives employees maximum flexibility and avoids conflict. But it fails to deal with the reasons for the denial. Moreover, all the aspects of the change have not been fully explained. The abruptness of the supervisor's comments on Day 11 creates added tension.*
Day 18:	Workers tell Mr. Smith, "If you want to sell out, you should just tell the owner of B. L. that we are all good workers, and if he doesn't agree to keep us, we'll all quit. Then he'll have no workers."	*The anger stage is clearly in full swing. Providing a rationale for why the applications need to be formally filled out is a little late at this stage and should have been done earlier. Furthermore, Mr. Smith still has not explained how this sale will affect the drivers. He assumes the workers should not be concerned, because he will still be their direct supervisor. The threats only exacerbate the situation until it builds into an interpersonal conflict.*

Chronology of events	*Analysis*
Day 20:	Mr. Smith and B. L. Disposal's vice president agree to meet with employees to discuss how the change will affect them and to answer any questions.	
Day 21:	Employees want guarantees about what exactly everyone will be doing and that everyone will keep their same job and responsibilities. The new owners assure them that they will all keep their jobs if they turn in their applications. But new workers will be brought in as well, mainly to do administrative work in the office. The workers are happy to hear they will keep their jobs, but confused about why office workers are needed.	*This is a textbook example of the negotiation or bargaining stage. They are promised their jobs if they turn in their applications.*
Day 24:	The drivers ask Mr. Smith why more office help is needed. He tells them that they (the drivers) will need to complete more detailed route reports so the business can bill and manage time more effectively. Additional office workers are needed to process these reports. The drivers are furious that they will have less freedom than before with these new responsibilities. The result: they do not turn in their applications.	*They revert back to the anger stage. The drivers still feel lied to and do not trust the new owners.*
Day 26:	Mr. Smith and B. L. inform the drivers that if their applications are not submitted in one week, they will begin to hire new drivers.	
Day 28–36:	Hesitantly, the drivers turn in their applications. The drivers will not talk to Mr. Smith or other managers, because they feel betrayed. They barely talk to each other.	*The depression stage has set in. Mr. Smith may have done the wise thing given the current situation. But the silence results more from bitterness than from sensitivity to the emotional state of the employees.*
Day 36–50:	The name "B. L. Disposal" begins to show up on the dumpsters and on the customers' invoices. The drivers are given the new forms they must complete and hand in every day to the office staff. Everyone begins talking again, and slowly relationships return to normal.	*Acceptance, finally. Maybe not wholehearted acceptance, but acceptance, nevertheless.*
Six months later:	All the drivers are filling out the correct forms.	
One year later:	In the break room, drivers discuss how easy it is to do the route sheet and how much less customers complain about mistakes on their billing statements.	

▷ Level 1—Contextual Analysis
▷ Level 2—Audience Analysis
▷ Level 3—Strategic Design
▷ Level 4—Tactical Preparations

Although the model might appear to be static, it is really rather fluid. Indeed, the focus is on asking the right questions in the right order rather than a series of how-tos. The specific action plan emerges from the dynamic interplay of critical communication principles and the answers to these core questions. These are presented in Table 7.3.

Most companies spend 80% to 95% of their time and resources dealing with such questions as

▷ How many pages should the brochure be?
▷ Should we prepare a speech for the CEO?
▷ What day of the week should we release the announcement?
▷ Should we communicate our message over e-mail?
▷ Who in the organization should communicate about the change?

These are the "above the water-line," tactical issues concerned with determining the content of a message, timing, channels, and spokespeople. These are all legitimate questions, but they are really secondary. They are, in fact, indicative of a *tactical* rather than a *strategic* approach to communicating change. My experiences suggest that resources should be allocated in precisely the opposite direction. From 70% to 80% of resources should be devoted to the first three levels of planning: contextual analysis, audience analysis, and strategic design. When these issues are resolved, the tactical decisions are usually fairly simple and straightforward.

Contextual Analysis

Gravity beats rocket fuel every time. Eventually, rockets run out of fuel and succumb to gravitational fields. In a similar way, one must understand the contextual field in which a change is to be assimilated. If not, the change effort may be crushed by the weight of the status quo. Hence information about the written and unwritten organizational rules is essential in planning. External consultants can be at a distinct disadvantage when it comes to understanding the nuances of the organizational culture. The background knowledge about the organization serves as a base for understanding how the change might be perceived.

The historical communication patterns set the interpretive context for employees. In fact, one researcher has shown that employee reactions to change can be traced back to the organization's founding conditions. The company's origin somehow deeply imprints employees, even those subsequently hired (Boeker

Spokespeople   *Timing*

Messages   *Safety Valves*

Channels   *Tactics*   *Monitoring Devices*

Strategy

Audience Analysis

Contextual Analysis

Figure 7.3. The Iceberg Model

1989). As Sir Winston Churchill put it, "The longer you look back, the farther you can look forward. This is not a philosophical or political argument—any oculist can tell you it is true" (Manchester 1983).

The president of a small manufacturing firm related the following story. He was concerned about the rough financial times his company would soon be experiencing. Some cost-saving measures would have to be implemented, but layoffs were not even discussed. The president considered himself a moral and straightforward person. Therefore, he felt he had an ethical obligation to inform his employees of the news. In due course, he called a meeting of all employees to discuss some of the difficulties ahead as well as the requisite changes involved. In good faith, he mentioned that there were no plans for layoffs and employees would be dealt with "as fairly as possible under the circumstances." So far, so good. Or so it seemed.

Within a few days the entire plant was buzzing with rumors about an impending plant closing and wage reductions. In fact, there was not a bit of truth to either rumor. The president was completely bewildered. He felt he had told the employees the truth and was honest about the situation. How could such vicious rumors spring from so noble of intentions? Weeks of meetings took place in order to quell fears. Still, for months, morale and productivity suffered.

TABLE 7.3 Thought Process for a Strategic Communication Plan

Planning Level	Questions
Contextual Analysis	1. Have employees readily assimilated other changes?
	2. Is the change congruent with the culture?
	3. Is the change seen as noncomplex and manageable?
	4. Is the change seen as advantageous over past practices?
	5. Are the benefits readily observable?
	6. Will key relationships be adversely affected?
Audience Analysis	1. What are the major groups of employees that will be affected by the change?
	2. How will each group be affected?
	3. What are the most likely points of resistance of each group?
	4. What are the communication preferences of each group?
	5. Who are the key opinion leaders (the "lions") of each group?
Strategic Design	1. What are the tentative communicative goals for each of the audiences?
	2. What are the common goals for the general audience?
	3. What is a unifying theme that energizes and motivates employees?
	4. How should communication resources be allocated, based on the audience analysis?
	5. What is a general structure for achieving the goals and championing the theme?
Tactical Analysis	1. What channels should be used?
	2. What are the key messages?
	3. What are the "safety valves"?
	4. What should be the timing of the various communications?
	5. Who should communicate the messages?
	6. How should the process be monitored?

Upon deeper probing and a year's worth of hindsight, it became abundantly clear why employees came away from the meeting with precisely the opposite message that the well-intentioned president had so sincerely sought to communicate. Employees had never before had a companywide meeting to discuss any issue, much less this kind of anxiety-producing news. Hence they legitimately, although incorrectly, reasoned that "things must be really bad" if the president "had to" call a meeting of this type. There was the feeling that management "must not be telling us all they know." Like a virus in an unhealthy body, rumors and inaccurate inferences naturally flourish under such conditions. Had meetings like this been held on a regular basis, the possibility of such an interpretation would have been minimized. The context of the situation spoke louder than the actual message. The president was bewildered because he focused on the inner message—his actual words—but had no understanding of the context in which employees interpreted the words. Both the employees and the president erroneously focused on only one part of the actual communication event. Pure intentions do not always guarantee perceptions of integrity.

The moral of the story is that when instituting a change, managers must carefully consider the context in which employees interpret the message. The context may prove more powerful than the message itself. This incident also provides vivid proof of how important it is to continually update employees on corporate news. Furthermore, it may mean that in order to institute a change with full employee support, management may need to apologize for past errors in failing to communicate effectively. A successful future can be built only on the firm foundation of the past. Rosabeth Moss Kanter (1983) expressed it thoughtfully:

> The architecture of change thus requires an awareness of foundations—the bases in "prehistory," perhaps below the surface, that make continued construction possible. And if the foundations will not support the weight of what is about to be built, then they must be shored up before any other actions can take place. (p. 283)

In short, the context of interpretation is etched as much by action as by words.

Ultimately, the contextual analysis is an attempt to anticipate possible resistance points. We use the following questions to guide the discussion of the contextual issues (Rogers 1995).

Historically, have the employees readily assimilated other changes? The scenario discussed above clearly demonstrates how history affects the speed with which changes are assimilated. If employees have not readily adjusted to other changes, then the current change will more likely run into significant resistance. However, examining the nature of past failures can provide useful insights into how to proceed. In fact, success breeds further success. Organizations that have successfully assimilated past changes tend to absorb new ones more efficiently. Why? The employees have learned how to effectively manage the change process with all its emotional strains and setbacks. Without that kind of history, employees need not only to assimilate the change, but also to learn about the change process, thus doubling the duty, but clearly not doubling the fun.

Is the change congruent with the culture? Changes seen as an extension of the culture are more likely to be embraced. Those that are not congruent will create more resistance. For instance, even the term *reengineering* may induce resistance, because employees see it as a radical departure from the "way we do things around here" (Deal and Kennedy 1982). But if the planners use another label—one more in line with the culture—resistance might be minimized. In one situation, we renamed a reengineering project as CI^2 (Continuous Improvement squared), because employees were used to the CI lingo and would have bristled at a term like *reengineering*. If employees see changes as alien to the culture, change initiators would do well to reconsider the endeavor.

Is the change seen as noncomplex and manageable? More complex changes are often resisted. Even if the changes are perceived as complex, there are ways to break down the task and make it appear more manageable. These tactics include the use of planning charts, outlines of key project phases, and scaled-down models of new products or processes.

Is the change seen as advantageous over past practices? This is often the trickiest issue to overcome because employees may feel that any change is an indictment of their past work practices. In a manufacturing plant, we helped introduce a major structural change of reporting relationships that created more accountability. One of the consistent refrains was, "We made the numbers in the past, we're achieving our goals now, why do we need to change?" Ironically, the very managers who said this were those who had consistently complained about the general lack of accountability at the plant. Their lament was basically, "If it ain't broke, why fix it?" Even the verbally skilled have a difficult time effectively communicating such seemingly contradictory messages as

1. In the past, the previous systems worked effectively.
2. Yet now the situation has changed and new practices are needed.

However, this may be the exact message that needs to be relayed to employees.

Are the benefits readily observable? Change for change's sake is rarely welcomed. There is often a need to present the conceptual benefits of a change as well as the practical ones. This may involve a physical demonstration of the benefits. One telemarketing firm provided a mock-up of the new scanning technology that was going to be introduced to its customers.

Will key relationships be adversely affected? One of the least discussed resistance points involves the impact of the change on social relationships. Changing the physical layout of an office may alter interpersonal relationships. Those employees who routinely see one another for casual conversations may not have such opportunities with a new office plan. Organizations that are moving to "virtual offices" often find this issue impinging on the ultimate success of the venture.

A strategy will begin to emerge as these questions are discussed. In some cases, a "no" response to any of the above questions can be turned to a "yes" with a small modification, such as renaming a "reengineering" project. In other cases, the plan cannot be altered. Therefore, more aggressive plans might need to be initiated to address the concerns. For instance, organizations that are heavily reliant on telecommuting may create quarterly retreats for those employees "residing" in their virtual offices.

Audience Analysis

What is persuasive to one person may not be persuasive to another. This is the fundamental principle of audience analysis. The objective at this point of the planning process is to isolate key groups of employees that may be directly and indirectly affected by the change. This may prove more difficult than it appears at first glance. For instance, many downsizing efforts have failed to reach long-term productivity goals, because organizations have not planned the communication to the "survivors;" those employees left after the cutback. These employees often have deep fears about their future, which, in turn, decrease their effectiveness.

Determining the key groups of employees will vary with the type of change. There are a lot of ways to slice the pie. When an organization alters a benefits package, age may be the key variable. With a job redesign issue, the critical variable will most likely be job classification. A flextime proposal may affect employees with children differently than those without children.

After the key groups have been isolated, four critical questions need to be answered.

1. How will each group be affected by the change? The final Halloween of the last millennium was scarier than usual for Hershey Foods. They did not deliver enough treats, such as Hershey Bars and Butter Cups, to their regional suppliers. Hershey could not pull off the ultimate trick: successfully integrating a $112 million computer system into their operations. It was supposed to modernize and expedite the entire order and distribution process. It did not. Technical problems confounded the experts, but how the change was communicated also played a significant role (Nelson and Ramstad 1999). How would the new computer system affect suppliers? Distributors? The ultimate consumer? Hershey, like many others, failed to understand fully the implications of the change for the various groups. Wise managers pay attention to how different groups are likely to interpret the change. What will it mean to them—not only in terms of job duties but also emotionally?

2. What are the most likely points of resistance of each group? Answers to this question flow directly from the previous point. One tactic is to ask employees to identify their concerns. Typically, they will discuss generic issues, such as economic loss, inconveniences, and workload shifts. But they are often hesitant to bring up the other concerns that are more emotional in nature, such as perceived loss of status, social disruptions, and anxiety over the unknown or insecurities like "Can I really do this new job?" Or, these concerns may surface in a dysfunctional way in the form of vicious rumors. Change initiators cannot assume that employees will be able to identify and articulate all of their own concerns. Wise planners take this into account.

3. *What are the communication preferences of each group?* Different groups may prefer their information in different forms or through different channels. Electronic mail may be a proper delivery system for younger employees, but not for older employees who may feel uncomfortable with that channel. Likewise, statistics might prove a proper way to make an argument for employees in the finance department, but not for those in the marketing department, who may be more persuaded by stories or critical incidents.

4. *Who are the "lions"?* The lions rule the tropical as well as organizational jungles. Influence is unequally distributed in an organization and is not necessarily tied to job titles. Often, the viability of a change will rest on the reactions of key opinion leaders. Therefore, it may be important to look at the individual persuasive preferences of key individuals who will, in turn, influence others. This may include creating a list of the lions in each group and developing tactics to exert influence on those individuals.

The audience analysis coupled with contextual analysis provides most of insight necessary for the challenging task of creating a strategy.

Strategic Design

The well-known military historian B. H. Liddell Hart (1967) once wrote that "in strategy, the longest way round is often the shortest way home" (p. 5). Communication strategies are no different. Planning a strategic communication process takes both time and effort; it is the "long way round." But it is also the smoothest, simplest, and most effective way to implement change. Typically, changes are communicated in a haphazard, "short way"—a "catch as catch can" philosophy. There is a better way. This section discusses five steps you can take to implement change smoothly.

1. Develop Tentative Communicative Goals for Each of the Audiences

Figure 7.4 provides a worksheet we use to summarize the audience analysis phase and start the strategy-making phase. Typically, the concerns of each group naturally lead into the development of specific communicative goals.

Consider the following situation: A small medical clinic with seven branch offices decided to change its phone system. Under the old system, patients called a specific office and any available personnel answered the phone. It often took several iterations before the patient was connected to the appropriate person. The new system would allow patients to call a single clinic number, answered by a dedicated operator, who would then connect the caller to the appropriate personnel. This was designed to improve office efficiency and provide more convenient patient care. We anticipated that not everyone would see it that way. Therefore, we split the audience pie into unequal pieces and created unique objectives for each audience. Table 7.4 presents a shortened version of that planning document. Note that although we identified a few unique goals for each audience, there were some that overlapped, which nicely leads to the next step.

2. *Glean a Common Set of Goals for the General Audience*

Typically, a few objectives emerge out of the specific goals derived for each group. In the case of the medical clinic, the general goals of the communicative campaign were fairly obvious:

▷ Provide reassurance that medical care will remain the same or improve.
▷ Demonstrate the ease and efficiency of the system.

These goals, in turn, suggest a starting point for making all the tactical decisions about what to communicate, how to inform people, and when to do it. The goals also set up the next strategic step.

3. *Develop a Unifying Theme That Energizes and Motivates Employees*

The goals need to be shaped into a memorable and motivating theme. The leadership team of the clinic decided that "Challenge 2000" nicely suited all the audiences, implying technological progressiveness and cutting-edge medical care while linking to one of the core clinic values. After all, what patient, young or old, would not want physicians "on top" of the most recent advances?

Consider another, more legendary case that exemplifies developing a unifying theme. When Stanley C. Gault became the CEO of Rubbermaid, he took the company from modest success to "superstar" status. He did it by becoming the "No. 1 quality controller." He constantly talked to consumers about Rubbermaid's products, and was known to order the redesign of a product based on one customer's complaint. He said, "On quality I'm a sonofabitch." He has a reputation for becoming absolutely "livid" about poor quality workmanship. Yet, as one observer put it, "Ultimately it's Gault's infectious pride in Rubbermaid's products, rather than his wrath, that motivates his troops. When it comes to encouraging quality, passion at the top counts as much as engineering precision at the bottom" (O'Reilly 1990, p. 43). In order for employees to buy into change, they must see a

MetaComm Change Analysis

Planning Guide

Audience	Impact	Resistance Points	Resistance Level			Channel Choice	Knowledge Base			Lions	Objectives
			High	Medium	Low		Need	Remedy	Drawbacks		

Figure 7.4. Planning Worksheet

TABLE 7.4 Audience Analysis Planning Guide

Audience	Concerns	Goals
Older patients	"Will I have the same access to care?"	Provide reassurances that care will be the same or improved.
	"Will I be able to adapt to the new phone system?"	Demonstrate the ease of the new phone system.
	"Will I be able to break out of my old habits?"	Restore confidence in their ability to handle changes.
		Show how the new phone system is more convenient by providing them more direct and quicker access to the desired staff.
Younger patients	"Will I have the same access to care?"	Provide reassurances that care will be the same or improved.
	"Will this make scheduling office visits more efficient?"	Underscore the efficiency of the new system.
Medical Staff	"Will I be able to get my job done more efficiently and effectively?"	Demonstrate the efficiency of the new system.
	"Will the transition to the new system be burdensome?"	Highlight the employee's role in the transition.
	"How will this impact patient care, particularly for the elderly?"	Describe specific benefits and potential concerns for elderly patients.
	"Will I be able to learn the new phone system?"	Discuss the training that will be provided.
Physicians	"Will I be able to get my job done more efficiently and effectively?"	Demonstrate the efficiency of the new system.
	"Will the transition to the new system be burdensome?"	Underscore the support system for the change.
	"How will this impact patient care, particularly for the elderly?"	Describe specific benefits and potential concerns of elderly patients.
	"Will I be able to learn the new phone system?"	Discuss the training that will be provided.

vision of the future, even if it is a bit of a clouded one. They must know the global goals, the possibilities, and hopes implicit in the change. In short, they must be collectively inspired by the change.

How? Leaders energize by creating a few simple rallying points. In a deeply insightful article, David Nadler and Michael L. Tushman (1989) suggest,

> Successful long-term changes are characterized by a careful self-discipline that limits the number of themes an organization gives its employees. As a general rule, managers of a change can only initiate and sustain approximately three key

themes during any particular period of time. The challenge in this area is to create enough themes to get people truly energized, while limiting the total number of themes. The toughest part is having to decide not to initiate a new program— which by itself has great merit—because of the risk of diluting the other themes. (pp. 199–200)

This is exactly what Gault did at Rubbermaid. He gave employees a vision, in part through his well-known antics, but more importantly by "preaching" a value that everyone in the organization could relate to—quality. Clearly, sermons alone will not do.

4. Allocate Communication Resources According to the Audience Analysis

In order for change to be sustained, three questions must be answered affirmatively:

1. Is there a need for the change?
2. Is this change the remedy for the concern?
3. Have the drawbacks to the plan been resolved?[1]

Because audiences have limited attention spans, choices need to be made about what issues to emphasize. If their needs are not met fairly quickly, the campaign could stall at the denial stage. For instance, if most employees are already convinced that a new office building is needed, it makes little sense to provide detailed analysis of the rationale for the construction. Instead, the focus of the strategy should be on *how* the remedy meets the corporate needs while avoiding any major downside. On the other hand, a company attempting to make a significant change in its health care benefit when employees do not need or want to change has a different focus. In this case, the strategy involves addressing the three distinct questions, first alerting the employees to the staggering financial burden of the existing plan on the company.

To this point, we have discussed a lot of what may seem to be defensive measures. But it is important to think about the fundamental rationale or rallying cry that will ultimately sustain the change. For one plant, we chose the acronym CFA (Coordinator Focused Accountability) as our banner to support a job redefinition plan. The choice of this acronym was strategic on two counts. First, this company had a strong culture built around the value of CFQ (Customer Focused Quality). Second, the term *coordinator* referred to the employees who actually initiated and championed the change. This was a strategic choice in that it contrasted sharply with a previous plan that was proposed and implemented by top management.

5. Develop a General Structure for Achieving the Goals and Championing the Theme

Persuading employees is a process. This means that one e-mail message or cleverly designed brochure will not be enough. It takes time and many communicative acts to get employees to "buy-in" to change. This is usually a rather helter-skelter and messy enterprise. As previously discussed, employees have a fairly standard set of reactions to change, starting with denial and ending with acceptance. What makes this messier is that different employees and groups may be experiencing those emotions at various times during the change process. Thus, change initiators must be highly flexible in approaching the various groups.

The general structure might take the form of phases. When employees first understand the need or necessity of change, they are more likely to embrace a solution. But after the *alert phase,* they need to be convinced the issue has been properly analyzed. During the *analysis phase,* change initiators need to let others understand their thinking. How was the need detected? How was the situation analyzed? What are the alternatives? Once these questions are sufficiently answered, the change initiators can discuss the specific proposal. This final *proposal phase* often presents a special challenge, because many employees will still be skeptical of the underlying need for the change. In fact many change initiators are astonished at how frequently they must repeat the rationale for the change. So they should be prepared to till that soil one more time. The alert phase prepares the ground while the analysis phase cultivates the soil. The change initiator sows the seed in the proposal phase, but no one can guarantee that every seed will sprout. Yet the phased strategy increases the odds that the change will develop deep roots in the organization.

Tactics

The tactics are the how-tos, the operational plans that emerge from the strategy. There are six areas to consider in developing tactics. Some standard rules of thumb in developing each tactic are highlighted below.

Channels

Typically, it is better to use multiple channels of communication, because it increases the probability employees will hear about the change. One university announced most of it changes via electronic mail. Officials were befuddled as to why there was "uneven" buy-in by the faculty. They failed to account for the fact that, at the time, only half the faculty had terminals in their offices. Using multiple channels helps ensure that everyone "gets the word." Additionally, different media are more useful for presenting certain aspects of a change. A print medium can better show a new office design than oral channels. Yet oral channels can be more useful in fielding employee questions. Hence the different channels should be used so as to exploit their various strengths. Moreover, the redundancy helps continually to remind employees of the vision behind the change.

Likewise, "rich" channels are usually better for nonroutine communication. Rich channels, such as face-to-face meetings, allow for rapid feedback and quick adaptation to employee concerns. It is very difficult to ascertain whether employees are still in the denial stage if the change is announced via corporate memorandum. When change is instituted in a large organization, the same principle applies. A group meeting, of course, could not be held with all employees, but a more dynamic alternative could still be selected. For instance, when AT & T was reorganized, thousands of Southwestern Bell employees and their families were linked via satellite and treated to a televised discussion about the planned changes. Although the cost was considerable, the benefits were great: deeper employee understanding of the change, greater commitment to the vision, and less employee anxiety. These results could not have been achieved through a less dynamic channel such as an employee newsletter. Why? Because the dynamic channel allows for more timely and effective feedback. Moreover, the very expense of a dynamic channel sends a powerful symbolic message that management cares about effectively communicating with employees.

Message

Professional communicators use many principles in constructing messages but several are particularly noteworthy at this juncture.

First, try to link messages to the audience's preexisting thinking routines. For example, when we communicated to employees about the need to cut costs in their health care plan, we compared the situation to a family expense crisis. This was something to which they could easily relate. We oriented our communication around the following theme: "As a parent, what would you do if your children were in the habit of buying their clothing from an expensive department store if they could get similar clothing less expensively?" This proved particularly persuasive, because our audience analysis revealed that most of the employees had teenagers and that their leisure activities were oriented around family matters.

Second, always discuss the upside and downside of the change. There is a tendency to oversell the change by stressing the positives. However, in the long run, a reasonable discussion of the downside proves useful. Why? Because it provides a more realistic assessment of the change and allows for employee input. Employees may be in the perfect position to solve some of the potential problems. Moreover, sharing concerns can create a climate of trust. Miller and Monge's (1985) noteworthy field study of an office layout change provides further empirical support of the importance of sharing both kinds of information.

Third, directly address likely resistance points. The more nonroutine the change is perceived, the greater the probability that there will be some resistance (see Figure 7.5). Although management often initiates change, only employees can sustain it. Prudent managers recognize this and prepare accordingly.

One note of caution: the issues perceived by management as possible concerns may not be the actual concerns of employees. In fact, employees may not even mention the real source of their angst. The audience analysis performed previously provides a particularly useful antidote. The generic employee concerns include job security, job stability, loss of wages, social disruptions, inconveniences, and anxiety over the unknown (Lawrence 1969). Some scholars have identified another set of potential resistance points (see Table 7.5). They argue that organizations, like nations, go through various developmental stages and different organizational impediments occur during each period (Gray and Ariss 1985). Therefore, the wise manager anticipates these various issues and develops appropriate responses to each concern.

One useful tactic is to respond to each potential objection point-by-point. The CEO of a small telemarketing firm used this approach in announcing a plan to change the telemarketers' responsibilities. In one part of his speech, he said,

> Some of you may be concerned about wages under the new system. This is a legitimate concern. But let me assure you that there will be no wage reductions under the new plan. In fact, our projections show that with the added revenues, your salaries will actually increase. Others of you may be concerned about layoffs. This has never even crossed my mind. In every single change we've instituted in this company's twenty-year history, we have always ended up adding personnel.

Note that the CEO accomplished four very important objectives in this excerpt. First, he clearly identified the potential resistance points, which legitimized the employees' anxieties. Second, he categorically denied each one. Third, he not only denied them, but said exactly the opposite would happen. Finally, he provided some kind of evidence to back up each of his claims. The speech must have worked, because the CEO reported that this was the most smoothly implemented change in the company's history.

In a variation on this theme, some companies simply issue a set of common questions asked about the change and provide answers to each item. Either approach works, powerfully counteracting resistance and building support for a change.

Fourth, remind employees that not everything is changing. Employees often panic if they perceive the "entire world is turning upside down." They need anchors of stability. Mooring or linking the change to established organizational values,

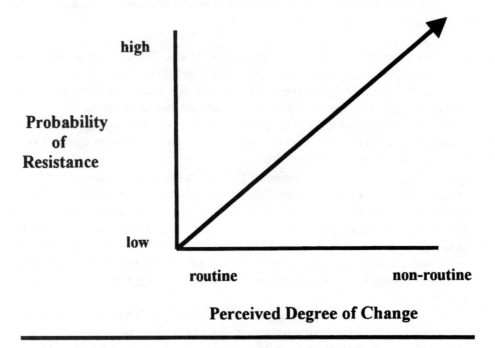

Figure 7.5. Probability of Resistance to Change

customers, or mission statement, helps. So does reminding employees that they have sailed in these kinds of waters before. Employees, like sailors, seek inspiration from their past successes. A confident affirmation may not calm the sea, but it can quiet the spirit.

Fifth, publicize initial successes. Change initiators who demonstrate success early in the process persuade others to jump on the bandwagon. It does not take much—an article in the newsletter, a phone call to a key person, or a kind word in the hallway, any little nudge of encouragement. These simple acts signal that change initiators are building a coalition to institute the change while whispering to the bystanders, "Get on board, or get run over."

Safety Valves

No matter how persuasively the change has been advocated, employees will usually have some doubts. There will probably be some dissent regarding parts of the plan. Change initiators need to "harvest the dissent," which involves proactively soliciting worker concerns about the change in a supportive environment. If management does not harvest the dissent, others will. In one dairy plant,

TABLE 7.5 Resistance Points at Organizational Stages

Organizational Stage	*Identifying Characteristics*	*Possible Resistance Points*
Birth and early growth	Emphasis on entrepreneurship	Uncertainty about CEO's reaction
		Diminished CEO control
	Heavy influence of "founding fathers"	
		Change of corporate vision
Maturity	Creation of standard operating procedures	Interdepartmental differences
	Institutionalized vision	Protection of "turf"
	Solidified departmental responsibilities	Control of resources
Decline or redevelopment	Downturn in competitive environment	Employee indifference and lethargy
	More bureaucratic structure	Concern over impact on established careers
	Quest to reshape corporate vision	Change in power relationships
		Employees need crisis to propel action

the plant manager announced major policy changes on bulletin boards and in plantwide meetings. He was perplexed that "nothing I say ever gets done." The reason why was that he never harvested the dissent—he would not entertain any significant questions about the new policy. This was a perfect opportunity for a few malcontent union workers to harvest the dissent themselves, in a nonconstructive manner, and stymie change efforts.

Therefore, it is important to include safety valves for employees to express their concerns. The key principle is to legitimize their concerns, no matter how far-fetched they may be. A simple but powerful technique is merely to ask employees to voice their concerns and record them on a flip chart in a nonevaluative fashion, consequently legitimizing, depersonalizing, and de-emotionalizing employees' ideas. Only after all the issues have been recorded are any of the problems debated or discussed. Moreover, the list can be transformed into a series of "Questions and Answers" that can be distributed to all employees within twenty-four hours. This helps ensure that there are no misunderstandings, and creates a vehicle through which employee concerns can be handled. There is also a powerful secondary message: "Your anxieties are legitimate." Change initiators, inspired by their visions, often resist this seemingly sloppy enterprise because it appears to tarnish their conception. Yet the focus of change is not to garner kudos but to get employees to quickly accept the new vision.

Timing

Timing is the tactical issue that has been least studied. Typically, major changes should be announced so that everyone hears about it close to the same time, thus partially restraining the grapevine. The stages of employee reactions can also provide a rough guide to timing. A frequent timing mistake is to make announcements to employees without building in time to actively harvest the dissent. One of the best ways to learn about timing is by examining what *not* to do. A recently hired vice president of a 250-employee paper manufacturer was given the task of redesigning a comprehensive benefits program. He did a brilliant job, devising a way to increase employee coverage while cutting corporate costs. He worked in virtual seclusion until it came time to announce the plans to the employees. On Monday, he distributed a notice to all employees announcing the meeting for the following Friday (see Figure 7.6). The VP thought the employees would be excited about his new plan. Because employees had never met this VP, they did not know what to expect and many were apprehensive. To make matters worse, a small story appeared in a local newspaper about a plastics plant (located in the same industrial complex) cutting back on their benefits. Rumors then started to circulate that benefits were going to be cut back at the paper manufacturer. The new vice president began the meeting by dwelling on the benefits of the plan to the company. Although he did mention that there would be "increased benefits" to all employees, he never specified what they were. He ended by saying that all employees would receive written documentation of the plan in two weeks. He did not ask for questions. That was it, the meeting was over. Employees were bewildered. By the following Monday, wild rumors were flying. Employee satisfaction and productivity hit an all-time low. It took two other meetings called by the CEO and months of reassurance to quell employee anxieties.

What went wrong?

1. Most likely, there was too much time between the announcement of the meeting and the actual meeting. Employee suspicions and fears were naturally aroused, particularly when dealing with a virtually unknown vice president.
2. The VP was insensitive to the employees' context of interpretation, which was influenced by other "unrelated events" (the newspaper story) during the week. In fact, he could have used the story to his advantage by opening his presentation with a reference to the story and then saying that just the opposite was happening here.
3. By dwelling on the benefits to the company, he implicitly communicated that the organization's interests were more important than the employees' were.
4. In addition to not providing a safety valve, he compounded the problem by having a meeting on Friday. Employees were desperately searching for more information, but over the weekend the only place they could turn

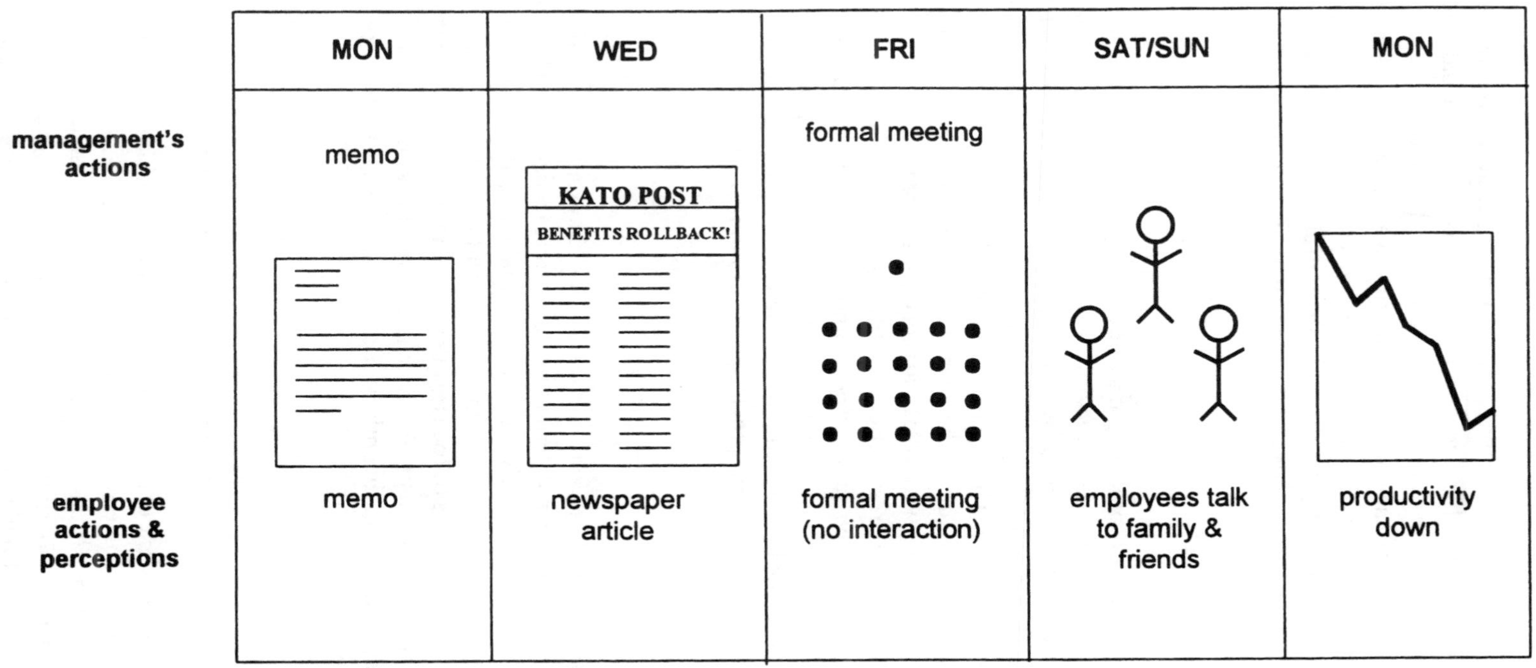

Figure 7.6. The Impact of Timing on Meaning

was to friends and relatives, who no doubt exacerbated the issue with their own fears. There was no official place to get formal information during this time period. Rumors were bound to spread.

5. The written summary of the information was released too late to answer employee questions. In sum, with the exception of setting a single time to disseminate the information, this VP completely failed to communicate the change in an effective and timely manner.

Spokespeople

Who communicates something may be as important as what they say. Those perceived as more credible persuade others more easily. Therefore, change initiators need to select carefully those who will announce and sponsor changes. In a medical clinic, we asked all the physicians to be involved in the announcement of an organizational change. They were not all equally skilled presenters. However, demonstrating solidarity among the physicians was more important than oratorical performances. Yet we were able to arrange for the physician with the greatest charisma to kick off the presentation. A physician who was very precise and detail-oriented explained the actual process and stages of the change. Once again, change initiators may be such enthusiastic supporters that they fail to realize that they may not be in the best position to announce the endeavor. Clearly, the background analyses discussed in the previous section should assist in these decisions.

Monitoring Devices

During times of change, one can learn a lot about an organization. For instance, change initiators can determine who the real leaders are. They may more fully understand critical underlying organizational issues that may lie dormant in calmer times. This all adds to a deeper understanding of the organizational culture. Devices such as surveys or focus groups can be used to assess the effectiveness of the communication strategy. As the change initiators monitor the organizational responses, they can gather other ideas to continuously improve the communication strategy.

Conclusion

The Kennedy Center is one of the most beautiful and magnificent buildings in all of Washington, D.C. In some ways, it is a miracle that it ever got built, for there were objections from all quarters as well as troubling financial difficulties. In large part, the structure owes its very existence and continued success to one man, Roger L. Stevens. He fought most of the battles, and expressed some perceptive comments on change and success:

There's an irony implicit in anything that succeeds. From the vantage point of success, it looks as if it couldn't possibly have failed. So with the Center. Twenty years ago, there were any number of people here in Washington eager to tell us that the Center wouldn't work—that even if we could manage to get it built, it would stand idle most of the time. At the moment, the doomsayers are silent, but they haven't gotten away. Maybe I'll get a chance to rouse them one more time. (Gill 1981, p. 52)

As change progresses from one person's dream, to "our" dream, to "the way it always was" or "should be," the obstacles seem to slowly fade into hindsight. What will eventually be seen as inevitable, can only begin as an inconceivable dream.[2]

Notes

1. Debaters will recognize these as the key stock issues known as need, remedy, and disadvantage.

2. This chapter is based on an article by Clampitt and Berk (1996), which discusses other case studies.

CHAPTER EIGHT

Interdepartmental Communication

I can hardly consider specialization, in itself, evil. On the other hand, I am thoroughly convinced that much of the evil of our times is related to specialization and that we desperately need to develop an attitude of suspicious caution toward it. I think we need to treat specialization with the same degree of distrust and safeguards that we bring to nuclear reactors.

M. Scott Peck

The final memo was terse but lacked the previous punch, like a boxer's weary jab at the end of a long bout: "You guys just can't get it right, the lid still leaks." What began as a routine and friendly exchange of memoranda between the research and marketing departments was ending more like a slugfest with the heavyweights trading insults as if they were punches. Marketing wanted a plastic lid for their new frosting mix. And the research department dutifully developed one that, quite frankly, they were proud of because it was both inexpensive to produce and structurally sound. So the new plastic lid was ceremoniously sent off to the marketing department to be tested on the cans of frosting mix. The research team was soon to be disappointed.

Two days later, the research team received memo one:

Good work guys! The lid looks great and is plenty sturdy, but it leaks! Our "lovely" white frosting turns brown after a few hours with the lid on it. There must be something in the lid that leaks out. Can you see what you can do?

The tone of the memorandum was pleasant enough, but it was greeted with a mixture of puzzlement and disbelief. Despite their obvious predilections, the researchers tested and retested the lid. The results: negative. The lid did not, and indeed *could not* leak. In due course, the research team drafted an equally magnanimous memorandum to the marketing department suggesting that something might be wrong with the frosting.

The second round was not long in starting. Suddenly "greats" became "terribles," "the lid" became "your lid" and the friendly tones were replaced with hostile ones. The researchers chose not to respond in kind, but proceeded to conduct still more tests—again, nothing. They sent an appropriate, though less congenial note, to marketing providing the "final" results of their tests. Unfortunately, marketing did not choose to respond with such restraint, and a three-month battle ensued in which neither side showed a great deal of wisdom nor professionalism.

This kind of incident is in no sense unique. Skirmishes like this occur in countless organizations between an ever-changing variety of departments. Indeed, about 65% of the organizations we have surveyed had significant problems with interdepartmental communication. In fact, I feel that with continued specialization of jobs and job duties in the workplace, interdepartmental communication will be one of the greatest challenges facing management in the future. William Ouchi (1981), author of the widely acclaimed book *Theory z,* put it this way:

> An economic organization is not a purely economic creation: it is simultaneously a social creation. Like any social system, a work organization involves a subtle form of coordination between individuals. Each person and each group within an organization is indeed like an organ in the body. If the coordinating mechanisms between the eyes and the hands are disrupted, then harder work by either the eyes or the hands will fail to improve their joint productivity. Industry does not need managers or workers to toil more assiduously. Instead, the mechanisms of coordination between them must be more attuned to subtlety of relations that are essential to their joint productivity. (p. 199)

In sum, although communication between departments is problematic in most companies, it is also an essential source of productivity.

Therefore, this chapter explores the nature of interdepartmental communication problems and provides strategies and tactics to address this issue. Incidentally, the mysterious "leaking lid" controversy was resolved. More on that later. A little hint, though: a key part of the message involved the use of the term "leaking lid."

The Nature of Departmentalization

Departments in an organization are what rooms are to a house. Departments divide. Departments separate. Departments specialize. And departments create barriers. The word *department* comes from the French word *departir,* which means to separate. Four particular "separations" are critical when examining interdepartmental communication problems.

1. Generally, Departments Perform Separate Functions

Henry Ford's successful production methods forever changed the way organizations do work. Before mass production, cars, like most products, were built one at a time. Henry Ford, of course, changed all that. For example, using old technology it took eighteen minutes to assemble a flywheel magneto, but by using the moving assembly line, the time was cut to five minutes. This change greatly affected production levels. In 1909, the company manufactured about 14,000 cars. By 1914, production rose to 230,000 per year (Stewart et al. 1999). The inevitable by-product of these spectacular results was the adoption of similar techniques throughout the United States and Europe.

Obviously, tremendous benefits have been reaped through the use of mass production techniques. Efficiency has improved, production has increased, and profits have soared.

Yet, as with any change, there are certain benefits of the old order left by the wayside. In this case, the advantages of the preindustrialized society included (a) employees who had an intimate knowledge of the entire product, not just a portion; (b) employees who psychologically identified with their job, not merely with a paycheck; and (c) employees who naturally made suggestions, not simply followed orders. These are the great communication challenges wrought by mass production techniques. In short, communication was simpler and more efficient before the assembly line.

Mr. Ford's ideas migrated into all modern organizations through the functional division of responsibility often masquerading under the rubric of a departmental name. Rarely will any one person in an organization be able to describe in any degree of detail the responsibilities and duties of personnel in other departments. Even when departments think they are using the same procedures, they can, in fact, be using very different ones. For example, controllers in one department of Pitney Bowes found that their version of the Lotus 1-2-3 software was different from their colleagues in other departments. Because they worked with different versions of the spreadsheet, they could not combine their results. In frustration, they turned over the whole business to an outside vendor (Carroll and Wilke 1989). This is a far cry from the days before Mr. Ford and his Model T. Ironically, the production efficiency gained through simplicity and standardization decreased the efficiency of communication by creating complex networks of departments that had to coordinate their actions in spite of their uniqueness.

2. Generally, Departments Are Physically Separated

Usually, the accountants work in one part of the building and the marketing representatives work in another location. Walls, stairs, or other physical barriers often separate departments. The net result is that the physical setup serves to facilitate communication *within* the department by creating barriers *between* departments. Interdepartmental communication is often sacrificed for the advantages of intradepartmental communication. Consequently, employees from different departments are only vaguely familiar with each other and they have only a minimal understanding of the equipment, ideas, and difficulties of their colleagues.

3. Generally, Departments Are Separated Through Accounting Procedures

Each department has separate accounts and separate budgets. Most expenses are charged to departmental accounts, not general accounts. One production line employee, when questioned about her reluctance to help fellow workers in another department, said, "It don't count" (sic). Further probing revealed that she received no compensation on her daily production quota sheet for such activities. In fact, such activities were recorded in a column designated as "down time." Hence her efficiency rating and the department's decreased whenever she "committed" interdepartmental communication. Such accounting procedures create a startling set of conceptual blinders that profoundly alter the relationships between departments.

4. Departments Separate Employees Through the Authority Structure

The chain of command is set up so that employees report to a single individual. Accordingly, among other activities, the boss evaluates employees' performance and often determines their pay scale. It is, of course, not very surprising, that given such circumstances most employees have an allegiance to their supervisors. In some cases, the commitment to the boss is so great that corporate goals are sacrificed at the expense of departmental goals (see, for example, Eisenberg et al.1982). What is good for the department is not necessarily good for the company. Yet employees must please the boss in order to get promoted. Indeed, the federal bureaucracy is a perfect example of departmental allegiances being valued more than corporatewide commitments (see, for example, Kissinger 1979). Waste, conflict, and poor decisions are the natural consequences. It is not surprising the word *department* was first used in governmental circles. In short, the authoritative structure of most organizations creates disincentives to communicate across departmental boundaries, and in some cases punishes those who do so.

Potential Problems of Departmentalization

There are benefits gained by organizing around departments, such as efficiency and the effective management of complex tasks. Yet managers must also recognize the potential consequences. If efforts are not made to bridge the inherent gulfs between departments, then a variety of serious problems can ensue. Lack of coordination creates difficulties in dance studios as well as in organizations. A few of these are discussed below.

Untimely Communication

One of the most serious consequences that can occur when departments fail to communicate is that the customer walks away dissatisfied. In one analysis of an airline's communication networks, we found that customers would frequently call the reservations agents and ask about new fares only to be informed that the fare did not exist. Upon further investigation, we found that the marketing department would send out advertising about new rates to customers and the media. Yet marketing belatedly informed the reservation agents of the changes and, in some cases, failed to inform them at all. Marketing perceived their primary function as communicating to the public and felt only a secondary responsibility to communicate to departments internally. Clearly, the department fulfilled their primary responsibility at the expense of the broader and more important concern: customer relations. For some very obvious reasons, the net result was that customers chose other airlines. Amazingly, marketing was bewildered as to why the company lost customers when they offered such low fares. Thus, the internal communication problems were reflected in the external image of the company.

The "Silo" Mentality

"I just do what I'm told." A comment like this often signals a "silo" mentality, where employees are only concerned with their own narrow departmental issues. The inescapable conclusion is that these employees are utterly unmotivated and, in some cases, deeply bitter. Their potential is squandered away. Why? There are many reasons, but one of the most frequent involves a rigid adherence to the departmental structure. These employees are not encouraged to offer suggestions for improvements and they rarely know what their colleagues actually do. They may question why the company has certain procedures and policies. The corporate response: "That's company policy." Employee reaction: Work to minimal standards. Reasoning: "I can't see why we do things the way we do, so why try?" Analysis: An unfortunate waste of human potential.

Overlapping Responsibilities

As a consumer, few events are more frustrating than getting the runaround. Why does this occur? Primarily because people in the different departments only know about their own particular functions and responsibilities. But, ironically, the source of confusion can be that the duties of one department overlap with those of another.

In one firm that we audited, the interviews revealed considerable tension between the customer service department and the telemarketing department. A typical complaint from the telemarketing employees was, "Customer service is interfering with our accounts and it seems underhanded; taking our accounts when they shouldn't be." When customer service employees were questioned, they were equally upset: "They keep transferring calls down here that they could easily answer themselves." One interviewee pinpointed the problem by noting that the telemarketing reps were forbidden to communicate with customer service employees except by memos, which often took too long. In this instance, as with many interdepartmental communication problems, the departmental responsibilities were not clearly defined and the problem was exacerbated by the lack of an adequate communication channel across the divisions.

Excessive departmentalization often results in a company wasting a tremendous amount of time. At the airline previously discussed, one individual reported this intriguing incident:

> During the first part of February, the schedule change and data service departments spent several man-hours developing a computerized method to analyze aircraft seating capacities. When ready to implement the changes, we discovered that most of these changes had already been handled in a manual mode. Thus, all our efforts were negated. One hand did not know what the other was doing.

Such lamentations reveal that not only did the company waste the time of all those employees, but also demoralized and frustrated them. Thus, the price of interdepartmental communication problems is paid at the individual and corporate level.

Unnecessary Conflict

Recall the "leaking lid" episode. What began as a typical exchange of memos between departments escalated into full-scale hostilities. In many ways the conflict was avoidable if each department had followed some simple steps that will be discussed later. In fact, the situation could have been handled in a manner that promoted greater understanding and mutual respect. Instead, polarization was the result.

This is not uncommon. One creatively designed study examined how employees tended to handle conflict during intradepartmental as opposed to interdepartmental conflicts (Putnam and Wilson 1982). The results were that conflicts between departments were highlighted by strategies that were more confrontational and controlling, which can lead to greater antagonism. In one sense, such expression might be useful if critical issues that are not normally brought out were discussed. On the other hand, such arguments frequently result in bad feelings. Then the departments may take a myopic view of the problem in a win-lose frame of mind. Although one department might "win," ultimately the organization, as a whole, loses.

In summary, the net result of these problems—untimely communication, overlapping responsibilities, a "silo" mentality, and unnecessary conflict—is less than optimal organizational performance. But an even more serious consequence may result: employee safety may be endangered. Consider the case of Mr. Hinojosa, a father of two, who was working for a contractor at a gas well and was attempting to dismantle a fifteen-foot tower by placing a chain around the tower. Yet the twenty-two-year-old Hinojosa did not know that another contractor had removed two of the four bolts holding up the tower. As a result, the tower fell, paralyzing him for the rest of his life. The judgment: a jury subsequently awarded him $64 million. The tragedy not only destroyed a man's life, but also wreaked a financial hardship on the company (Langley 1986). The lesson is that effective interdepartmental communication is not a luxury, but an obligation.

Contributing Factors

A number of conditions tend to accentuate the problems inherent with departmentalization. The factors discussed below create even greater barriers between departments, something like adding a hedge of thorns to a fence already separating two homes.

Language Differences

Even today, the haunting Biblical story about the Tower of Babel can still provide insight.[1] The tale records that God wanted to ensure that his people did not dishonor him by building a monument to themselves:

> Now the whole world had one language and a common speech. . . . But the Lord came down to see the city and the tower that the men were building. The Lord said: "If as one people speaking the same language they have begun to do this, then nothing they plan to do will be impossible for them. Come, let us go down and confuse their language so they will not understand each other." So the Lord scattered them from there over all the earth, and they stopped the city. (Genesis 11.1, 5-8)

The instrument used to stop the building was not some divinely ordered thunderbolt or meteor shower or even a ghastly plague. Rather, it was a singularly effective and powerful tool: compelling the people to speak different languages. Equally, though less deliberately, language dissimilarities prohibit modern organizations from achieving their goals.

The difficulty of communicating in an unknown tongue, like Chinese, immediately comes to mind when talking about language difficulties. Yet what I am speaking of confounds in a far more subtle and pervasive, if no less formidable, way. Accountants have a language of their own. They speak of *debits, credits, liquidity,* and *yield.* Computer programmers have their own vocabulary of *bytes, bits, CPU, hardware,* and *software.* Even communication scholars have their own obscure language, including words such as *dialogics, cybernetics,* and the *Elaboration Likelihood Model.* These are the critical language barriers within organizations. People in different departments quite literally speak a different language. They use different jargon, acronyms, and even describe the same things in different ways. This is not all bad. Jargon, acronyms, and specialized meanings for words are all ways for specialists to communicate efficiently and precisely with one another. The problem occurs when trying to communicate with the nonspecialist.

Additionally, the expert has more specific knowledge and makes more precise distinctions than the novice. "Horsebreeders have various names for breeds, sizes, and ages of horses; botanists have names for leaf shapes; interior decorators have names for shades of mauve; printers have many different names for different fonts, naturally enough" (Pullum 1991, p. 165). In a literal sense, experts perceive phenomena differently than nonexperts. They see things that nonexperts do not see. They use names and categories the novice does not use. In short, the experts recognize more specificity in their area of specialization than nonexperts. Similarly, departments act as resident experts in their organizational domain. Hence they experience the same problems that all experts have when communicating with nonexperts.

Purchasing agents face an unusual challenge in this respect. They are constantly ordering materials that have an almost infinite variety of peculiarities. One agent, for instance, received a memo from the engineering department requesting ten ¾-inch screws because the ⅞-inch screws "didn't work." Sounds simple, or at least it did to the engineers. Now consider the purchasing agent who has to thumb through an assortment of catalogs, select a vendor, and decide on these kinds of features:

1. Left or right twist
2. Flat head, round head, or hex
3. Type of alloy used
4. Head type screwdriver or Phillips
5 Tolerance/strength
6. Length
7. Used for metal, wood, or plastic

The engineers in this particular company simply had no idea about the degree of specificity needed to order a seemingly "simple" item. To the engineers, a "screw" represented a single concept. To the purchasing department "screw" was a multidimensional concept. In this instance, the agent had to call the engineers to get answers to all these questions. But this was no easy matter, because of the difficulties contacting the engineers. The net result was a needless delay for both the purchasing and engineering departments.

Office Design

Office design may well create the subtlest barrier to effective interdepartmental relationships, because it subconsciously restricts natural communication impulses. Winston Churchill once said, "We shape our buildings, thereafter they shape us" (Humes 1980, page 269). To a great extent, office design determines who has access to whom by creating barriers to some departments and bridges to others. In some fascinating research at MIT, Thomas Allen (1967) revealed that people more than ten meters apart have only an 8% to 9% probability of communicating at least once a week, versus a 25% chance at five meters (see Figure 8.1). Of course, this is only one of many studies about the effects of office design on communication (see, for example, Ornstein 1989). Because each office is unique, special factors have to be considered in each organization to make changes that will facilitate more effective communication between departments.

The same company that had the rigid communication guidelines for the telemarketing representatives also had a unique office design. The telemarketing department was physically separated from other departments to such an extent that the telemarketing reps would not talk to other employees for weeks. Despite having a joint lunchroom, employees from different departments huddled around their individual tables. The telemarketing reps vividly characterized the situation: "There is zero communication between upstairs and downstairs. It is like the stairs are a wall or no-man's land. 'The Great Stairwell,' we call it. We up here can't bother them downstairs."

The Great Wall of China for centuries separated China from the rest of the world physically, culturally, and intellectually. In much the same way, "The Great Stairwell" in this business separated telemarketing from the other departments. This office was designed in this fashion for sound "functional" reasons, such as telephone hookups, but the layout failed to consider some significant interpersonal communication issues. In any event, such design decisions, whether intentional or not, unfolded into some rather disquieting implicit messages to employees and contributed to the difficulties between the departments.

Priority Differences

In addition to the formidable barriers caused by language differences, departments also have different priorities. What may be the first priority for department X may be the last priority for department Y. Ordinarily this may not be a problem, except when department X is dependent on department Y. A destructive sequence of impatience, tension, and distrust may even be set in motion.

One industrial laundry firm we investigated had gone through this exact sequence of events, which eventually led to lower productivity and employee morale. Industrial laundry firms deliver clean linen to other business, such as hotels or hospitals. The operation can basically be broken down into three interdependent phases: The dirty towels, rugs, and uniforms are brought into the plant by the driv-

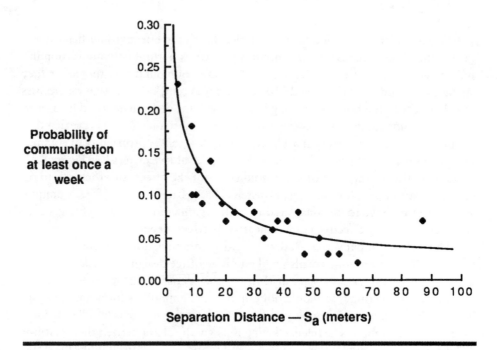

Figure 8.1. The Effect of Location on Communication

ers (Phase 1), cleaned (Phase 2), and delivered back to the clients (Phase 3). The main priority in Phase 2 is to make sure all the laundry is properly cleaned. The priority of drivers in Phase 3 is to make sure the right items are delivered to the proper clients as efficiently as possible. In order to do this, the drivers like to arrange the items precisely in the trucks before the actual delivery, much like a mail carrier. In this company, the cleaning personnel loaded the trucks for the drivers. There was constant tension between the two groups, because the drivers felt the laundry was not arranged "properly," to ensure the speediest of deliveries. Tension led to distrust, which led to even further problems. Simply, the employees who did the cleaning were not sensitive to the priorities of the drivers.

Structure of Rewards and Punishments

A rigid departmental structure places the sole power to reward and punish employees in the hands of the boss. When communicating across departmental boundaries, there are few direct rewards or punishments that can be meted out by supervisors in other departments. Thus, communication efforts across departmental boundaries have less urgency for employees.

Pat, an engineer in a large firm, simply refused to share information with a colleague in another department because Pat felt the other engineer, Sean, would take the credit for developing a more efficient technique. Did Pat incur any punishment for the refusal? No, because Sean's boss had no power over Pat. Only when Pat's boss asked for the requested information did the engineer comply. Meanwhile, valuable time had been lost. Moreover, Pat was not even warned about such behavior. Why? Sean's supervisor could not complain about Pat without Pat's supervisor being understandably protective. Thus, the reward/punishment structure inherent in most companies actually creates barriers to interdepartmental communication. Even when the communication climate is more positive, sharing information across divisions is seen as a favor and can ultimately lead to a bartering of information.

Adherence to Rigid Procedures

Frequently, past abuses of open and free communication between departments result in rigid managerial control of the communication channels. One communication audit of a small telemarketing firm revealed that the procedures used in communicating between departments were quite restrictive and hindered worker productivity. If telemarketing representatives had a question about a product, they had two options. First, they could ask their managers. This strategy rarely worked, because most of the telemarketing representatives knew the products better than their managers. Second, they could draft a written request to the appropriate person in the organization. In practice, the policy prohibited direct verbal communication between the persons who had questions and those who could supply the answers. One employee summarized the results of the policy:

> We have to be able to get information about products, credit, and computer runs right away. We used to be able to call most people on the phone, but in the last month we have been restricted from doing this and have to send memos. This delays things for hours and sometimes days before we receive an answer. This hinders us in our productivity and sales. We end up taking the static for loss of sales. . . . A lot of things could be solved faster by a single phone call. All this paperwork slows everything down and also loses sales.

When questioned about why this policy was implemented, upper management pointed out two salient factors. First, telemarketing employees were taking too much time from other employees by constantly calling to ask questions. Second, the answers to the telemarketing representatives questions were frequently in the written material that they had at their work stations. In an apparent overreaction, the pendulum had swung too far to the side of rigidity. In general, most companies have some legitimate needs to restrict communication between departments, but these procedures cannot become so rigid so as to hinder achievement of corporate goals.

Complexity of Communication Relationships

A phenomenon that could be called "the addition/multiplication factor" appears deceptively simple. When an organization *adds* departments, it *multiplies* the number of communication linkages. An arithmetic increase in departments geometrically increases the number of communication linkages. The implications of this are really quite profound. For instance, a company that has two departments has only one communication link between the departments. When the company adds another department, the communications linkages increase to three. Add a fourth department, and the linkages increase to six. Figure 8.2 shows the dramatic increase in linkages that occur when only one more department is added to the organization.

The problem is that many top managers see the addition of a single department as a small structural change, without recognizing the dramatic increase in linkages. Instead of just adding one more department to coordinate with, the company dramatically increases the number of linkages needed to coordinate their activities. A rigid policy to control communication between departments is one possible response to an unwieldy number of communication links. The other response could be to open up the system, like the free market, and let each department fend for itself. Information overload, office politics, and information bartering are often the results of this extreme. Thus, by failing to take into account the linkages factor, many top administrators unwittingly create interdepartmental communication problems.

What to Do?

Diagnosed problems are not solved problems. How can interdepartmental communication problems be effectively managed? The strategy for improving communication between departments hinges on four ideas.

1. Rally Employees Around Common Goals and Values

Bruce Moorhouse (2000), Manager of Corporate Communications at 3M, clearly articulated the central challenge:

> People think either holistically (simultaneous thinking) or in a linear way (sequential thinking). The challenge for us as leaders is to get organizations who are full of sequential thinkers to think more holistically across departments and divisions. We want them to ask, "What is best for the organization as a whole? not, What is best for me, or my department, or my division?"

A common goal or value provides a flag that all departments can rally around. It is transcendent. Customer service usually fits the bill in for-profit organizations.

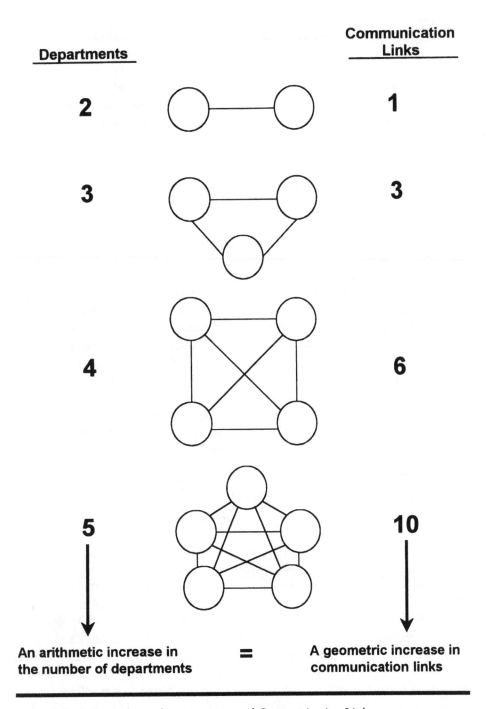

Figure 8.2. Relationships of Departments and Communication Links

Competitors can also become a source of inspiration, as in "At Avis, we try harder." Turf battles usually occur because departments fight over scarce resources, prestige, and any number of other factors. But who really wins? Who loses? Even though a particular department may "win," the customer usually loses. The competitor may even win. Customer service or a competitive threat should inspire and bridge the gaps between departments. Usually, executives must raise the flag and bring together the troops. Then the departments can fight battles worth winning.

2. Make Cooperation Between Departments a Priority

At one time or another, Continental Airlines suffered from every fatal malady any organization could endure: bankruptcy, union-management strife, executive turnover, stock slides, and consumer disgust. You name it, they had been through it. Could anyone turn the beleaguered airline around? Gordon Bethune, a former Navy mechanic, did. And he did it in just five years. Continental is now profitable, the stock value has improved dramatically, and customer disgust has turned into delight. How did he do it? One of the four key initiatives was a simple but effective campaign built around a "Working Together" slogan. He made cooperation between departments, the union, and management a priority (O'Reilly 1999). Flight attendants feel confident enough to resolve a problem on the spot with the catering service in order to meet core goals, such as on-time service. In the old days, resolving conflicts like this was someone else's job. Gordon might even help a baggage handler load up the plane in order to push the plane onto the tarmac on time. That is "working together," in both word and deed.

3. Reconcile the Inherent Tensions Between Information Providers and Consumers

Just as a dancer balances creative impulses within musical constraints, managers must balance the needs of information seekers and providers (see Table 8.1). The communication system must not be overly constrained, as is the tendency of Arrow managers. Yet it must avoid the Circuit manager's inclination of a completely open system, which may lead to information overload. An effective communication system avoids wasting the time of information providers and receivers. It is counterproductive for a system to be so open that employees are expected to answer the same question ten to fifteen times a day. Employees get weary answering the same questions day after day, especially when the information is readily available in a written form. The perfect system would block all redundant information requests, but allow every unique or special inquiry. This ideal will, no doubt, prove elusive. The objective is to develop sensitivity to the needs, desires, and problems of other departments. After all, today's requester may be tomorrow's provider. Frustration by either party ultimately results in discontent for all.

TABLE 8.1 Constraints in Sharing Information

Concerns of Information Providers	Concerns of Information Consumers
It takes time to answer questions.	Information is needed to complete tasks.
Information dissemination is a responsibility.	Sometimes, it's easier to ask someone than to look up the answer myself.
My priority should be answering nonroutine inquiries.	Sometimes, making a routine request for information is a way for me legitimately to get the attention of someone whom I couldn't normally contact.
Providing information also facilitates receiving information.	They might tell me something I don't know.
It takes time to document everything.	I just want to make sure the information is current.
	I want to confirm the written information.

4. Create Organizational Processes and Procedures to Manage Interdepartmental Conflicts

For over twenty-five years, Dr. Barry Usow practiced medicine, treating thousands of patients on a variety of urological matters. Like most physicians, he practiced medicine on a case-by-case basis, prescribing medicine for some patients, and performing surgery on others. Instinctively, he approached his new job as Chief of Staff at St. Luke's Hospital in the same way. An organizational problem would arise and he would address it. Another conflict would occur and he would deal with it. Soon, he learned that the managerial world was not at all like the medical world. He revealed,

> You can't make much progress working case-by-case; you can't schedule hospital problems like patient visits. There would be an emergency every minute of the day. I eventually surmised that by setting up mission-driven committees staffed with the right people, different departments naturally learned to work together more effectively. My role was to make sure that the right processes were in place, not to try to resolve every problem. (Usow, personal interview)

In short, healing interdepartmental rifts usually requires patience and the right environment—not necessarily radical surgery.

How to Do It?

Strategic clarity does not guarantee tactical competence. Therefore, the final section of this chapter discusses fairly specific activities that have proven useful in resolving interdepartmental problems. Some of these initiatives require less effort than others do. Selecting the appropriate response depends on the severity of the interdepartmental problems.

Minor Effort Projects

The projects discussed below can help foster a deeper sensitivity on the part of employees as well as provide more specific information about departments across the organizational boundaries.

Job Switching. Few projects can more effectively force employees to come to grips with their colleagues' work situations than job switching. The basic idea is that employees from various departments switch jobs for several days to get a feel for the other person's job. Employees can see firsthand how their actions affect another department.

The industrial laundry firm discussed earlier used this technique with remarkable success by having plant workers ride with the drivers who delivered the linens to customers. After five of the sixty plant workers participated in the program, some dramatic changes occurred. The tension between the departments slowly dissipated. Amazingly, without any explicit appeal, the plant workers started to arrange the linens in the trucks in a very precise way to make it easier for the drivers to do their job. The power of such quick and vivid firsthand experiences can replace hundreds of rules, exhortations, reports, and countless hours of training.

Companywide Seminars. A companywide seminar that involves frontline employees as well as top management personnel can provide a rich and unique opportunity to foster effective interdepartmental communication. Many topics are of interest to personnel at all levels of the organization, such as conflict resolution or basic communication skills. Skillful seminar leaders can help bring out the perspectives of the various departments and organizational levels in such a way that everyone develops greater sensitivity to the big picture. If the seminar involves some sort of case study or project in which there is group work, the wise seminar leader would encourage people to work together who would not normally get the opportunity to do so.

For instance, a basic communication skills workshop was conducted for all personnel at a financial institution. In each session there were employees representing various departments from tellers to top-level managers. This was one of the few opportunities for employees from across the organization to get together. One employee reported that such seminars allowed time to develop a "lingo link" that helped bridge departmental barriers. Although not one of the major objectives, a pleasant benefit of the seminar was that top management became aware of a particular issue that tellers were facing on a day-to-day basis. Changes were made that may not have been considered had the tellers' concerns been forwarded through normal channels. Additionally, management, by their presence, was subtly communicating that they valued training of this type and that they were still learning just as they expected of their employees.

Interdepartmental team building can also prove useful. Bank employees from two departments that were consistently experiencing communication difficulties found this to be a successful experience. They began the session with the administration of a personality profile, the Myers-Briggs Type Indicator, which revealed some intriguing differences between employees in terms of behaviors and thinking styles. The profile proved to be an excellent primer for a more detailed discussion of the interdepartmental difficulties. Why? Because it legitimized the differences and provided a more objective way to discuss the difficulties. The result was an action plan developed by the departments that helped ease tensions.

Coauthored Articles. Developing opportunities for people from two different backgrounds to work on a project can frequently provide the impetus for departments to change their attitudes toward each other. This project is simple in design, but more difficult in execution. Employees from two different departments are asked to coauthor an article on a topic of interest. The article could be published in a scholarly or trade journal, or even the corporate newsletter; the more prestigious the publication, the better.

In one chemical research firm, a member of the marketing division coauthored an article with the researcher who developed the product. The article was published in a trade journal. Both individuals reported a renewed respect for the other's expertise. Furthermore, the marketing department now had an important advocate within the research department who was able to explain a marketing perspective. The reverse was also true, which, in the long run, aided in the overall coordination of corporate policy.

Brainstorming Sessions. Many times, other departments can provide useful insights into difficulties that another department experiences. Setting up sessions between departments in which each unit shares its problems can be a creative experience. The agenda need not be formal. For instance, the marketing department of a research firm noted that the plastic carriers used to transport cats and dogs on airplanes often chipped and broke on the corners. They recognized the marketing possibilities and mentioned this to the research department in a brainstorming session. Subsequently, they designed a new and elegantly simple animal carrier that created a nice little success in the marketplace. What makes this case extremely interesting is that normally the research department either thought up their own ideas or, more often, top management developed project ideas. In this case, reversing the communication pattern led to convincing results. Many executives might be quite surprised at the workable ideas that could be generated in the various "corners" of their corporate world.

Quizzes. One organization that was experiencing some rather dramatic turf wars asked a consultant for some help. The consultant assembled all the department heads, and asked them to describe their core responsibilities. No problem.

Then he inquired if there were any surprises in the meeting thus far. There were none. Then he asked, "How healthy are relationships between departments?" Silence. In one-on-one interviews, they would quickly reel off a dozen complaints about other departments, but in a group setting they conspired in their silence. They did, however, at least demonstrate that they could work together, even if it was unintentionally.

In a flash of insight, the consultant thought of a way to break through the silence. He asked all the department heads to write down five things everyone in the room should know about his or her unit. He then said to the assembled silent conspirators, "I'm going to compile all these facts into a test. How many of you are going to get 90% or better on this quiz?" Everyone's hand quickly shot up. The next week, they took the thirty-item quiz. The result was that their collective confidence was completely shattered. The average score was barely above 50%. This proved to be the crucial event that turned their silence into genuine dialogue about the turf wars. Interestingly, almost 90% of the items on the quiz dealt with how long it took to complete certain tasks. Amazingly, these basic facts had never been clearly communicated. In short, the quiz provided a much needed educational experience. Similar tactics can prevent unnecessary interdepartmental misunderstandings before they occur. For example, a regular feature in one company's newsletter is a ten-item true/false quiz highlighting a particular department.

Interdepartmental Agreements. Marriage counselors sometimes negotiate agreements between sparring partners to get the relationship back on track. Some companies use a similar tool to resolve interdepartmental rifts. The bickering departments negotiate an accord that respects the interests of both parties, stipulating the responsibilities and duties of each unit. Typically, someone formally drafts up a written statement of mutual understanding—nothing fancy, overly formalized, or comprehensive. Why? Usually the process of creating the agreement proves more useful than the accord itself. In fact, being overly specific usually guarantees that the accord falls apart. If there are too many provisions, the department can pick and choose what points of the agreement to follow. Then the bickering starts all over again. Better to choose a few items that have the greatest chance to resolve the major concerns.

Tracking Organizational Processes. What would happen if you stapled yourself to a purchase order in your organization? From this vantage point, you might gain a deeper understanding of why interdepartmental conflicts occur. In fact, several of Harvard Business School's finest proposed this very activity as way to better serve customers, seize business opportunities, and improve corporate performance. Their research yielded the following conclusions:

> In field visits to 18 different companies in vastly different industries, we invariably found a top marketing or administrative executive who would offer a simple, truncated—and inaccurate—description of the order flow. The people at the top couldn't see the details of their OMC [Order Management Cycle]; the people deep

within the organization saw only their own individual details. And when an order moved across departmental boundaries, from one function to another, it faded from sight; no one was responsible for it or the customer. (Shapiro, Rangan, and Sviokla 1992, p. 115)

My associates and I replicated their study in a number of organizations, reaching similar conclusions. But we added a twist: We used the results to improve interdepartmental communication by creating a dialogue with all those who helped construct the OMC diagram. Often the group realized that the procedure could be simplified by taking out steps. At other times, the group recognized that adding a particular piece of information could greatly speed up the process. And almost always the group gained a greater understanding of the entire process and the constraints of other departments. In short, mapping out the OMC proved to be a wonderful tool to improve both interdepartmental communication and customer service.

Show-and-Tell. Most school children eagerly look forward to show-and-tell day. On those days, their excitement is unbridled and their curiosity overwhelming. What new electrical gizmo will Elton bring in? Can Taylor's bow shoot real arrows? Will Martha's cat really dance? The premise is simple: each child brings in something of interest to show the class, and then talks about it. At that age, "talking about it" whips up almost as much fun as bringing something. That changes with age, of course, as self-consciousness weaves its inhibiting spell.

Many an organization would do well in reviving this old Friday afternoon tradition. I never cease to be amazed at how little we actually know about what our colleagues are doing on a day-to-day basis. In many cases, a university professor knows far more about a former colleague at a college a thousand miles away than about someone from another department whose office is located right next door. But this is the nature of the modern organization.

Recall the plastic lid case at the beginning of this chapter. After the research department was thoroughly disgusted with marketing and vice versa, they decided to have one final bout. Each brought their respective documents to show how the other side was wrong and misguided. Predictably, the arguments that had hitherto been expressed in other forums were vented in the face-to-face encounter. At one point, someone from marketing pulled out a can of frosting, removed the vacuum-sealed aluminum covering, and placed the plastic lid on the can. The meeting concluded indecisively with both sides claiming victory and neither admitting defeat.

As is often the case, what is communicated unsuccessfully with statistics and arguments can be clearly and vividly communicated with one simple demonstration. By happenstance, the research department took the can of frosting back to the office. Lo and behold—it turned brown over night. The very next day, research had the answer. What had happened was that the lid was porous to air molecules, and the air had interacted with the frosting causing it to discolor. Research was right; the lid did not "leak." Marketing was right; there was a problem with the lid and frosting. Yet both were wrong. Neither department attacked the problem in the most effective manner. One simple but powerful demonstration could have resolved the difficulty without needless strife, frustration, and wasted time. So it was the grade school game of show-and-tell that stopped the adults from arguing like little kids.

Major Effort Projects

For many firms, the projects reviewed above may be the only solutions needed. Yet, for other businesses, more radical measures are needed because the interdepartmental communication problems are more deeply ingrained within the current organizational structure.

Job Rotation. As distinguished from job switching, job rotation involves becoming familiar with another department's jobs and responsibilities, and actually performing them over long periods of time. There are no specialists. This year's production manager was the personnel manager three years ago, and this year's marketing manager was the previous production manager. And so it goes. "At Canon, critical people move regularly between the camera business and the copier business and between the copier business and the professional optical-products business" (Prahalad and Hamel 1990, p. 91). Why? It is a quest to develop "core competencies." The central idea is that the company seeks to develop fundamental know-how that can have a wide variety of applications. The key is for the company to strategically bring together corporate knowledge in order to develop or enhance products and services (Hamel and Prahalad 1994). This kind of program provides managers and employees with an amazing amount of detailed knowledge about functions of departments and the company as a whole. Beyond sensitivity, managers develop a commitment to the company instead of their specialty. Moreover, researchers have shown that changing jobs can actually result in increases in employee performance, innovativeness, and job satisfaction (Keller and Holland 1981). William Ouchi (1981) describes how the Japanese utilize such a program:

> Sugao will enter in a management training position, spending perhaps a year just meeting people and learning his way around while working on various assignments. Then he will be sent out to a branch to learn bank operations including working with tellers and managing the flow of information, paper, and people. From there he will be brought back into headquarters to learn commercial banking, the process of loaning large sums to major firms with whom the bank maintains relations. Then back to yet another branch. . . . Ten years will have passed and Sugao will gain his first major promotion, perhaps becoming a section chief. In this capacity he will move again. . . . By the time he reaches the peak of his career, Sugao will be an expert in taking every function, every specialty, and every office of the Mitsubeni Bank and knitting them together into one, integrated whole. (pp. 29–30)

In such a program a lateral move is not seen in the typically negative light, but rather as a radiant opportunity to learn more about the complexities of the company. Although, at first thought, it may seem that employees in rotated jobs might experience more ambiguity about their roles than those who do not rotate, researchers found exactly the opposite (Keller and Holland 1981). Perhaps, by knowing more about the big picture, employees know more about their specific role in the organization.

Redesign Accounting Procedures. Most accounting systems are simply blind to the necessity of interdepartmental communication. Generally, employees are not rewarded for such efforts, and the budgetary constraints actively discourage such attempts. Yet, at some restaurants, the waiters and waitresses work as teams. A restaurant can promote the team atmosphere by asking all employees to pool their tips. Hence customers never have to look for "their" waiter or waitress, because everyone works together. Such a simple change in accounting procedures has a tremendous impact on the level of customer service (Keidel 1988). In short, if a company chooses to become serious about interdepartmental communication, then some major changes will be needed in the accounting procedures that will reward employees both monetarily and in terms of performance evaluations (see, for example, Kaplan 1984).

Office Redesign. As previously discussed, the physical layout of a business can dramatically alter communication patterns. Whether intentionally or unintentionally, office design fosters certain communication events and discourages others. The overriding issue managers should consider is whether the office layout is conducive to communication between departments. Frequently, the changes can be quite minor but have a relatively major impact.

The telemarketing company that had some interdepartmental communication problems (aided and abetted by "The Great Stairwell") could not, at the time, take out the stairwell or change buildings. Yet there was one saving grace. All employees ate in the same lunchroom. Even here, however, the office design conspired in the downfall. The lunchroom had twenty small round tables that could seat four or five people. Guess who sat with whom? The telemarketing reps sat with telemarketing reps, the marketing personnel sat with marketing personnel, upstairs with upstairs, and downstairs with downstairs. "The Great Stairwell" was still intact even in a common lunchroom. The solution was to put in longer tables, like long picnic benches, and stagger lunch hours so employees would have to eat lunch with people in other departments. Informing the employees about the purpose of this change, accompanied with the development of a strong communication policy, proved successful.

The CEO of Viant, Bob Gett, believes in the power of architecture. When competing against the likes of McKinsey and Andersen Consulting, his company needs every advantage it can get. "Gett believes that up to 50% of breakthroughs on projects—'bursts of brilliance'—occur when people run into one another and begin talking" (Welles 1999, p. 116). What to do? Viant's offices were designed to create "knowledge accidents," those wonderful times when experts crash into one another, solving a critical problem in some novel way. But accidents do not just happen; you can engineer them by minimizing walls, eliminating offices, and creating handy conference rooms for those spur-of-the-moment meetings. Through these efforts and others, Gett has created one of the hottest, most integrated, and successful consulting businesses in the world.

Job Description Modifications. Few organizations have interdepartmental communication built into job descriptions. Honda is one exception. In their Maryville, Ohio plant, there are only two job classifications: assembly and maintenance. Honda workers perform many different tasks, which is inconceivable in other auto factories that have up to 100 classifications (Koepp 1986). This approach permeates everything Honda does. Job descriptions are left purposely vague:

> My boss gave me the best advice I've ever received. During my first week, I commented on how difficult it was for me to understand what my actual job was. He looked at me silently for a few seconds and then said in a low voice, "Your job is everything." That was it! Not another word and he walked away. It took me a while to realize what he meant and how right on target he was. (Shook 1988, p. 129)

Such job descriptions may induce some degree of anxiety, but are unlikely to create departmental blinders. Typically, job descriptions are narrowly confined to departmental responsibilities, not corporation-wide ones. In sum, job descriptions may send the clearest messages to employees about the organization's commitment to effective interdepartmental communication.

Cross-functional Teams. When members of a closely-knit departmental team put off communicating with the rest of the organization, they prevent others from understanding the design principles that guide their decision making. Cross-functional teams try to circumvent this natural organizational problem by bringing together people from different departments to manage a project. Researchers have found that these teams can dramatically cut the costs and decrease the time needed to develop new products (Maccoby 1999). Companies that use cross-functional teams tend to get products or services to the marketplace sooner than their competitors (Jassawalla and Sashittal 1999). Cross-functional teams also have been used successfully in a wide variety of other situations, ranging from purchasing computers to resolving factory problems (Avery 1998). A note of caution: Cross-functional teams are not a panacea; they require special leaders with superb interpersonal communication skills.

Parallel Development Cycles. Traditionally, departmental relations were set up to run like a relay race—one department finishes its job and hands off the project to the next group. If there were problems, the race would start all over again at the

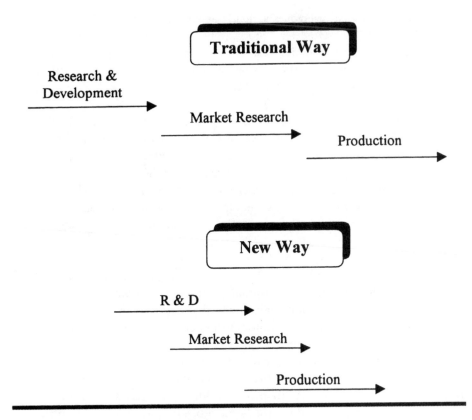

Figure 8.3. Ways of Organizing Work

beginning of the process (see Figure 8.3). More recently, innovative companies like Toyota and Microsoft have set up concurrent or parallel processes (Sobek, Ward, and Liker 1999). For instance, the marketing and engineering departments might work on a project at roughly the same time (Iansiti and MacCormack 1997). Or different design teams might concurrently work on different parts of a major software project, like Microsoft Word.

The benefits of this approach are more rapid innovation, greater flexibility in product designs, and an improved ability to respond quickly to marketplace changes. Making this process work requires some special communication plans. Microsoft, for example, uses what has been aptly named the "synch-and-stabilize" strategy:

> The essence [of synch-and-stabilize] is simple: Continually synchronize what people are doing as individuals and as members of teams working in parallel on different features, and periodically *stabilize* the evolving product features in increments as a project proceeds, rather than once at the end of a project. Microsoft

people refer to their techniques variously as the "milestones," "daily build," "nightly build," or "zero-defect" process. The term "build" refers to the act of putting together or "integrating" partially completed or finished pieces of a software product during the development process to see what functions work or what problems exist. (Cusumano 1997, p. 11)

These routine communication cycles between teams (or departments) foster solid relationships. The speed of the feedback cycles helps ensure that misunderstandings and incompatible assumptions are quickly discovered. Naturally, daily conflicts will occasionally emerge from such a process. But that beats starting an entire project over because departments either infrequently or inadequately communicated. In short, the company wins the race to the consumer by eliminating the hand-offs altogether; everyone arrives at the finish line at approximately the same time.

Organizational Restructuring. Perhaps the most extreme step that could be taken would be to alter the organizational structure in some way to facilitate communication. Some organizations have found that a change in reporting relationships can indeed provide the impetus for more effective interdepartmental communication. Sometimes, combining departments, altering job responsibilities, or even splitting some departments may prove to be effective strategies.

A highly successful insurance firm, Aid Association for Lutherans, for years had three separate sections: health insurance, life insurance, and support services. The result was that agents calling the home office frequently talked to dozens of different personnel in order to make minor changes in a policy or check the status of a claim. One corporate reorganization was designed to allow a single team of twenty or thirty employees to serve a certain geographic group of field agents. Thus, a team dedicated to particular agents completes the hundreds of tasks that used to be performed by a seemingly faceless group of corporate employees. Now, the agents deal with only a small team and are not overwhelmed by the home office bureaucracy. The results are a reduction in processing time of applications and a major increase in productivity. By changing and expanding job responsibilities, corporate employees experience slightly more stress, but agents and clients clearly experience less (Hoerr 1988b). This dramatic change in corporate structure helped the organization coordinate its efforts more effectively, which should be the focus of interdepartmental communication efforts.

One of the more radical proposals involves creating a matrix organizational structure. The idea is relatively simple. Certain employees in the organization report to two managers instead of just one. A marketing specialist, for instance, might report to a manager on the West Coast and another one on the East Coast. Or, a quality control engineer might report to the production manager as well as the product manager. There is one top manager who oversees the entire process. Certainly, this facilitates communication between departments, but it takes a special organization and unique individuals to make the idea work. Training is a must because of ambiguity over responsibilities and a tendency to manage for the short term. The aerospace industry was the first to try the concept; now, it is used in a wide variety of organizations, including hospitals, banks, and research firms. It is a serious step, though, and needs to be carefully thought out.

Conclusion

Most organizations, to some degree, have difficulties with interdepartmental communication. Unfortunately, the problem is frequently overlooked and, even when recognized, often the symptoms are treated instead of the causes. To a large extent the problems are unavoidable in business because of the penchant for rigid departmentalization. However, even under these conditions, some significant changes, as discussed above, can enhance communication between departments.

Avoiding unnecessary conflict, low performance, time delays, and decisions that work at cross purposes are compelling reasons for taking active measures to improve interdepartmental communication. Yet one question remains: At what cost? Are there any dangers in encouraging interdepartmental communication? In a word, yes. An overly integrated organization can stifle creativity and innovation, and develop a tendency for "groupthink." Frankly, given the ingrained belief in the wisdom of departmentalization, these possibilities are remote.

Slower decision making is a more likely consequence of fostering interdepartmental communication. As many Japanese businesses have discovered, decisions will typically take more time to make because all the departments have to be consulted and allowed input into an impending change. But that time is often more than compensated for by swift and smooth implementation. Nevertheless, a more rigidly departmentalized company may be able to react more quickly than one that is not.

On the balance, though, the benefits of effective interdepartmental communication far exceed the costs. Misunderstandings can be reduced, antagonisms avoided, cooperation encouraged, and sensitivity promoted. And, in the end, a supportive communication climate can be developed and maintained.

In a sense, communicating across departmental boundaries is like taking a voyage into an unknown land. Daniel Boorstin (1983), in his magnum opus *The discoverers,* writes passionately about the real goal of the "discoverers:"

> The ability to come home again was essential if a people were to enrich, embellish, and enlighten themselves from far-off places. . . . Getting there was not enough. The internourishment of the peoples of the earth required the ability to get back, to return to the voyaging source and transform the stay-at-homes by the commodities and the knowledge that the voyagers had found over there. (p. 158)

So too, communication between departments seeks to enrich, embellish, and enlighten the lives of individuals throughout the entire company. The frontier these days is not geographical, but rather technological and managerial. But a trek into another department's cognitive landscape often proves as elusive and vexing as any journey into an unknown land.

Note

1. In Hebrew, the word *Babel* sounds like the word for confused.

NINE

Communicating the Innovative Spirit

Everything that can be invented has been invented.

Charles H. Duell, Director of
U.S. Patent Office, 1899

Loyalty to petrified opinion never broke a chain or freed a human soul.

Mark Twain

He was like so many innovators who yearned for change and looked to the future with a wide-eyed eagerness. He was young, energetic, a bit brash, and had an infectious enthusiasm for life. He had a favorite saying that inspired not only him, but also those around him: "Some men see things as they are and say, why? I dream things that never were and say, why not?" This is the spirit of innovation. And it was that spirit that emboldened the thousands who supported him. Tragically, his life was cut short at the hand of an assassin.

Yet, even in the anguish and despair of that moment on June 6, 1968, there was a glimmer of hope. The vision—his vision—still lived. Even today, there are those who dream dreams and have the courage and tenacity to bring them to reality. Robert F. Kennedy never had that chance. But he would cheer on those who did. He understood the innovative process and how to foster the spirit of innovation. That is the focus of this chapter.

Misconceptions

A host of misconceptions plague the innovative process. Some of the more important ones are discussed in detail below.

Myth 1: Innovation Is Risky

Managers and organizations often resist innovation because of a fear of the unknown. Innovative practices, by definition, are not tested, tried, and proved; they are not traditional. Results cannot be guaranteed. There can, in fact, be "failures." The safe course appears to continue to do what the organization does well. Thus, managers often assume that tampering with past successes can incur unnecessary risks. Why change if everything is going well?

Yet this pseudo-argument begs the question; the answer is implicit in the question. Logically, one could just as easily ask, "Why not change?" After all, the successful company or manager is in a better economic and political position to experiment than those who are less successful. Indeed, those who ask, "Why change?" are already standing on shaky ground, because they do not really understand the source of their success.

Entrepreneurs tend to be highly innovative. But, contrary to popular belief, entrepreneurs do not tend to be big risk takers. The press often covers those who are, but careful research on the attributes of entrepreneurs generally reveals that their propensity for risk-taking is not much different from the general population (Brockhaus 1980). Other characteristics, such as the need for achievement, autonomy, self-esteem, and independence tend to be far more predominant in entrepreneurs. A tolerance for ambiguity, high energy levels, and assertiveness are other unique attributes of the entrepreneur (Collins and Moore 1964). In short, entrepreneurs may be robust and exciting human beings, but they are not some kind of organizational Evel Knievel.

In the long run, corporations risk more by *not* innovating than they do by innovating. The near collapse of the U.S. steel industry is a case in point. For years, major U.S. manufacturers took a pass on the minimill technology while competitors embraced the innovations. The result is that today minimills produce most of the rods, bars, and structural beams in North America (Christensen 1997).

But the risks of not innovating go beyond the domination of a particular market. The very survival of the economic system is dependent on innovation. Around 1909, Bell Telephone conducted a study of how many telephone operators would be needed if telephone usage continued to increase at the present rate at the time. They concluded that between 1925 and 1930, every female in the United States between the ages of seventeen and sixty would have to become a telephone operator (Drucker 1985). That scenario, of course, was untenable. Yet, within two years, automatic switching devices were developed. The lesson is simple: Innovation is a necessity, not an option. Furthermore, scholars have analyzed the financial results of firms that heavily invest in research and development efforts. They discovered that those companies recognized for being on the cutting-edge significantly out-perform other less innovative competitors in terms of stock prices, earnings, and productivity (Deng, Lev, and Narin 1999). In short, the perceived risks of innovating quickly fade upon deeper examination.

Myth 2: *Innovation Is Always the Product of the Revolutionary "Big" Idea or Grand Scheme*

Innovation is not always the product of revolutionary ideas. Although there are some innovations that appear to be of this ilk, such as the Wright Brothers' airplane, these in fact tend to be the exception rather than the rule. The "little" ideas, the minor modifications here and there, or the addition of this or that feature, are the greatest sources of innovation. Here is a sampling:

> ▷ One employee at a Texas Instrument plant suggested using larger spools of wire to decrease the number of trips made to replace the used spool. The result: A time study showed an annual increase in productivity around 15% ("Organizing for productivity" 1981).
>
> ▷ An employee at a small paper converting plant suggested that someone begin work one-half hour early in order to warm up the cutting machines. The result: The elimination of five man-hours a week of idle time for that division.
>
> ▷ During the 1950s, Allen Grant, the president of Glen Raven Mills, asked his wife, Ethel, "How would it be if we made a pair of panties and fastened the stockings to it?" She thought it was a grand idea. The result: pantyhose ("Nights of the garter are over" 1989).

In each case, these seemingly minor innovations have reaped huge dividends.

Likewise, many of the greatest scientific discoveries were the product of the seemingly inconsequential. For instance, Louis Pasteur became intrigued by an experiment that had gone "bad" when his calcium tartrate solution became turbid because of some mold. "Most chemists would have poured the liquid down the sink, considering the experiment as entirely spoiled" (Dubos 1976, p. 107). Not Pasteur, who used such a seemingly trivial event to launch into his prodigious innovations of pasteurization and immunizations for contagious diseases. Pasteur once reflected on "the infinitely great power of the infinitely small" in the world of bacteria, fungi, and the like (p. 45). Perhaps he spoke in another sense, as well, and was characterizing the entire process of innovation.

Myth 3: *Innovation Is Solely the Product of a Few Great Minds*

Tangled in the web of the "big idea" theory of innovation lies the belief that innovation can be done only by a select set of gifted individuals. Certainly some innovations, such as genetic engineering or the silicon chip, would not have been possible without the genius of a select few. But this does not mean that all innovations are the product of the gifted. Examples abound of the "ordinary" individual coming up with some special and useful new innovation. Even the supposedly uninformed customer can sometimes be the source of useful innovation. For instance, Clearwood Building, Inc., a San Francisco–based construction company, simply listened to customers' complaints about their competitors. Then the company revamped their service to alleviate the more common complaints about contractors, such as poor manners, beat-up trucks, and workers who track dirt across the carpet. Their service level became the epitome of professionalism, with spotlessly clean trucks and employees dressed in jacket and tie. This may all sound a bit "obvious," but it worked. Within two years, annual revenues jumped from $200,000 to $1 million (Galante 1986).

Another problem with the "great mind" theory of innovation is one of perspective. Rarely are the great minds recognized as such in the beginning of their careers. In fact, it is usually just the opposite. Who would have thought that two college dropouts tinkering with electronic components in a garage would have launched the personal computer revolution? Of course, that is exactly what Steven Jobs and Steven Wozniak did with Apple computer. The label of "innovative genius" is almost always attached after the fact.

Innovators may not necessarily be blessed with an apparent intellectual prowess. Rather, intellectual curiosity and drive are more important. Most great scientists have an IQ score of at least 120. Yet after that point there is little relationship between IQ and scientific success. "A scientist with an IQ score of 130 is as likely to win a Nobel Prize as one with a score of 180" (Beveridge 1980, p. 93). Likewise, grades in school may not be a useful predictor of potential. Einstein and Darwin are two classic examples of poor students who clearly achieved some scientific fame. On the other hand, there are those who carried straight As in school, but never had a creative idea in their life.

Organizations that wait for the "great minds" to propose innovations almost always wait until the innovation proves to have a high likelihood of success. By then, the competitors recognize it and also jump at the chance. By virtue of the fact that "great minds" are labeled after the fact, most companies fail to exploit a host of innovative opportunities within their grasp. For nine years Chester Carlson tried to sell his idea of xerography to over twenty companies, such as RCA, Kodak, and IBM. All rejected the innovation, reasoning that there was no need for a machine that does the same thing as carbon paper (Jacobson and Hillkirk 1986). Of course, Xerox is now a corporate giant. The crux of the matter is that innovative opportunities abound in organizations, whether at Xerox or the local flower shop. Potentially, anyone could propose a useful innovation. Hence the great challenge is to encourage the innovative spirit in employees but still be able to separate the wheat from the chaff.

Those who, by word or deed, endorse either the "great mind" or the "big idea" theory of innovation are frequently seeking to justify their own complacency. They are trying to deny their responsibility to innovate. They will not accept the burden of an occasional "failure." The logic goes as follows: One cannot fail if one attempts nothing. They seek the safe course. Ultimately, they do so at their own peril and the company's, as well.

Myth 4: *Innovation Is Product-Focused*

Most discussions of innovation center on the invention of new products like the electric light bulb or personal computer. The entrepreneurial heroes typically praised tend to have invented some gadget or device. The school history books take note of the genius of Alexander Graham Bell, Benjamin Franklin, Eli Whitney, and Robert Fulton. Clearly, they deserve attention, because they have contributed greatly to our lives. Yet this is only one narrow band on the entire innovative spectrum.

There are other great innovators who, though not heralded in the history books, have equal significance. Few Americans would recognize the name of Rowland Hill. Yet he is often credited with "inventing" the modern postal service in 1836. Postal systems have existed since antiquity, but Hill suggested a new approach: a postage rate that was uniform across Great Britain. He also proposed that the sender pay the fee and attach a stamp to the letter, just as it is done today. But it was not always that way: previously, the cost was computed according to the weight and distance and paid by the recipient. Such service was, at the least, inconvenient and costly. Hill's proposal changed all that and was a smashing success. Yet he invented no product or new gadget; rather, he invented a new method that has been enjoyed by countless millions since then (Drucker 1985). Surely he deserves mention in the innovators' Hall of Fame.

Or, consider what Hanes did with L'eggs pantyhose. They did not invent pantyhose, but they were they first to sell them at the grocery store. Like most manufacturers, Hanes sold pantyhose at department stores, which women visited on the average of once every six weeks. However, marketing research found that women visited grocery stores about twice a week. Thus, by placing those funny shaped plastic eggs filled with pantyhose next to the razors and candy at the checkout stand, Hanes greatly increased the probability of purchase. And that is exactly what happened. The stock increased six-fold after the introduction of L'eggs (Lynch 1989).

Each year in Japan, the Edward Deming prize is given for the best quality improvement of the year. Deming (1986), an American, introduced to the Japanese a variety of ideas developed by scholars in the United States. Deming and his followers developed the concept of quality circles, which allow the workers actually doing the job to come up with more productive ways to complete the task and solve other job-related problems. Deming might be said to have meta-innovated, because he introduced a new way to encourage innovation. In sum, innovation that is not product-based is a vital part of the economy. New approaches to service, learning, marketing, management, advertising and even innovations are equally essential. In fact, despite all the press about high technology, I believe the most unexpected innovations in the future will be in the area of these so-called "soft sciences."

Myth 5: Creativity Is the Same as Innovation

Some executives argue that the reason new ideas never surface in their organizations is because their employees are not creative enough. Sometimes, these employees are then dutifully packed off to some seminar to give them a dose of creativity. Here, the employees learn of their latent creative powers that have never been tapped. And, sure enough, the employees find that they are indeed more creative than they ever thought. How can one fault such an approach? Yet this method falls short on two accounts.

First, lack of ideas is rarely the problem in organizations. In fact, the problem is usually just the opposite. Employees, if given the chance, have too many ideas to act on effectively. And this explains why so many ideas can be generated at these creativity seminars. Most human beings are naturally creative if properly challenged. In the organizations we have audited, the employees almost always have numerous ideas to improve operations. Not all the ideas are feasible, but many are. Yet, when asked why they do not share their ideas with anyone, the most frequent response is that management does not listen. The real problem is listening, not creativity.

Second, some employees erroneously believe they are innovative if they can think up a lot of new ideas. This may be the essence of creativity, but not of innovation. Rather, innovation means carrying the idea to fruition. Nothing is more frustrating than talking to an "idea person" who has no idea about how to implement one.

Professor Lindeman, one of Winston Churchill's long time advisors, knew the difference between creativity and innovation. In 1916 many airplane pilots died in violent nosedives. "The Prof," as he was called, worked out the mathematics of a new maneuver that would bring the planes out of the tailspin. "The pilots said it wouldn't work. The Prof taught himself to fly, took off without a parachute, deliberately set the aircraft down in a spin, and brought it out so successfully that mastering his solution became required of every flier" (Manchester 1983, p. 781). Here is a man who was a true innovator, because he was willing to stake his very life on an idea.

In the final analysis, those who believe creativity is innovation are fundamentally unclear about the true nature of innovation. To this issue we now turn.

What Is Innovation?

Innovation is more than a good idea. It is a process that can be thought of in four stages:

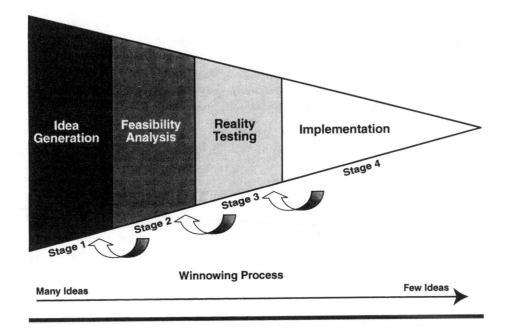

Figure 9.1. Innovation Process

▷ Stage 1—idea generation
▷ Stage 2—feasibility analysis
▷ Stage 3—reality testing
▷ Stage 4—implementation

The process is one of winnowing down the possibilities to the select few that can be really useful to the organization (see Figure 9.1).

Idea Generation

The first stage, idea generation, is the one most typically associated with innovation; it is the point of pure creativity. The emphasis is on the generation of novel ideas. One of the more effective techniques that can be used at this stage is brainstorming. Often done in a group setting, people are encouraged to think of wild, bold, and new ideas in a nonevaluative setting. The more far out, the better. Feasibility, logic, and practicality are *not* the guides; instead, intuition, ambiguity, and speculation reign supreme (see, for example, Oech 1983). As mentioned before, most employees have a wealth of creative ideas that could prove useful. Indeed, after extensive study of creative and noncreative research and development employees, a group of psychologists have concluded that the greatest difference between the groups was that "the creative people thought they were creative and the less creative people didn't think they were" (Oech 1983, p. 122). Organizations stifle creativity in a variety of subtle ways, such as by not recognizing employees who have useful ideas or not having a forum to make suggestions. The central challenge for managers is not to demand inventiveness, but to release employees' latent creativity by removing the inhibiting factors. Ingenuity must be cultivated in the organizational culture, much like tending a garden. Ideas will not sprout instantly, but under the right conditions and with proper care, a rich harvest can be reaped.

Feasibility Analysis

In Stage 2 of the innovation process, the question becomes, Which of the multitude of ideas generated are really feasible? Is it possible actually to create the product or execute the idea? Many of the ideas generated in Stage 1 will be eliminated at this point, because they fail to meet this test. Experiments or test-runs are often conducted at this juncture in order to determine if a product can actually be made. For example, computer simulations of design changes of an airplane may be used. Prototypes can be built and tested. A new advertising campaign could be test-marketed. Frequently the results indicate that the basic idea or design needs to be rethought and the entire process can begin again. Whatever strategy is used, fundamentally, the tests are designed to determine if the idea is a real possibility.

For example, in the early 1970s, Philips, a Dutch company, suggested that it might be possible to use lasers to play audio and video recordings. Many U.S. corporations, such as RCA and Zenith, worked for years only to abandon the project as hopeless. Sony and Philips did not abandon the idea, and they launched the entire compact disk revolution that made vinyl records a collector's item. For most companies, the idea never got past the feasibility stage (Stage 2). For Philips and Sony, persistence paid off; they not only introduced an innovation, they introduced a revolutionary one (Browning 1986).

Reality Testing

The most difficult hurdle of all for any idea is what might be called *reality testing*. Are corporate resources available to produce the innovation? Can the new service be rendered with a reasonable profit? Does the new procedure really save money or improve productivity? These are the toughest questions of all. The fundamental concern revolves around making a reasonable return on investment. For instance, in an unusual lapse, IBM allowed Reduced Instruction Set Computing (RISC) to "languish" for years in the pipeline, only to have competitors, such as Sun, commercialize it (Buderi 1999). Stories like this are not new or surprising. Why? Because wisely addressing the return on investment question requires considerable expertise, luck, and prescience. Information will usually be incomplete. And many innovations take a long time to be reality tested. Consider the difficulty in assessing the economic viability of introducing a new prescription drug. The feedback loop extends over many years. New ideas that are introduced internally may appear more successful than objective evidence indicates because of the *placebo effect*. That is, employees will often make something work simply because they thought up the idea, which may not reflect marketplace realities.

Organizations also have their own idiosyncratic reality tests that are determined by the unique corporate culture. An idea that may be embraced in one culture might not stand a chance in another organization that does not have the culture to sustain the idea. Moreover, the political structure of the organization may be part of the reality test. An idea needs to be filtered to the right people at the right time in order to succeed. Indeed, someone who develops a successful innovation not only needs a workable idea, but also the political backing in the organization to push it through to the implementation phase.

Implementation

Seemingly, if an idea has survived the feasibility and reality tests (Stages 2 and 3), then implementation (Stage 4) should be a foregone conclusion. Experience does not bear out this conclusion. In one organization, we found that only 60% of the ideas formally accepted were actually implemented. Another study suggested that the nature of the innovation itself as well as its symbolic significance had a major impact on whether an idea actually got implemented (Meyer and Goes 1988). The ideas that are frequent victims are the ones generated at the lowest levels of the organization. The reason is that implementation frequently depends on other people to initiate the action. For example, in an attempt to increase productivity, one paper mill employee suggested a change in the way a drum was cleaned. The idea was evaluated and deemed cost effective. Approval was given and budget allocations were made. But for some reason the purchase was never made and the idea never implemented. Neglect, time constraints, and other priorities take their toll. The irony, of course, is that an idea that has survived the most difficult hurdles fails to become a true innovation because someone neglects to finish the last few yards of the race.

Implications

There are four important implications of this process view of innovation.

First, differing criteria of evaluation are used at the various stages of the innovative process. In the first stage, judgments tend to be made in terms of novelty. Creativity is often measured in terms of how bizarre or different the idea is. This is perfectly acceptable at this stage, but it does not mean the idea will translate into innovation.

For instance, railroads have for years tried to deal with the curvature of the countryside by blasting through mountains and blowing up hills and slowly rounding the tracks. Even with these measures, trains are notoriously slow. Why not develop a train that can take the corners at a high rate of speed while keeping the passengers upright and riding like a cork in a bottle of water? Why not develop a tilting train? Now that is a truly novel idea and exactly the "innovation" the British government funded. No other train had been designed along these lines. It was an exciting and new concept. But it never really worked. The British government sunk fifteen years and $75 million into the project with little or nothing to show for it (Newman 1986). Novel idea, yes; a successful innovation, no. The tilting train failed to meet the important test of feasibility.

Even if an idea proves feasible, that does not guarantee workability. For example, the oceans contain billions of tons of gold. Polymers have been created that can sift the gold from ocean water. However, production costs make the process financially untenable. Hence the idea is novel and possible, but not workable. It fails on the third criteria. Faced with a roadblock at any of the stages, innovators have two alternatives: abandon the idea, or rework the entire process until eventually the idea crosses all the hurdles.

Second, organizational barriers can occur at any point in the innovative process. The problems encountered at one stage are not the same as those at another stage. In fact, the organizational policies or attributes that allow seeming success at one stage of the process may actually inhibit the process at another stage. Typically, organizations that are high in complexity, low in formalization and centralization, provide a rich environment for innovation in the initial stages, but present difficulties at the implementation stage. This seems reasonable, because complex but loosely organized companies would allow frequent and varied communications across departmental and organizational boundaries. Thus, a great number of ideas should be spawned in such interactions. Yet getting the employees together to do something different would prove difficult because of the very same diversity. On the other hand, a more centralized and controlled structure does not fully encourage communication across organizational boundaries, and therefore inhibits idea formation (Dougherty and Hardy 1996). Yet such a structure would be able to quickly implement a new idea if one should be approved (see, for example, Lawrence and Lorsch 1969). Therefore, executives need to learn how simultaneously to encourage new ideas and to maintain a structure that can rapidly implement the ideas. Striking that balance requires special skills.

Managers must use different tactics at each juncture of the innovative process. Indeed, the Circuit manager tends to excel at the initial stages of the innovation process, whereas the Arrow manager excels at the latter stages. The effective manager acts like an "idea shepherd," protecting ideas from various attacks along their journey. Flexibility and savvy are the key weapons. Table 9.1 reveals some of the more common difficulties encountered at each stage. In the idea generation stage (Stage 1), the difficulties tend to revolve around developing an environment of creativity. Communication across departmental boundaries is essential, as is receptivity on the part of supervisors. In the feasibility analysis stage (Stage 2), the issue becomes getting the ideas on an agenda to actually be tested or seriously analyzed. In the reality testing stage (Stage 3), building commitment for the idea

TABLE 9.1 Barriers to Innovation

Stage	Evaluation Criteria	Critical Questions	Organizational Barriers
Idea Generation	Novelty	Is the idea novel?	Highly structured organizational climate
			Authoritarian communication style
			Too many rules and regulations
			Extreme power differences
Feasibility Analysis	Possibility	Is the idea possible?	Lack of corporate resources dedicated to research
			Lack of commitment to research
Reality Testing	Practicality	Does the idea produce a reasonable return on investment?	Short-term focus
		Does the idea fit with organizational objectives?	Inadequate research on the potential return or marketability of idea
		Does the organization have the start-up capital for the idea?	Resistance to change
Implementation	Activity	Has the idea been acted on?	Too many priorities
			Nobody has responsibility for the implementation
			Overconsultation with involved parties
			Highly unstructured organizational climate

becomes the core challenge. Managers need to demonstrate that the idea will actually work in a cost-effective way. In the final stage, implementation, managers need to motivate, persuade, and perhaps cajole people into doing what the organization has approved.

Third, the time line for the innovative process is elastic. In some cases, the four stages can take a matter of days. In other cases, the process may take years. A new office filing system may take only a week from conception to implementation, whereas the design of a new microchip may take years. As J. A. Morton (1971), a former vice president at Bell Telephone laboratories, said, "Innovation is not a single, simple act" (p. 49). Therefore, the cost of innovation will vary greatly depending on the type of idea. The filing system, if a failure, can be easily changed, whereas an entire company's well-being may be based on a new microchip. The degree of thoughtfulness needed at each stage changes in proportion to the time invested. More prudence and thought are required for innovations with a longer timeline. Service organizations, such as marketing or advertising firms, can try a wealth of new ideas with less concern for failure than can an automobile manufacturer. Service organizations should emphasize and encourage creativity (Stage 1). A traditional manufacturing firm proposing a new product has to be more careful; consequently, the emphasis should be on proper research and development (Stages 2 and 3).

Fourth, an overemphasis on any one stage can become problematic. If innovation consists of more than just a lot of novel ideas, it also requires more than research on feasibility testing. Innovative companies must also face the tough questions of reality testing and implementation. For instance, during a five-year span, Campbell Soup Company bought into the lure of the creativity panhandlers and introduced 334 new products. While there were successes, there were some dismal failures. The Pepperidge Farm division, for example, lost $9 million in one year. The CEO decided that "Campbell may have done too much innovating too fast" (Schwadel 1985, p. A1). In short, the products were creative and possible, but failed at the implementation stage because of some inadequate reality testing. In a broader sense, the problem was an overemphasis on the creativity part of the innovative process.

Measuring Success and Failure

At one time, artificial intelligence (AI) was considered the next great frontier in the computer industry. The basic idea was very simple: teach computers the rules by which human experts make decisions. The so-called "knowledge engineers" went about this task by interviewing acknowledged experts in some area (Schank 1984). The goal was to understand how experts made decisions so that this information could, in turn, be programmed into a computer. For instance, how does a physician go about determining what type of blood disease a patient might have? Or, how does an investment counselor decide the type of financial portfolio a client needs? These are the kinds of questions a knowledge engineer tackled by extracting a series of decision rules from the expert.

The most intriguing part of the entire process was where the problems or bottlenecks tended to occur. It might seem reasonable to assume that the greatest difficulty would be in developing the proper software; that is, translating the expert's knowledge into a programming language the machine could understand. Or, at first glance, the great difficulty might appear to have been one of developing proper hardware to handle all the complexities. But neither concern proved all that problematic. Rather, the really tough problems were getting the experts to articulate what they knew. Apparently, most experts operate on the basis of an intuition gleaned from years of experience. The experts know how to make the proper responses, but do not always know how they arrived at those responses. In a nutshell, they do not always know what makes them successful.

Most organizations face the same dilemma. Survival depends upon at least a modicum of success, but companies are not always clear about the source of their success. Even more opaque to organizations than their failures is a deep understanding of their achievements. Ultimately, those companies that desire a long-term innovative spirit must have a proper perspective on both success and failure.

What, then, is failure? What is success? Perhaps the most useful perspective is to look at success and failure along two dimensions instead of just one. Figure 9.2 diagrams four possible quadrants in which a given innovation might fall.

Potential Success

Quadrant one is labeled *potential success,* because one learns from the "failure." Consider the events surrounding the successful launch of a Bell Labs satellite: In 1962, Bell Labs launched the Telstar 1 satellite. It was thoroughly tested and re-tested in the best of their tradition. Yet even with the most carefully tested notions, failure often lies hidden in the background. One day before the launch, the Soviets secretly conducted a high-altitude test of a nuclear device. The satellite was shut down within seven months because it was not resistant to radioactivity. A failure, yes; a complete failure, no. Why? Because Bell Labs learned from the "failure." A year later, they launched a satellite, Telstar 2, that could successfully function even with radioactivity in the atmosphere (Morton 1971). Thus, Bell Labs transformed a failure into success by turning the mishaps into a learning opportunity.

In every "failure" there is some knowledge to be gained. This may sound like some platitude of a motivational speaker, but the cold hard facts remain that those organizations and people who ultimately prevail learn from their "mistakes." And those who do not are at the whim of happenstance.

Enduring Success

The sources of enduring success are both producing useful ideas and knowing why they are successful. Certain people seem to have this uncanny ability, like Thomas Edison or Benjamin Franklin. Organizations, even more than individual inventors, need to understand their successes in order to pass along their knowledge to others. IBM, for example, seems to appreciate this fact of innovative life. They have shown over the years sustained growth and development. They continue to introduce successful products and services despite occasional "failures"— such as the PC Junior, which is really another example of a potential success. IBM's consistent profitability flows from a deep understanding of the corporate values necessary for success. Thorough employee training in the "IBM way" helps ensure

Knowledge Level

		High	Low
	Positive	Enduring Success	Temporary Success
Results			
	Negative	Potential Success	Failure

Figure 9.2. Innovation Successes and Failures

that the attributes of success are sustained. IBM constantly conducts research, even on the products that are successful. They seek to understand their success as well as their failures. Why is this so important? Because companies are not always successful for the reasons they think they are successful. This leads to the third quadrant.

Temporary Success

A temporary success occurs when the results obviously meet or exceed expectations but the organization does not understand why the success occurred. Temporarily, money—maybe lots of money—can be made, but the results are not enduring. Schwinn bicycles, for example, at one time dominated the market, but executives failed to act wisely as the market changed. Schwinn "failed to recognize that after those golden years the bicycle markets segmented, with new populations arriving to take to alternate forms of the sport" (Sobel 1999, p. 301). They essentially missed out on the mountain biking and hybrid markets.

So what? It could be argued that temporary success is better than no success at all. True enough. But that is a false dichotomy. The real question is, Why have temporary success when it is possible to have enduring success? The problem with temporary success is that no one knows how long the results can be sustained. Organizations that are temporarily successful do not have the corporate intelligence to cope with change. They are caught flatfooted when some change in the business climate occurs. Although they may be financially successful temporarily, the true source of future innovation is knowledge, not money (Gilder 1981). There also seems to be an ethical obligation for an organization to provide its employees as much job security as possible. The costs of temporary success may not be felt too deeply by those in top management, but are borne in the lives and families of those who work for the company.

Failure

True failure can only result when no knowledge is gained from an innovative experiment. Such a situation is almost always avoidable. The movie industry, for example, has had an almost sustained rate of box office "bombs" over the years. Is this the nature of the business? Maybe. Yet little research has been devoted to the characteristics of these box office failures other than on an individual basis. The collective knowledge yielded from such research could at least alter the probabilities of future box office failures. This state of affairs seems like a failure on two levels: financial results are less than spectacular and no one seems to learn from mistakes.

Implications

First, present success is no guarantee of future success. Just because an innovation has proven successful under one set of conditions does not mean it will continue to be. Oscar Wilde said it best: "Consistency is the last refuge of the unimaginative." For instance, in the electronics market, there has been a tremendous turnover in the industry leadership from the vacuum tubes of 1955 to the present day. Many of the companies are no longer even in business (Foster 1986). It may seem safe to keep doing what one does well. There is a measure of wisdom in this. However, there is another pull as well: the need to continue to change. Keeping a proper balance between the traditional successes and future potential successes is one of the important challenges facing management. After all, tradition is often the enemy of innovation.

Second, the actual innovation is but the tip of the iceberg. The knowledge base underneath the idea is the key to further growth and innovation. Even "failures" can add to the knowledge base. When conditions change, a new idea can spring forth from that knowledge base that substitutes for the old.

There may not even be an awareness of all the knowledge that sustains a successful innovation. The inventor of Ethernet and founder of 3Com, Bob Metcalfe (1999), said, "Most successful entrepreneurs I've met have no idea about the reasons for their success" (p. 56). The same could be said about successful innovators within organizations. But herein lies the opportunity for sustained success: continually pushing to get at even deeper levels of understanding provides the basis for still further innovation. Vaccines, for example, have been used for years to prevent deadly diseases, but only in more recent years have scientists begun to understand why a vaccine actually works. As the reasons for success emerged, so have other treatment regimens. So it is with most innovations. Indeed, this is precisely the challenge facing the knowledge engineer.

Third, fostering meaningful dialogue sparks learning and knowledge creation. The implicit rules that govern organizational discussions greatly influence the degree to which knowledge emerges from technical successes or failures. Managers who rule through intimidation induce an unwillingness to hold meaningful discussion. Paul Winch, the Senior Innovation Manager at Good Humor Breyers, adopts just the opposite approach. Perhaps his choice of diversions has something to do with it. He has written a novel, plays in a rock band, and even composed a local classic tune, "Cheesehead Girl." That is a pretty intriguing resume for a guy with a Ph.D. in Physics. He spurs on the innovative spirit of his employees by allowing discussions to veer "off the topic." As a result, light bulbs start turning on. He summed up his philosophy like this: "In the long run, a stimulating discussion beats a meticulous plan every time" (Winch 2000). In short, he engenders trust and comfort, so that employees can discuss honestly the reasons for successes or failures.

Stop and Go Signs

Stop signs regulate the flow of traffic; they tell people when and where to stop. With too few stop signs, the streets are unsafe. With too many, advancement slows. Either extreme is disastrous.

Organizations also have stop and go signs. They may not have red, yellow, and green lights, but they are just as real and have just as much effect on the flow of organizational events. The corporate policies, rules, regulations, procedures, organizational structure, and the day-to-day interactions in meetings, conversations, and memoranda are all varieties of these organizational traffic signals. If there are too many stop signs, then innovative efforts come to a grinding halt. If there are too few, then there is chaos. The objective, then, is to design a system that (a) does not impede the flow of innovative ideas; (b) increases the probability of a safe and speedy passage for useful ideas; and (c) decreases the probability that the poor ideas proceed to the implementation stage. Only through careful and thoughtful planning can each of these goals be achieved. The more important guidelines for successfully setting up the organizational traffic signals are discussed below.

Develop a Formal Corporate Policy on Innovation

A policy statement in the employee handbook can be a useful starting point. Here, a commitment to innovation can be made in black and white. The very process of developing this policy statement forces management to articulate goals and commitments. The initial training of employees can also stress the necessity for innovation. Even the corporate philosophy should have a sentence or phrase about the organization's position on innovation.

But policy statements are no guarantee of action. There must be mechanisms for implementation, some of which are reviewed later. Employees must see the link between the specific programs and the policy. This demonstrates that the company is willing to practice what it preaches.

Require and Reward Innovation

One of the more radical steps an organization or manager can take is to make innovation a requirement of the job. For example, 3M sets divisional sales targets in terms of new product development. Approximately 30% of an operating unit's sales should come from products developed in the last four years (Mitchell 1989). Bonuses are also tied to this yardstick. It works. They market more than 50,000 products worldwide ranging from Scotch® Tape to Thinsulate™ Insulation.

The formal evaluation system also plays an important role. Companies reward activities they value. Employees know this, and react accordingly. Financial rewards have proven successful, but there are other and often more meaningful rewards such as personal recognition. Innovators can be recognized in company newsletters, trade publications, and the local media. Stories about innovators not only provide recognition, but also show others in the organization what the company really values.

Rewarding individual innovators is not the only tactic that can be employed. After all, the objective is to spur on the spirit of innovation throughout the entire organization. Why not recognize an entire unit, department, or division that is particularly innovative? This might encourage the teamwork so necessary for successful innovation. Why not carry it a step further? Could the entire company be recognized for its innovative spirit? It might seem like "tooting your own horn," but that is exactly what Allied-Signal, Inc., did with a full-page spread in the *Wall Street Journal* (see Figure 9.3). This ad sends a clear message to the public-at-large as well as Allied-Signal employees that the company values innovation. Moreover, the ad cleverly recognizes the authors of the patents. One can easily imagine Allied-Signal, Inc., scientists looking up their patent number in the newspaper, circling it, and showing the spread to family and friends.

Ironically, rewarding innovation often proves more meaningful for those who have not been recognized than it does for those who have been. The reward acts as a target, because it tells them what the attributes of success are at this company. Hence the size of the reward matters less the meaning of the recognition. In fact, a large award may implicitly send a message that the organization is only interested in the "big ideas."

Develop Company Programs That Encourage Innovation

Some companies, such as IBM, allow their employees to take sabbaticals to work in a new environment or teach in a college. By placing employees in different environments, they can meet new people, come across new ideas, and, hopefully, generate their own novel approaches. They can even pursue some projects on

There's strength in numbers.

Every one of these patents represents an original idea. A way to advance technology. Allied-Signal is proud to say that we own over 25,000 of these patented ideas. With 10,000 more pending. Last year alone, we were granted more U.S. patents than any other American industrial company except IBM and GE.

Allied-Signal is a research leader in such diverse areas as aerospace propulsion and guidance systems, automotive electronics, high-strength fibers, high-performance alloys and ceramics, and video graphics.

And we intend to stay a leader. With our thousands of scientists and engineers working constantly to advance advanced technology. Because one good idea leads to another.

Figure 9.3. Example of Praising Corporate Innovation

company time. For example, two IBM scientists, K. Alex Mueller and J. Georg Bednorz, toiled away on their project at their Swiss lab in between their normal duties. They were two of the principal scientists who set off the frenzy for superconductors, which are substances that conduct electricity without resistance. At one point, Bednorz was so excited about the project that he was spending up to 30% of his time on it. In the end, they told not only management, but also the world about this revolutionary idea (Hudson 1987).

Other major companies have model programs that encourage innovation as well. 3M has a program that allows employees to spend up to 15% of their time working on their own innovative project with little or no direct managerial control. Indeed, the almost ubiquitous Post-it® Notes are a direct result of this rule, and now account for millions of dollars of revenue. And 3M takes it one step further with its Genesis grants. Employees can apply for up to $85,000 in seed money to carry their projects past the idea state.

Another program that has been successful involves keeping a written record or log of all suggestions and the actions taken on those ideas. The list is then circulated around the company. Timeliness is also important. Walter Scott of Motorola, Inc., said, "Any employee's recommendation for new methods or change should get a reply in 72 hours or less" (Barks and Bennett 1979, p. 35). Providing a timely response and maintaining a written record demonstrates a corporate resolve to harness the innovative potential of its employees. A note of caution: recall that generating ideas is only one stage of this process.

By financing and sponsoring these kinds of activities, a company sends a message to employees that it is willing to invest the money necessary for innovation. The financial backing shows that innovation is more than just rhetoric. Although these programs provide no guarantee that employees will come up with useful ideas, it does increase the probabilities. That is the bet management makes.

Train Every Employee to Be an Innovator

Employees should realize that innovators need more than a lot of good ideas. Recall that idea generation is only the first step in the process. Some organizations unwittingly overemphasize Stage 1, and then become overwhelmed with the sheer volume of ideas. Additionally, employees who know the objective standards by which to judge an idea are more likely to propose useful as well as responsible ideas. An idea can be judged novel but not practical, or practical but not feasible. The employees whose ideas stall at one stage or another can also feel a certain amount of fulfillment, and should be encouraged to keep on trying. Moreover, training about innovation demonstrates that the organization takes innovation seriously. And this may be the most important message of all.

Thus, it usually makes sense to make employees in some way responsible for the winnowing process. Employees are going to have to set their own priorities and decide which ideas are really important. Some people will turn back; the ideas will not be pursued. Others will take the detour and brave the rocky course. The joint venture of Toyota and GM, NUMMI (New United Auto Manufacturing, Inc.), discovered the power of this notion. The "suggestion form at NUMMI makes very explicit the criteria by which the suggestion is going to be evaluated and encourages workers to evaluate their suggestions themselves using these criteria" (Adler 1999, p. 43). Consequently, the average employee makes about six suggestions per year, and over 90% of them are adopted. Compare these statistics to the typical company: Only 8% of U.S. employees make any suggestion at all, and only 25% culminate into some action (Adler 1999, p. 43). The lesson: invest in the employees, and they will invest in the organization. If not, opportunities will walk out of the door everyday.

Innovation is a matter of probabilities. Failures are to be expected, just as every batter expects to strike out. The only losers are those who do not get up to the plate in the first place. Even then, a batting average of .400 is considered exceptional. So too with ideas; a certain percentage will always go awry. The key is to keep on trying. Certain financial loses are to be expected, but they are necessary in order to have a chance at winning. Thus, if an idea does not exactly pan out, there need be no recriminations. Everyone hits foul balls.

Eliminate Lengthy Proposal Procedures

The paperwork involved in proposing or even pursuing a project can be a major roadblock to innovation. Employees often feel stifled when asked to fully justify ideas; they may be working on a hunch. In the first place, many of the questions cannot be answered fully until later in the innovation process. Second, many relevant questions cannot even be anticipated. Moreover, the message sent to employees by requiring extensive paperwork is that results must be guaranteed and failure is unacceptable.

Streamlining the documentation process may be a good start, but other procedures warrant examination. The administrative procedures for proposing and implementing an idea can become cumbersome. How many organizational levels does an idea have to go through to get the green light? Can any of these levels be eliminated? Can some ideas simply be approved and initiated on the spot? How long does an idea take to wind its way through the administrative process— months? weeks? hours? What can be done to speed up the process? Addressing these tough questions can help eliminate the natural barriers to innovation and smooth the bumpy road.

Foster Informal Communication

Paperwork and administrative regulations are often initiated in organizations to provide some control of organizational events. What will be the regulative mechanism if these are scaled down? Informal communication can fill the gap. Managers can keep up-to-date by informally communicating with employees about projects or new ideas. Often, this kind of "checking up" proves more informative than endless reams of paperwork.

Informal communication encourages discussion across departmental boundaries and formal lines of authority. More useful ideas seem to be spawned in such a free-flowing environment. Why? In part, because these discussions expose organizational problems, concerns, and needs, all of which are begging for innovative solutions. As Professor Markides (1997) of the London Business School put it,

> Strategic innovation occurs when a company identifies gaps in the industry positioning map, decides to fill them, and the gaps grow to become the new mass market. . . . Gaps appear for a number of reasons, such as changing consumer tastes and preferences, changing technologies, changing governmental policies, and so on. (p. 12)

Employees need to know where these gaps are before they can creatively address them. Additionally, in a supportive environment colleagues can informally critique employee ideas. This helps the employee "save face," because no one records a formal rejection. Moreover, informal criticism provides valuable information about where improvements are needed and, at times, solutions to dilemmas.

Bill Gates, the innovative founder of Microsoft, credits the use of electronic mail as one of the keys in keeping his company on the creative frontier. If someone has a brainstorm, he or she can immediately flash the idea to others for their reactions. He says, "It sparks interest" (Field 1988, p. 86). Adding blackboards, sketchpads, and small conference rooms in the workplace has also proven helpful in encouraging more informal communication (Peters and Waterman 1982). Electronic mail, blackboards, and sketchpads have one common characteristic: mistakes can be quickly and easily corrected. Therefore, speculation, change, and creativity are encouraged. Deletions or additions can be readily made. This is the spirit of informal networks—quick feedback with little fear of change. There are few repercussions when changing an idea in an informal situation. Formal documents are less easily amended. And that is why it so important to set up an informal communication environment.

Learn How Properly to Reject Novel Ideas

Dr. Orlando A. Battista (1984) was asked to develop a fine structure of nylon fibers to be used in tires. Instead, he came up with a white powder in a crystal form. His boss wanted to fire him. As it turned out, that would have been a major blunder. Other minds prevailed; he was allowed to pursue his strange substance, Avacil. The result is that today Avacil is used as a clotting agent for blood, as well as used in salad dressings, beauty creams, and a host of other products. All of this from a "bad" idea.

The art of dealing with a "bad" idea rests on a simple philosophy: An idea may fail, but people are not failures. Too many times employees who introduce ideas that do not work out are ostracized or labeled as kooks; in essence, they are treated as failures. Such practices send strong and discouraging messages to others who might have a useful idea: "The cost of an idea failing is very great." The logic continues: "It is, therefore, safest not to suggest anything." As a result, innovation is stifled. One wonders how many potential Battista's have been lost because a manager rejected the person along with the novel idea.

Typically, a new idea is evaluated in terms of whether it is good or bad, useful or useless, effective or ineffective. If an idea has problems, then it is rejected out-of-hand, just as Avacil initially was. This kind of evaluation process creates a false dichotomy, where an idea either hits or misses the target. Far too many ideas go unheeded and untested because of this kind of simpleminded thinking.

A more useful way is to look at an idea in terms of attributes or characteristics, some of which are good and some bad.[1] As seen in Figure 9.4, there are two primary ways to evaluate an idea. In the first case, some useful ideas, like diamonds in the rough, may be quickly cast aside because they do not appear in final form. In the second case, the idea is examined more closely, the characteristics of the idea are refined and discussed, just as a jeweler cuts and polishes the diamond.

Inevitably, managers will flatly have to reject some ideas. The worst possible method is to ignore the suggestion. There are countless ways of ignoring suggestions: changing the subject when the idea is brought up, nonverbally communicating disinterest, or simply not taking the time to listen to the idea fully. Ignoring an employee's idea discourages not only pursuit of that idea, but also any other ideas that might be really useful. The broader message is, "I don't have time" or "I don't care about your new ideas." Employees generally respond more positively to an honest and straightforward appraisal of the idea. Then they know precisely what criteria are being used in evaluating an idea. And they may even find some solution to the precise objection, thereby making the notion viable. In the long run, a frank appraisal might discourage pursuit of a certain idea, but it does not hinder the general pursuit of innovation. That is, indeed, precisely the message you wish to communicate.

In sum, implementing only one of the ideas suggested above will not transform a logjammed organizational system. The entire set of organizational traffic signals has to be examined. With a proper balance of incentives and policies, the organization can become a kind of innovative superhighway that creates a system in which ideas are quickly exchanged. The final case study presented below summarizes the dilemmas as well as the challenges associated with innovation.

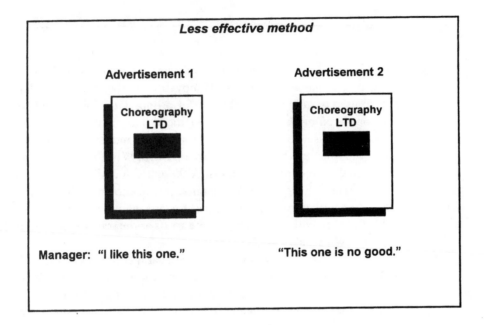

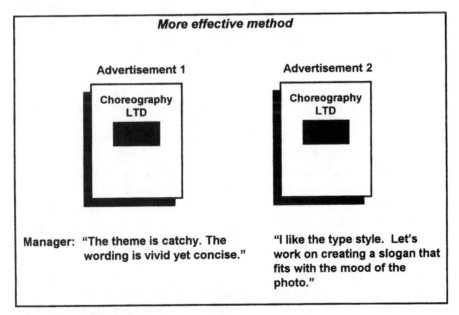

Figure 9.4. Evaluating an Idea

Blue Ribbons and Red Tape

Sir Winston Churchill is best known as a great statesman, author, or perhaps, a painter. Few know that he was also a successful innovator. His special genius led to a navigational tool used to guide pilots, the idea of dropping tin foil to confuse enemy radar, armor-plated buses, and even the artificial harbors used on D Day (Manchester 1983). He was also known as the father of the modern tank. It was Churchill, who, during the bloody trench warfare of World War I, thought of the tank as a practical means to end the madness. Although Churchill said that no single man could be said to have invented the tank, it was known at the time as "Winston's folly." And with good reason: He was the one who provided the idea and the money for the endeavor. But today, no one scoffs at the transformation of warfare wrought by "Winston's folly."

The invention of the tank teaches us lessons on several counts. As Churchill freely acknowledged in his memoirs, the idea was not entirely novel. H. G. Wells had speculated about such a vehicle as early as 1903. But, as suggested before, a novel idea—even a fictional one—is not an innovation. It is, however, a start. The tools used for the innovation were already well known. The technology for armor plating had been used in ships and the internal combustion engine had proven reliable, as had caterpillar tracks. The key was to combine the various devices into a new and useful weapon. This was no easy task. Similarly, many innovations are the product of the novel combinations of already existing ideas. Moreover, "Winston's folly" provides a splendid example of the hurdles faced by most innovators. He discussed the project at length in his memoirs of the First World War:

> I thus took personal responsibility for the expenditure of the public money involved. . . It was a serious decision to spend this large sum of money on a project so speculative, about the merits of which no high expert military or naval authority had been convinced. The matter, moreover, was entirely outside the scope of my own Department or of any normal powers which I possessed. Had the tanks proved wholly abortive or never been accepted or never used in war by the military authorities, and had I been subsequently summoned before a Parliamentary Committee, I could have offered no effective defence to the charge that I had wasted public money on a matter which was not in any way my business and in regard to which I had not received expert advice in any responsible military quarter. The extremely grave situation of the war, and my conviction of the need for breaking down the deadlock which blocked the production of these engines, are my defence; but that defence is only valid in view of their enormous subsequent success. (Churchill 1931, pp. 316–317)

Churchill's narrative of his decision offers three valuable lessons.

First, this passage illustrates the speculative nature of any innovation. Any number of different experts and committees had rejected the idea. No one thought it would work except Churchill. In a similar fashion, disbelievers often attempt to thwart innovators in organizations. Innovators naturally seem to run first into the scoffers, then the cynics, followed by the critics, and, finally, the surprised.

Successful innovators learn to sift the rhetoric from the reality. Often the corporate policy says, "We want innovative ideas," but the real meaning is, "We want innovative ideas *that work*." Countless white papers have to be prepared justifying the project. Prolonged analyses about the potential impact have to be drafted. In some cases, doing the paperwork takes more time and money than the actually testing of the notion. For instance, when the Israelis installed rearview mirrors in their F-4 Phantom jets, one American pilot remarked that in the United States it would take four years of research and development just to put in that rearview mirror. It took the Israelis one week. They just tried it out (Weisman 1986).

Churchill, like all successful innovators, recognized that there were no assurances. Someone had to take a chance, albeit a calculated one. Companies that refuse to take risks, often by tying up the process with endless red tape, stifle innovation. Moreover, they are operating under the delusion that the red tape will provide certainty, when, in fact, there can be no such thing. There must be room for "failure," and no amount of red tape can remove that basic risk. Campbell (1977) sums up the matter best: "The demand for predictable outcomes deprives many companies of unusual outcomes" (p. 90).

Second, note that Churchill was the First Lord of the Admiralty at the time when he proposed and financed the tank. Here was a man whose primary responsibilities was sea warfare, backing the research and development of a land-based weapon. He obviously strayed very far afield. Organizations that believe in innovation cannot stick to rigid departmental responsibilities. Often the very best creative ideas come from the cross-fertilization that occurs between departments. Sometimes a person from another department can have a perspective on a problem that no one in the department would even think of. Effective interdepartmental communication is a necessity for any organization that wishes to innovate.

The "Not Invented Here" syndrome contributed to the downfall of such companies as the bicycle manufacturer, Schwinn. Many organizations tacitly communicate that innovation should be done within the narrow confines of a particular job. Ideas are rejected out-of-hand because they come from the wrong department or outside the company. Managers communicate this message with comments like, "That's not really your concern." Sometimes the approach appears more reasonable, but the results are the same. Confining all innovation to the research and development department is one of the frequent practices of this ilk of management. Often, when companies are asked if they are committed to innovation, they respond by boasting about the number of dollars spent on research and development. Certainly, research and development contributes greatly to the innovative process, but other departments often have much to offer as well. The frontline innovators may be supervisors in contact with their employees. If new ideas are not harvested at this level, then the company cannot be said to be truly innovative. New ideas are like wildflowers: They can crop up anywhere, even in the Admiralty. Innovation is not the sole province of any one department or person; rather it should be a commitment of everyone in the organization.

Third, the saga of the tank demonstrates the necessity for someone to be the champion of the idea. Somebody must clear away the red tape, take the chance, and become an "idea shepherd." Furthermore, the person must be powerful enough or the organization flexible enough to allow this person the financial wherewithal to sponsor the endeavor (Meyer and Goes 1988). There must be some slack resources to commit to the idea, even when it is clearly outside the province of one's primary concern.[2] Churchill committed a considerable sum of money, and dozens of people devoted time and effort to the project. This is what it takes to transform an idea into an innovation.

Conclusion

At county fairs all across the land, blue ribbons are given for the best breads, jams, chili, and a host of other goods. The prizes do not go to those who follow the book. They go to those who dare to fail. After countless attempts and admitted failures, they succeed. Why? Persistence helps. But freedom—freedom to dream—is the critical factor. The freedom to change, to try something new, and even to "fail" emboldens the innovator. There are no real boundaries. Unfortunately, most organizations discourage tinkering while encouraging red tape. How can employees be free if they are tangled in the red tape? In the end, paralysis sets in; the red tape chokes off any chance for the blue ribbon. But the red tape can be cut, procedures streamlined, and innovation can triumph. Churchill did it and dedicated managers can, as well.

Notes

1. Theoretically, each attribute could even have a valence attached to it. Thus, a weighted score could be computed that would allow the innovator to further work on those features that are most problematic.
2. On the other hand, too many slack resources also inhibit innovation, because the organization lacks the discipline to pursue only those projects likely to provide added value. See Nohria and Gulati (1996).

TEN

Communication Ethics

It is strange that social scientists, who are by profession devoted to the application of reason to man's affairs, have been more impressed by the use and misuse of power than by the use and misuse of knowledge.

Harold Wilensky

If one peered into a crystal ball of managerial consciousness, how often would ethical concerns filter into major decisions—or even minor ones? What shape would those concerns take? Would they be clear visions or hazy apparitions? If managers even mention the subject of ethics, they do so with great fear and trepidation. Only in the last decade or so have business schools added courses on ethics to their curriculums. Most textbooks in organizational communication completely avoid the topic. There may not be an active conspiracy of silence, but there seems to be a tacit one. Why? There are many reasons, but three stand out in particular.

First, many managers believe that discussing ethics inevitably leads to imposing one's morality on others. The Western tradition grants people the widest possible freedom and individual discretion in forming moral opinions. Hence even seeking to persuade someone of the rightness or wrongness of a particular decision can be seen as a first step onto the sacred ground of individual discretion and responsibility. Consequently, managers often retreat to the safe ground, avoiding the discussion all together.

Yet governments have always imposed a type of morality on their citizenry. Laws are designed to prohibit certain behaviors, even though some members of society may deem these practices as ethical. The Mormon faith, for instance, at one time condoned polygamy. The U.S. government said otherwise, and enforced the law of monogamy. Similarly, organizations have certain rules and regulations that may be contrary to a person's ethics, such as prohibiting alcohol consumption on the job. Organizational rules and regulations, like laws, impinge on individual freedom. In short, organizations and managers do indeed impose their ethics on others.

Although philosophers may enjoy debating the question, "Do we have the right to impose our values on others?" managers do not have that luxury. They must ask, "Do I have a duty to impose my ethics on others in this situation?" Surely, in keeping with Western values, employees should be given the widest possible discretion for individual freedom. We will discuss the boundaries of this freedom later in the chapter. But here is the fundamental point: Avoiding ethical discussions because "one does not impose one's views on others" is, ironically, an unethical cop-out.

Second, ethical concerns appear to be irrelevant to the fundamental purpose of business. Do ethics have an impact on the bottom line? It would be nice to say that ethical behavior always results in increased profits or productivity, but that is simply not the case. Many corporations with high ethical standards have been overwhelmed by unscrupulous competitors. Employees who altruistically "blow the whistle" on unethical corporate practices frequently suffer financial strain, social ostracism, harassment, and medical problems (Kleinfield 1986). Bad things happen to good people and good organizations.

The tendency may then be to dismiss all arguments of an ethical nature as irrelevant. Yet simply because ethics may have little or no impact on the bottom line does not mean managers can ignore them. After all, employee job satisfaction has little direct discernible impact on productivity, but that does not mean employers should disregard it. Less satisfied employees are more likely to quit, miss work, and experience health problems (Locke 1976). Consequently, many researchers have successfully argued that job satisfaction is a legitimate organizational goal in and of itself. Likewise, an ethical standard of organizational behavior appears to be a legitimate corporate objective. Even though a concern for ethics may not be strictly justifiable in terms of the bottom line, there is ample reason on other grounds. Namely, that ethical behavior is valued for its own sake, just as are job satisfaction and profits. Good people like to work for good organizations.

Businesses are not simply cold money-making machines. Organizations are not just bastions of plenary productivity. People are the heart and soul of organizations. And these uniquely human communities must also be concerned with the human condition. Behaving ethically is one of the continual human struggles. Organizations cannot ignore such a fundamental human dilemma. To do so disavows part of the human essence. Ironically, one of the most famous champions of the profit motive came from a professor of *moral* philosophy—Adam Smith.

Third, ethical discussions are avoided because of the "it depends" philosophy. When confronted with case studies of ethical dilemmas, people frequently probe for further information. Nothing wrong with that. But sometimes they draw an erroneous inference from such an exercise; namely, that the uniqueness of the situation trumps deeper and more fundamental ethical principles. Consequently, discussions of fundamental ethical principles that apply across situations are trivialized.

A deep-seated belief in the "situational ethic" would clearly obviate much discussion of fundamental ethical principles. Yet, upon further examination, the "it depends" philosophy breaks down. Physicists have long known that the weight of an object depends on the gravitational field in which the object exists. A 180-pound person on earth weighs thirty pounds on the moon. Yet physicists did not stop looking for fundamental principles of physics because weight varied with gravitational field. Indeed, they became intrigued by the problem. In the same way, it may be frustrating to come to grips with the fact that the same action can be deemed ethical in one circumstance and unethical in another. But physicists did not give up when faced with such complexities, so why should anyone else? To be sure, there are difficult issues and all the answers are not discernible at this juncture in time. Yet we must seek to understand. The secrets of the universe lie behind physical complexities. Perhaps the secrets of the human condition lie behind the ethical complexities.

Integrity lies at the core of ethical complexities and moral life. Stephen L. Carter (1996), a Yale professor of law, argues that living a life of integrity requires three steps:

1. Discerning what is right and wrong.
2. Acting on what you have discerned, even at a personal cost.
3. Saying openly that you are acting on your understanding of right and wrong.

Therefore, this chapter unravels some of the complexities involved in distinguishing right from wrong in organizational communication.

Foundations

Three fundamental assumptions shape this discussion of ethics.

1. *Every Communication Decision Has Some Ethical Dimension to It, Acknowledged or Not.*

There are countless complexities involved in the communication process, but communicators initially face three simple choices: to speak, to listen, or to remain silent. Each choice implies an ethical decision.

A message sender chooses to disclose information, motives, or feelings to others. That choice inevitably involves an ethical element. Clearly, some messages should not be sent, such as those involving "insider information." To do so gives certain people an unfair advantage in the marketplace. But should one share a rumor about an organizational change with a colleague? Such actions are commonplace and appear to be less objectionable than insider trading. The timing and mode of communication add another layer of complexity to the ethical calculus. Is it ever wrong to tell the truth? Can one be too blunt? Should certain information be communicated only face-to-face? People inevitably make ethical judgments in choosing the timing, the subject, and mode of their communications.

Few would doubt that ethical concerns are inherent to the act of speech, but what about the act of listening? Alexander Solzhenitsyn (1978), winner of the Nobel Prize in literature, experienced both the oppression of the Soviet Union and the immoderation of Western Society. His peculiar vantage point allowed him to experience the distinctive problems of each society. In an address at Harvard University he cast his discerning eye on American society:

> Because instant and credible information has to be given, it becomes necessary to resort to guesswork, rumors, and suppositions to fill in the voids, and none of them will ever be rectified, they will stay on the readers' memory. How many hasty, immature, superficial, and misleading judgments are expressed every day, confusing readers, without any verification? The press can both stimulate public opinion and miseducate it. Thus, we may see terrorists turned into heroes, or secret matters pertaining to one's nation's defense publicly revealed, or we may witness shameless intrusions on the privacy of well-known people under the slogan: "Everyone is entitled to know everything." But this is a false slogan, characteristic of a false era: people also have the right not to know, and it is a much more valuable one. The right not to have their divine souls stuffed with gossip, nonsense, vain talk. A person who works and leads a meaningful life does not need this excessive burdening flow of information. (p. 680)

Unfortunately and perhaps inevitably, his deep insight and remarkable candor was never fully appreciated. He addresses not only the responsibilities of the speakers, but also the listeners. Simply because someone will speak to us does not oblige us to listen. Even choosing to listen means taking a moral stand.

Remaining silent might seem like the safest way to avoid ethical dilemmas. But even here there is no safe harbor. Remaining silent in the face of unlawful behavior or a potentially harmful situation presents a serious ethical decision. Silence signals acquiescence or perhaps tacit agreement, as many of the Watergate defendants surely found out. In sum, there are ethical considerations whether communicators choose to speak, write, listen, or remain silent.

2. Communication Ethics Inevitably Involve Both Motives and Impacts

We easily condemn people who lie to pull off swindles. Their deceitful motives lead to immoral results. Yet what happens when the good motives get mixed up with a questionable impact? For instance, a manager wanted to boost United Way contributions in his unit. A noble motive, no doubt. He proceeded to obtain salary information about each employee from the personnel department. On each employee's check he attached a note "suggesting a fair percentage gift." The means used to attain this noble goal are, at the least, questionable. Indeed, most employees felt this action was a violation of their privacy. The old adage, "The road to hell is paved with good intentions," still rings true. In short, noble motives are not enough; the ultimate impact of the actions must also be considered.

3. The Ethical Nature of Communication Must Be Considered Within the Context of Who, What, When, and Where

Suppose fellow employees discussed a project they were working on. This may seem perfectly ethical on the surface. After all, such discussions actually foster effective interdepartmental relationships; a worthy goal indeed. The problem may be that the discussion took place in a crowded bar and a competitor overheard the conversation. When the employees are confronted, they may well reply, "What did we say that was wrong? We weren't talking to a competitor." But this is, of course, the wrong question. The issue does not concern *what* was said or even *who* they were talking to. The ethical issue revolves around *where* the conversation took place. Herein lies the complexity of ethical issues—evaluations must be made on more than one dimension. Ethical communicators are not concerned with just *who* or *what* or *where* or *when,* but with all four dimensions simultaneously, just as a physicist looks at the movement of a particle in four dimensions.

Ethical Dilemmas

Managers face many ethical dilemmas. Some of the more vexing ones are discussed in detail below.

Secrecy

Secrets are held for honorable and dishonorable reasons. In her thoughtful book *Secrets,* Sissela Bok (1982) defines secrecy as "intentional concealment." Her definition does *not* imply moral judgment. Indeed, she comments that

> secrecy is as indispensable to human beings as fire, and as greatly feared. Both enhance and protect life, yet both can stifle, lay waste, spread out of all control. Both may be used to guard intimacy or to invade it, to nurture or to consume. And each can be turned against itself; barriers of secrecy are set up to guard against secret plots and surreptitious prying, just as fire is used to fight fire. (p. 18)

Here then lies the challenge for the manager: to determine when secrets are justifiable and when they are not.

The engineer who remains silent about potentially catastrophic product failures has abrogated moral responsibility. Such a duty should not be taken lightly. The makers of asbestos who knew of the potential health hazards of their product were morally culpable. Secrets can have a clear and detrimental impact on decision making and consumer safety.

On the other hand, organizations have a legitimate need to protect certain information. If competitors, for example, gain access to proprietary research and development, they can produce that product for a much lower net cost because they do not have to pay the research and development expenses. Consequently, businesses would have little incentive to innovate, thus not only hindering the company, but also slowing the general technological advancement of society.

Yet there must be limits to even trade secrecy. Too much secrecy about trade practices creates just as many problems as too little. Having access to a wide range of new ideas provides the grist for the innovative mill. Dr. An Wang (1986) believes that the great speed of computer technology development in the United States and Great Britain can be attributed to the openness of laboratories and the lack of secrecy clamps imposed by the government. In the haphazard ricochet of one person's ideas against another's, new insights emerge. Innovation materializes in the rebounding of ideas whizzing through a community, as they bounce from conferences to the university, then to the business world, to government laboratories, to private research facilities, to publications, and back again. When the clamp of secrecy tightens too much, the interactions constrict too much. And the net results are all too predictable—lack of innovation. The weak innovative heritage of the Soviet Union and China are the quintessential examples.

Thus, problems are evident at either end of the spectrum. Too much secrecy bogs down the creative process. Too little secrecy removes incentives. There is a middle ground of sorts. Patent and copyrights allow for information to be used and generally circulated while providing a modicum of protection for companies, researchers, and authors. For example, Gillette used patents to "secure and sustain a market hold" on some product lines; other companies use a thicket of patents to "develop very favorable partnerships and licensing relationships" (Rivette and Kline 2000, p. 58). Texas Instruments, for example, has earned billions of dollars from licensing revenues.

Sometimes a thicket of patents hinders but does not stop competitors. Changing some minor aspect of a product may be enough to circumvent a patent infringement lawsuit. Moreover, litigation is time-consuming and costly. Even simple patent disputes have cost upwards of $1.2 million (Shulman 2000, p. 72). Even then, less than 30% of the patent infringement lawsuits are settled for the plaintiffs. However, about 50% of suits involving trade secrets have stood up to judicial scrutiny (Bok 1982, p. 140). Hence many companies have started using trade secrecy agreements to protect innovative ideas. Therefore, one of the continuing dilemmas for Western society is how to avoid the stifling effects of either extreme of the secrecy continuum.

Whistle-Blowing

Any employee who goes public with information about corporate abuses or negligence is known as a whistle-blower. The challenge for managers is to find ways to make whistle-blowing unnecessary. Corporations and managers legitimately expect employee loyalty. Only under extraordinary circumstances should such obligations be cast aside. Greed, jealousy, and revenge motivate some whistle-blowers. That does not mean they are necessarily wrong, but it does cast doubt. Some are simply misinformed. Some confuse public interest with private interest. Certainly the community has a right to know about corporate practices that are potentially hazardous, yet courting the whistle-blower too aggressively can be problematic. After all, Stalin, Lenin, and almost every despot encouraged widespread "whistle-blowing."

Stifling criticism through autocratic measures may work in the short-term, but might reap discontent in the long-term. The objective then is not for the organization to squash dissent, but rather to have some procedure to handle complaints and concerns internally rather than externally. The open-door policy provides one avenue. This policy allows employees to take a grievance to their supervisor first, and then up through the chain-of-command until they get satisfaction. But more than once the open door has become a trap door. For example, three engineers working on the San Francisco Bay Area Rapid Transit System (BART) complained to their managers about potential safety problems, but to no avail. Their theoretic predictions proved ominously accurate. Several years later, the control system failed and one of the trains crashed into a parking lot for riders. After further pursuing the matter, the engineers were fired. They had trouble finding jobs elsewhere and experienced a host of other hardships. Sadly, these were the consequences for criticism that was right on the mark (Baum and Flores 1978).

On the other hand, some employees choose to "swallow the whistle" rather than discuss matters with the very manager who may be part of the problem in the first place. The result is that potentially valuable information never surfaces, depriving many people of the choice to make reasonable decisions. With the default of many savings and loans in the late 1980s, one has to wonder how many employees "swallowed the whistle" (see, for example, Berg 1987). Although the open-door policy proves useful in many situations, it does not always meet the needs of the potential whistle-blower. Open-door policies inherently stress power relationships rather than corporate citizenship. Grievances are framed by the needs of the chain-of-command rather than by the merits of the individual case. Hence appeals are rarely investigated or impartially considered. In short, both swallowing the whistle and blowing it can be problematic. Therefore, the central challenge for organizations revolves around how to properly channel employee dissent.

Leaks

A leak is like anonymous whistle-blowing. The accused does not know who or why a person has chosen to release certain information. Politicians have used leaks for years to send up trial balloons, stall a plan, or even defame an opponent. Employees may also leak information to the press for honorable or dishonorable reasons. Leaks may cause organizational plans to be altered or forgone altogether. Leaks can be a form of political maneuvering in the organization or a way to sabotage the career of a colleague competing for a job.

Are leaks ethical? In one sense the ethics of leaking information is the same as whistle-blowing. Indeed, the preventive measures are about the same. However, one distinction casts a dark shadow over the propriety of the leak; namely, that the person who leaks information cannot be cross-examined. This often casts doubt on the credibility of the claim (Near and Miceli 1995).

For example, a supervisor at Georgia-Pacific received an anonymous letter accusing a worker of being drunk in public. The supervisor fired him and reported the incident to 100 employees at a meeting. The state appeals court awarded the employee $350,000 for defamation of character (Hoerr 1988a). Clearly, this worker never had a chance to respond to the charges. This hit-and-run tactic makes it difficult to assess the veracity of any claim and the motives of the accuser. Therefore, using a leak is particularly dubious in nature and should be undertaken in the rarest of circumstances.

Rumors and Gossip

Is there anything inherently wrong with sharing news about the birth of the supervisor's baby? What about speculating on an affair the supervisor is supposedly having? Or what about passing on an unconfirmed report of a corporate takeover? Rumors and gossip seem to be an inevitable part of everyday corporate life. Even though rumors and gossip often travel through the same networks, there is a distinction between the terms. Rumors tend to focus on events and information, whereas gossip focuses on people. The manager faces a two-fold ethical dilemma: First, should gossip about other employees be listened to? Second, what should be done about rumors in the organization?

Managers appear to be on slippery ethical ground when they listen to gossip about fellow employees. Even though managers usually treat the information as "yet to be confirmed," the juicy tidbit may cloud judgments about that employee. The information has a way of creeping into performance evaluations and promotion decisions, even if unintended. Moreover, the information may be completely inaccurate. Why would someone want to make a decision on the basis of inaccurate information? Consider this case: A new manager heard about one of his employee's sons having a drug problem. He decided not to promote the employee, reasoning that if this mother "couldn't control her kids, then how could she manage a department?"—a dubious assumption at best. (I wonder if a father would be held equally accountable.) Of course, he never said that, *per se,* but the assessment of her "leadership skills" was considerably lower than the other candidates. Such practices appear unethical on several accounts. First, the employee could never confirm or deny the information, even if it could be shown to be relevant. Thus, there was no mechanism for correcting the inevitable distortion. Second, the manager did not have access to the same type of information about all the other candidates. What if the manager found out that the son of another candidate was a drug dealer? No doubt such information would have altered the rankings of the other employees. The supreme irony was that this employee's son was not on drugs but helping other kids get off them.

In fairness, others take another position on this issue. Blythe Holbrooke, the author of *Gossip: How to Get It Before It Gets You* (1983), says, "A commanding knowledge of gossip and gossips gives you the edge in conversation and helps keep you clear of potentially damaging situations at work" (p. 5). Other social critics have argued that gossip allows people to develop their moral sensibilities. By gossiping, people develop and expose their moral judgments. Gossiping about the boss's affair surely indicates a moral condemnation. Lance Morrow (1981), *Time* magazine's social commentator, wrote:

> In gossiping, people try to discover their own attitudes toward such behavior and the reactions of others. It is also a medium of self-disclosure, a way of dramatizing one's own feelings about someone else's behavior, a way of asserting what we think acceptable or unacceptable.... Gossip is the layman's mythmaker and moralist, the small, idle interior puppet-theater in which he tries out new plays, new parts for himself. (p. 98)

If so, this moral training is often done at the expense of running roughshod over other peoples' reputations. Is this really fair? There must be a better antidote.

Indeed, rumor mongering could be justified on similar grounds. Rumors can have a disastrous effect on corporations. Procter and Gamble spent years and thousands of dollars fighting a rumor that their corporate symbol represented the devil. Rumors that McDonald's added worms to its meat in order to increase protein content lowered sales in some states. Both rumors were unequivocally false. But clearly the impact was great. Passing along such hearsay seems ethically unjustifiable. The seminal research in the area was done by Allport and Postman (1947), who studied rumors during wartime. They found that rumors were passed from person to person, and hence distortion was inevitable. Allport and Postman identified three fundamental ways in which the information is distorted. First, *leveling* may occur, which means that details of the original message are left out. Second, *sharpening* may happen, in which certain parts of the message are overly highlighted. Finally, *assimilation* may occur, in which case communicators twist the information to fit some preordained prejudice or predisposition. What parts of the rumor have been leveled, sharpened, or assimilated? Managers have no way of knowing. Thus, no one can really be sure what type of distortion has taken place.

But the critical point is that some distortion is inevitable—and this leads to the ethical dilemma.

Rumors are more apt to occur in ambiguous situations in which people have a high interest in the topic. Announcing that "changes" are forthcoming in an organization without providing any specifics cultivates the perfect environment for rumors to flourish. Passing along unverified information in these circumstances may seem like an effective way to cope with anxiety. Even though an organization will never be able to control rumors entirely, the best antidote is providing timely information, even to the point of admitting when something remains unknown. In a crisis situation, the key is immediately to develop a highly credible channel of information that people believe will provide accurate and timely information. Johnson & Johnson used this approach, with exemplary results, when handling the Tylenol tampering case. Some organizations even have rumor control hotlines where employees can call to check out any unconfirmed reports they have heard. Maybe some of these ideas sound a bit idealistic. Employees find rumors and gossip almost as irresistible as the mythological Sirens whose beautiful voices lured sailors to their death. The allure seems inevitable. Perhaps, but remember the sailors in Homer's *Odyssey* easily resisted the temptation. They had plugs in their ears.

Lying

Of all the ethical dilemmas discussed thus far, lying would appear to be the least morally perplexing. Most would agree that "one ought not to lie." A lie is a false statement intended to deceive. Yet lies in business are more common than many would care to admit. A letter similar to the one in Figure 10.1 was sent to a small group of executives in a major organization by a corporate lawyer. Within days, hundreds of employees had "mysteriously" received copies. The bold-faced admission of past deception had a predictable effect on morale; anger, cynicism, and apathy resulted. Those who dealt with this lawyer, no doubt questioned the veracity of all his past comments. He moved ever so close to the linguistic "black hole" discussed in Chapter 2. Like most lies, this one harmed both the deceiver and those deceived.

Good intentions are frequently used to justify duplicity. The white lies that are uttered to flatter or to avoid hurting someone's feelings are of this ilk. Some people even argue that certain "little lies" are inconsequential and have "little" actual impact. However, the very people who vigorously defend a falsehood on such grounds are rarely comfortable with others telling them "white lies." Moreover, there can be some long-term unintended consequences. Consider the tale of the "broccoli soup:" A couple, married for thirty-five years, sought the help of a marital counselor. In one of the final sessions with the counselor the following conversation took place:

> *Husband:* And another thing—Why do we always have broccoli soup on Tuesday nights? I hate broccoli soup!
> *Wife:* I hate it, too!

ACME Oil Company
Legal Department

January 15

To: All Managers
From: Wm. G. Howard

Re: Pension Litigation

During the pendency of this litigation, we have had numerous inquiries about the status of the case. Recently, rumors have surfaced that the case has settled. These rumors were further fueled by a misleading broadcast on CNN reporting that a settlement had been achieved. In the past, when calls were received from former employees, we suggested that ACME respond by saying that no settlement negotiations are underway between the parties.

On November 28, the plaintiffs tabled their first settlement proposal. [. . .]

If you have any questions on this matter, please call me directly.

Figure 10.1. Example of Objectionable Corporate Memo

Husband: Then why do you make it?
Wife: I only make it because I thought you liked it. Don't you remember, the very first meal I ever cooked you? It was broccoli soup. I asked if you liked it. You said you loved it.
Husband: I only said that to be nice to you.

For thirty-five years they both ate broccoli soup, which they both hated. I wonder how many "broccoli soup" management practices are stirred up by little white lies.

Therefore, even white lies should be avoided. There are usually more ethical alternatives. For instance, Judith Martin, "Miss Manners," once counseled a reader about how to handle inquiries about her rather large diamond wedding ring. The reader was often asked by inquisitive acquaintances, "Is it real? How many carats is that? What does your husband do?"

Such questions are often met with little white lies, anger, or bewilderment. Miss Manners offered a "gem" of a response. She advised that the answer to the first two questions should be, "I'm so glad you like it," and to the third, "Charming things, as you can see." These are more than clever responses. They are at once honest and polite, while effectively communicating that the information is "none of your business." When faced with situations that might invite some little falsehood, managers would do well to think of such appropriate and effective retorts.

Even if some lies are used for the best of intentions, scholars have discovered that most falsehoods are uttered for less altruistic reasons. In one study, researchers found that 76% of lies benefited the liar, 22% benefited the person lied to, and 2.5% were told for a third party (Camden, Motley, and Wilson 1983). Equally alarming was the finding of another researcher, who determined that 75% of lies told in the workplace are directed at superiors (Hample 1980). Because most falsehoods are self-serving, supervisors might question the validity of information received from some subordinates. Lying inhibits the free flow of potentially valuable information that could be used to change a policy, alter a procedure, or mitigate potentially serious situations. For example, when an employee lies about actions during a crisis, the true cause of the disaster may never be known. Thus, the potential for recurrence increases.

The bottom line is that lying breaks down trust between individuals, shaking the very foundation of our discourse. How does one communicate in a community of liars? Which remarks can be trusted? Which cannot? Sissela Bok (1978) insightfully summarized the issue:

> The veneer of social trust is often thin. As lies spread—by imitation, or in retaliation, or to forestall suspected deception—trust is damaged. Yet trust is a social good to be protected just as much as the air we breathe or the water we drink. When it is damaged, the community as a whole suffers; and when it is destroyed, societies falter and collapse. (pp. 26–27)

In short, when words lose their power, only force remains.

Euphemisms

Lenin reportedly once said, "If you want to destroy a society, corrupt the language." By definition, a euphemism is using a less offensive expression instead of one that might cause distress. Using the expression "passed away" instead "died" is one of the more common examples. This usage is no doubt understandable. Yet frequently a euphemism becomes the first cousin of a lie. A purchasing agent has a far easier time accepting a "consideration fee" than a "bribe." Petty office theft gets passed off as merely "permanently borrowing" the item instead of "stealing." People use these terms to obscure the truth not only from others, but also from themselves.

Yet euphemisms cannot be universally condemned. The user's motivations and the impact of such language need to be carefully evaluated. When used to rationalize unethical activity, such as bribery or theft, there is little justification. The deeply contemplative Dag Hammarskjöld (1978), the former Secretary General of the United Nations, poignantly wrote of what should be our attitude toward language:

> *Respect for the word* is the first commandment in the discipline by which a man can be educated to maturity—intellectual, emotional, and moral.
>
> Respect for the word—to employ it with scrupulous care and incorruptible heartfelt love of truth—is essential if there is to be any growth in a society or in the human race.
>
> To misuse the word is to show contempt for man. It undermines the bridges and poisons the wells. It causes Man to regress down the long path of his evolution. (p. 112)

Ambiguity

Because all language contains some degree of vagueness, there might be some question about why the subject should be discussed in this chapter. Yet ambiguity, like secrecy, can be used for ethical or unethical purposes (Bavelas et al. 1990). For example, an employee asked his superior about the possibility of promotion and was told, "We have the very best in mind, but we can't discuss it now." The supervisor implied that the subordinate would, in fact, be promoted. That was one possible interpretation and the most reasonable one. But what the manager actually meant was that he had "the best" in mind for the company, which meant that the employee would be fired. That, of course, was another possible interpretation. There can be no doubt that only the most cynical of employees would come away with the latter interpretation. Was such a statement an ethical way to stall further discussion? When later confronted with the true facts, the employee justifiably felt lied to. Technically, this may not have been a lie because it was not a "false statement." The *intent,* however, was clearly to deceive.

With a lie, the onus of responsibility for veracity clearly rests with the sender of the message. Even when someone chooses to remain silent, the onus of responsibility falls on the secret keeper. But with ambiguity, where does the responsibility rest? That is not clear. There can be no question that in this example, deception was the obvious intent and indeed the effect. In this sense, the manager's action was unethical. Moreover, there were legitimate alternatives open to the manager. If he wanted to stall on the issue, then he could have simply said, "We will have to discuss it later." Such an expression implies no commitment and does not lead the employee astray.

Communicators are to some extent held responsible for possible misinterpretations (Austin 1961). This means that managers must be aware of the probabilistic nature of communication, and need to consider not only their intentions, but also how their messages might be misunderstood. Communicators have a responsibility to anticipate at least *some* of the possible interpretations of their remarks. This does not mean that speakers are responsible for *all* possible misinterpretations, because any remark can be twisted into thousands of different meanings. Their responsibilities are confined to reasonable misinterpretations.

Purposeful vagueness or equivocation can be ethical as well. Managers may equivocate when setting up certain tasks in order to encourage creativity. Employees are more likely to come up with new ideas when asked to come up with "a new marketing strategy" than when told in highly specific terms what the strategy should be like. Equivocation can be an effective and legitimate persuasive tool. Professor Lee Williams (1976) of Southwest Texas State University has done extensive research on the topic and found that

> In contrast to the tenet advocated since antiquity that all issues should be addressed clearly, this study indicated that under certain circumstances the speaker might be wiser if he used deliberate vagueness. . . . If the speaker knows that certain issues are disagreeable and if he feels that the circumstances seriously limit the probability of successful persuasion, then equivocation appears to be the best alternative available. It provides the speaker with an effective means for avoiding premature exposure of his innermost feelings, it leaves the receiver with a neutral to moderately favorable disposition, it minimizes the chance of recalling the disagreeable issues, and it avoids negative connotations that might jeopardize future persuasive attempts.

Hence managers, when considering difficult issues, might legitimately use equivocation as a strategy.

Equivocation also serves a useful function of uniting people while allowing diversity. Corporate slogans are one of the best examples. The company with a "commitment to excellence" can aspire to "excellence" in hundreds of different ways, but the slogan allows for some semblance of corporate unity. Ambiguity also allows for freedom to maneuver when circumstances change. Dr. An Wang (1986), the founder of Wang Laboratories, encouraged employee commitment with the philosophy of "providing specific solutions to clients' problems." He did not make a commitment to a specific product, *per se*. Thus, when he decided to move out of the calculator market—one in which the company had enjoyed great success—and into the computer market, he was being completely consistent. If the change was perceived as a total shift of corporate position, then the strategic move would have been met with even more resistance than it was. Indeed, Wang's move proved prescient. Although values are necessarily ambiguous, the commitment to the values endures long after the passing fancy of the marketplace. Such commitments engender trust and stability amidst the turbulent seas of technological change. Skillful executives discern when ambiguity is necessary and when it is not.

Apology

Inevitably, managers and organizations are involved in situations that require an apology. This special communication challenge calls into question the motives or reputation of a manager. Such concerns strike at the very heart of managerial effectiveness. If managers' motives or reputations are suspect, so is their credibility and, ultimately, their ability to influence others.

Every apology is unique. However, there are two basic strategic responses to a perceived or actual offense. First, a manager might seek to *reform* perceptions of the offense by denying the allegations, clarifying the situation, or identifying with independent, credible sources. For example, one manager was accused of making racist comments at an off-site party. When questioned by the vice president, the manager not only denied that the episode occurred, he also encouraged the VP to question colleagues, who were minorities, about his racial attitudes. Clearly, the manager was seeking some independent verification of his position. Second, a manager might seek to *transform* perceptions by placing an incident in a broader context of events, or show that the incident was an aberration (Ware and Linkugel 1973).

The fundamental issue in choosing between the reforming and transforming strategies involves responsibility. Is the manager going to accept responsibility for the incident or not? The appropriate strategy depends on the incident. But regardless of where the responsibility for the episode lies, the manager or organization must take responsibility for resolving the situation. The Tylenol tampering case began with the death of a woman who took two Extra Strength Tylenol capsules. An unknown terrorist had perpetrated the crime; Johnson & Johnson was not directly responsible for the mishap. However, Johnson & Johnson did have a duty to respond to the situation in a responsible and decisive way. Tylenol continues to sell well despite the incident because the "apology" was handled effectively (Benson 1988).

When an organization accepts responsibility for a mishap, effective communication can limit the damage and actually build the corporate reputation. Consider AT & T's response to a major service disruption that affected long distance service across the United States. Clearly, this kind of difficulty threatened AT & T's reputation. However, after a brief period of confusion, AT & T handled the situation with aplomb.[1] The letter in Figure 10.2 was the centerpiece of their strategy.

This letter provides an appropriate model for an apology on the following levels:

1. *It was timely.* In less than five days, the letter appeared in major U.S. newspapers.

AT & T
Robert E. Allen
Chairman of the Board
550 Madison Avenue
New York, NY 10022

Dear AT & T Customer:

AT & T had a major service disruption last Monday. We didn't live up to our own standards of quality and we didn't live up to yours.

It's as simple as that. And that's not acceptable to us. Or to you.

Once we discovered the problem, we responded within minutes with every resource at our disposal. By late evening, normal service was restored. Ironically, the problem resulted from a glitch in software designed to provide backup in a new signaling system we were installing to bring even greater reliability to our network. It has now been fixed.

We understand how much people have come to depend upon AT & T service, so our AT & T Bell Laboratories scientists and our network engineers are doing everything possible to guard against a recurrence.

We know there's no way to make up for the inconvenience this problem may have caused you. But in an effort to underscore how much we value our relationship with you, we've filed with the FCC to offer a special day of calling discounts on Valentine's Day, Wednesday, February 14:

> Discounts all day for residence and business customers on most out-of-state calls made on the AT & T public network throughout the U.S. and on international calls to all 158 direct-dial countries.

We've also extended the provisions of our AT & T 800 Assurance Policy to cover this extraordinary situation.

For more than 100 years, we've built our reputation on superior quality, reliability and technological innovation. Our goal is to ensure that you always regard us that way.

Sincerely,

R. E. Allen
Chairman

Figure 10.2. Facsimilie of a Corporate Apology

2. *It openly acknowledged the problem.* AT & T did not equivocate about the nature of the incident, but admitted it in the first sentence.
3. *It unambiguously accepted responsibility.* The letter cleverly acknowledged that AT & T caused the problem, while simultaneously suggesting that they had higher standards.
4. *It discussed action steps to prevent future occurrences.* AT & T's decisive action was vital in securing future customer loyalty.
5. *It was brief.* The letter did not go into a lot of detail that could detract from the central purpose of the apology, making it appear that AT & T was trying to gloss over the situation.
6. *It provided a type of restitution.* The Valentine's Day discounts could not compensate consumers for their problems, but it did show that AT & T was remorseful. Moreover, consumers were aware that this form of restitution had an impact on AT & T's bottom line, which meant they were willing to pay for a good reputation.

Clearly, the objective of this letter was to vouchsafe AT & T's reputation. They wanted to communicate that the service disruption was an aberration and not an indication of their service quality. In short, the AT&T letter was based on sound principles of an effective apology.

A Strategic Approach to Corporate Ethics

No one can absolutely guarantee that a corporation or its employees will behave ethically. Yet acknowledgement of occasional failures does not reduce our fundamental ethical responsibility. Organizations, like people, should strive for ethical behavior. This philosophical position implies certain actions in three basic areas: cultural, policy, and personal. Ethical organizations are created and sustained by individuals of personal integrity, operating in a culture of principle, and governed by conscientious policies (see Figure 10.3).

Corporate Culture

Throughout the span of history, the great philosophers and religious figures have penned works aimed at resolving the moral perplexities that face all human beings. There are a host of ethical quandaries that mankind has faced since the beginning of time, but there are three central threads running through the great debates: Mankind's relationship to God, to things, and to each other. Cultures have been deeply shaped by our struggles with these fundamental issues.

Yet, with modern computer know-how, a fundamentally new and different arena of ethical concern has emerged: our relationship to information. What are the moral principles that govern information management? Do we need an eleventh commandment about information? Building consensus on information values may be one of the greatest cultural challenges facing CEOs in the future. For

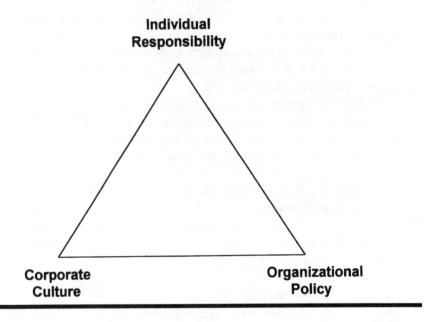

Figure 10.3. The Ethical Organization

example, some internet-based companies place "cookies" on customer's personal computers to facilitate information sharing and commerce, sometimes without informing the consumer. An unscrupulous operator might use the technology to track clients' consumer behavior without their consent.

Another issue involves the concept of *corporate due process,* which has a toehold in the business conscience. David W. Ewing (1989), a former editor of *Harvard Business Review,* defines the concept as "effective mechanisms and procedures for ensuring equity and justice among employees" (p. 4). Values are slowly emerging through the dynamic interplay of practice and philosophy. However, the very existence of an ongoing debate communicates the importance of the ethical concern. Indeed, the ethical organization must have a culture that symbolically signals its commitment. There are a variety of ways to do this, including the development of a set of fundamental operating principles that are widely circulated. For example, when Charles Brewer started MindSpring (now EarthLink), he used nine principles to guide the business. As shown in Table 10.1, over half of them relate to matters of ethics (Grimes 1999). But principles are not enough; principles must be translated into policy. To this issue we now turn.

Organizational Policy

Organizations face three critical policy issues. First, what information should be gathered? Second, how should that information be gathered? Third, how

---

TABLE 10.1 EarthLink's Core Values (a sample)

These are EarthLink's "Core Values and Beliefs." If we don't seem to be living up to them, call us on it!

▷ We respect the individual, and believe that individuals who are treated with respect and given responsibility respond by giving their best.

▷ We require complete honesty and integrity in everything we do.

▷ We make commitments with care, and then live up to them. In all things, we do what we say we are going to do.

▷ Work is an important part of life, and it should be fun. Being a good businessperson does not mean being stuffy or boring.

▷ We are frugal. We guard and conserve the company's resources with at least the same vigilance that we would use to guard and conserve our own personal resources.

▷ We are believers in the Golden Rule. In all our dealings we will strive to be friendly and courteous, as well as fair and compassionate.

---

should the information be used? Within the vortex of these circles of concern lies the essence of an ethical policy (see Figure 10.4).

Policy Issue 1: What information should be gathered? Because the cost of gathering and retaining data has steadily decreased, many organizations routinely gather information for which they have little use. Companies often reason, "Who does it hurt? Besides, it might be useful someday." Yet this cavalier attitude often runs roughshod over employee rights to privacy and may unfairly influence decision making (Burgoon 1982). There are important ethical considerations when one gathers information, and organizations need to consider carefully the implications of their procedures.

We can capture the complexity of this issue by examining the tension between who controls access to the information and who desires it. In particular, three fundamental parties are involved—employees or potential employees, the organization, and the community at large. A proper information policy should consider the often conflicting needs and desires of each of these three groups. Some of the more common dilemmas are identified in Figure 10.5.

What information does an organization legitimately need about employees? Some points of controversy are identified in Sector 1. Does an organization really need information about a person's marital status, employment of spouse, previous arrests, off-job behaviors, and health? Organizations routinely collect such information. For example, a society that believes "innocent until proven guilty" could hardly justify making a hiring or promotion decision on an arrest. Indeed, this is what the courts have ruled. Moreover, in most cases, the health background of an employee has little relevancy to promotion decisions. Hence a manager, when

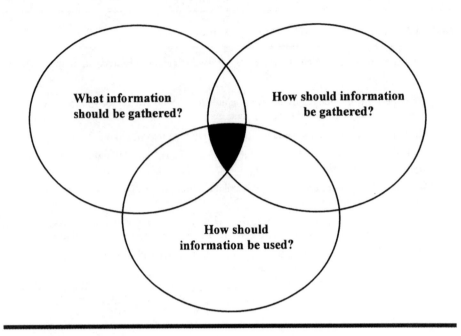

Figure 10.4. Organizational Policy Issues

making such a decision, should not even have access to this information, so that there is no possibility for it to influence decision making.

Other issues, such as the use of DNA screening and personality tests, present potential concerns for employees. Employee privacy and personal dignity lie at the core of all these issues. Organizations can eliminate many of these problems by asking a simple question: Is this information actually relevant to the decision at hand? If not, stop collecting it.

Sector 2 represents the quandary often faced by employees in resolving their respective responsibilities to the community and to the company. Employees need to have a clear sense of what they can and cannot discuss with members of the community at large. Organizations need to respect employees' freedom of speech while simultaneously protecting vital information. Employees should be aware that trade secrets, marketing plans, and the like are out of bounds. Making the community privy to internal policy disputes is another questionable activity, although employees of public agencies are allowed a little more leeway in publicly criticizing policy (Sanders 1986).

On the other hand, employees are ethically obligated to reveal corporate misconduct and consumer safety concerns if the corporation proves unresponsive. Many federal employees are protected under the Federal Whistle-Blower Protection Act (see, for example, Wald 1990.). The California Supreme Court has ruled that "the privilege ends where the public peril begins." Managers and employees alike should feel an ethical obligation to inform the public of events that might im-

Information Controlled By	Information Desired By		
	Individual	**Organization**	**Community**
Individual		• Medical Records • Purchasing Patterns • Marital Status • Off-job Behaviors • Personality Tests • Social Security Number **sector 1**	• Corporate Misconduct • Trade Secrets • Corporate Strategy • Policy Disputes **sector 2**
Organization	• Performance Appraisals • Personnel Files • Salary Projections • Private Management Files **sector 3**		• Recommendation Letters • Product Information • Employee Names, Phone **sector 4**
Community	• Affirmative Action Guidelines • Professional Standards • Legal Rights **sector 5**	• Competitor Strategy • Government Policies • Forthcoming Media Stories **sector 6**	

Figure 10.5. Dilemmas in Gathering Information

peril their safety. The code of corporate secrecy, although important, is subject to a higher code of societal responsibility.

Sector 3 addresses the degree of access employees should have to files about themselves. A number of companies allow employees to see almost all job-related and non-job-related information in their files. If they feel an error has been made, they can insert explanatory material. This policy of open employee files might sound burdensome to the organization, but few companies have found it so. Less than 1% of the employees at AT & T have asked to look at their files (Ewing 1983). Clearly, organizations need secrecy, but there is little need for metasecrecy—secrecy about the secrecy. That is, employees can be told what information will be screened from them and why. There are a few areas, such as promotional prospects or salary plans, in which the company might rightfully restrict employees' access to their records. If employees know the organization's rationale, they will usually support such policies.

Sector 4 represents the information the community-at-large desires about the organization. Publicly-held corporations have a legal responsibility to provide certain information to their stockholders, such as earnings, assets, and liabilities. Product information presents another arena of concern. Certainly, clear warning of potential hazards needs to be provided by the company. Another concern regards how much information about an employee can be released to outsiders without the employee's knowledge. IBM will verify that a person is an employee, the place of work, job title, and date of employment. Any information beyond this requires the employee's consent. Bank of America has a specific guideline prohibiting the disclosure of employee names and addresses to any other organization for the purposes of solicitation, even nonprofit solicitation (Westin 1980). Even disseminating company phone books to the public should be considered when examining policies in this area.

Sector 5 concerns information primarily under the control of the community-at-large that is desired by employees. Organizations have some responsibility to ensure that their employees are aware of laws and governmental policies that affect their well-being. Corporate newsletters often serve this function. Organizations also have a vested interest in fostering employee membership in professional organizations and societies.

Organizations quite legitimately seek information about the community-at-large. The environment has a tremendous impact on the business. Sector 6 presents some of the ethical decisions for the organization. How far should the organization go in trying to gather information about a competitor, consumers, the press, or government's future plans? These issues are particularly fuzzy, because the restrictions are more often in terms of *how* the information is gathered rather than *what* information is gathered. Placing a spy in another organization to steal trade secrets is expressly forbidden (see, for example, Ingrassia 1990). But restraints on the precise data-gathering techniques are unclear. Often, the attitude is "the more information, the better," but this is precisely the kind of stance that has led to so much concern about employee privacy. Hopefully, as businesses grapple with this issue, a reasonable consensus will emerge about what are the legitimate information needs of the organization in regard to the government and competitors.

Policy Issue 2: How should the information be gathered? Managers must be concerned with not only what information they gather, but also the means by which it is gathered. It is legitimate, for example, to appraise employee work. But is it ethical to tape employee telephone conversations in order to do so? What about reading their e-mail? Almost 30% of organizations do it today, and the practice will likely increase in the future (Bott 2000). Why? Because it is easy and legal. Maybe not ethical, but legal. In fact, almost two dozen employees were fired from a *New York Times* business office for transmitting bawdy and lewd e-mail messages (Carrns 2000). Would they have been fired for passing the same messages via the phone system or voice mail? These are the kinds of issues facing organizations today. There are two basic areas of concern.

First, organizations need a policy on what methods can be used to gather information about employees. Should an organization investigate employees without their knowledge? One survey of 126 Fortune 500 companies found that 42% secretly gathered information on employees (Solomon 1989a). The same survey reported that 57% of the companies used private detectives to investigate employees. Should drug tests be administered to employees? If so, under what conditions? Should employee phone calls be monitored? Should polygraphs ("lie detectors") be used on employees? These are the kinds of issues every organization faces. IBM, for example, has an explicit policy of not recording meetings or telephone conversations unless employees are informed of the practice. These vexing issues not only raise questions about employee privacy, but also send powerful messages about the degree of trust management has in its employees.

Second, organizations need a clear set of guidelines concerning the methods used to gather information about competitors. There are entire books published about the subject (see, for example, Fuld 1985). To what extent should a business go to secure information? Some firms have no problem with purchasing stolen documents. The law does, however. For example, Chien-Min Sung was accused of selling GE's secret formula for making industrial diamonds to a South Korean firm. The possible loss to GE was conservatively estimated to exceed $5 million (Ingrassia 1990). Tapping into another company's data bank is expressly forbidden. But what about using consultants to unwittingly provide information about competitors? Should trusted clients be pumped for information about the competition? The list of questions is endless. Clearly organizations need to have a clear policy on such matters. Fundamentally, the issue comes down to fairness. Most of the information needed about competitors can be legitimately gleaned from published sources that are widely available. That is fair. Other practices, decidedly, are not.

Third, organizations would be well-advised to set up due process procedures to air employee grievances. "Corporate due process is a dispute resolution procedure whereby a neutral agency or person has the power to investigate, adjudicate, and rectify" (Ewing 1989, p. 35). Some organizations use an investigator approach, but most use one involving an appeals board. Regardless of the approach, the intent remains the same: to provide employees with a vehicle for dealing with grievances outside the normal chain of command. Corporate due process provides a kind of organizational safety valve for employees. Why is it needed? Because some problems cannot be fairly resolved through the normal open-door policies. Grievance review boards typically disregard rank and status issues and focus on the merits of an employee's case. David Ewing (1989) has conducted some intriguing research on corporate justice, and suggests thirteen tests for an effective corporate due process system (see Table 10.2). A small but growing group of corporations, such as Honeywell, Polaroid, and John Hancock, are using such systems with great success.

Policy Issue 3: How should the information be used? Information, unlike property, can be lost without the organization knowing it. Unlike the thief who steals jewelry, someone could read a personnel file and leave no clue that a "theft" has even taken place.[2] In this sense, information security presents a more difficult challenge than protecting property. Once released, information is no longer under your control. What might happen, for instance, when you mail in a donation to a worthy cause? Your name may wind up on dozens of other charity mailing lists, which freely send you their literature and solicitations. Therefore, organizations need to consider carefully three fundamental questions.

First, who has access to information? Federal employees are governed by the Privacy Act of 1974, which allows them to examine their own personnel files. If an employee deems the information inaccurate or misleading, there are ways for the employee to correct or explain any of the material in the file. One survey found that 87% of U.S. organizations have adopted similar policies, which often result in a morale boost because of the increased sense of fair play and equity (Solomon 1989a).

Second, when can information be released? The U.S. government operates under The Freedom of Information Act, which sets a clear time line for the release of classified documents. Companies might well consider a similar sort of freedom of information act concerning corporate decisions and future planning. Such openness can help engender that intangible but powerful sense of employee trust in managerial decision making. In a crisis or time of uncertainty, employees feel more secure if there are guidelines about when information will be forthcoming.

Third, when should information be destroyed? Negative information in a personnel file often tags along with a person for years. This may unfairly influence decision making. For example, one executive was not given a promotion because his personnel file contained a note about "larcenous tendencies." It turns out that the characterization referred to a teenage prank (Solomon 1989a). How long should performance appraisals be kept on record? Is there really any need in keeping an appraisal from ten years ago? A manager deciding on two candidates for promotion might base an evaluation on an incident in the distant past, rather than a thorough examination of the candidate's more recent performance. Indeed, at IBM most performance appraisals are destroyed after a three-year period. Such a policy acts as a kind of statute of limitations. Employees need to feel that the "slate will be wiped clean" after so many years. Even God did not condemn Moses forever because he committed a murder in his youth.

Individual Character

Corporate culture and organizational policy are powerful forces that can mold the ethical spirit of an organization, but they are no substitute for the character of individual employees (see, for example, Pastin 1986). Thorton Bradshaw, a former president of Atlantic Richfield and chairman at RCA, was once asked about how to "infuse ethics into a huge organization." He responded,

TABLE 10.2 Ewing's Tests of a Due Process System

▷ Does the procedure make a difference?

▷ Is access to the system a right, not a privilege?

▷ Is the procedure simple and easy to use?

▷ Is the board or investigator independent of the chain of command?

▷ Does the ombudsperson or board have the power to get the facts on both sides of the case?

▷ Is retaliation kept to a minimum?

▷ Is the response of the tribunal or investigator timely?

▷ Is confidentiality preserved?

▷ Is the system visible?

▷ Are cases approached rationally and objectively?

▷ Are the processes and decisions predictable?

▷ Are staff people ready to help and advise employees with complaints?

▷ Are the rules clear?

> Well, I'm not sure it's a matter of infusing ethics into an organization, because I think most people that any good organization hires come with a set of ethics of their own, and live with because they're their own. What an organization should do—its objective should be not to twist or distort those ethics. (Freudberg 1986, p. 230)

Most employees want to behave ethically. Indeed, research indicates that when employees behave unethically they believe that others are often the cause. On the other hand, when they behave ethically, they cite personal values as the reason (see, for example, Baumhart 1961). Personal ethics emerge from the rich interaction between a person's religious values, family background, and professional standards. Yet an employee's supervisor also significantly affects personal ethics. As Raymond C. Baumhart (1961) argued in *Harvard Business Review,* "If you want to act ethically, find an ethical boss" (p. 3). Employees often feel compelled to adopt the values of their supervisors. This places an extraordinary burden on managers to foster ethical behavior.

How can managers successfully impart ethical standards? Typically, employees are trained in what specific activities to avoid. Is this necessary? Perhaps, but there is another way. Ethics is more than a list of "thou shalt nots." Employees yearn for values they can believe in. "The value of an ideal is that it shifts attention away from what we know does not work and onto what we want to accomplish" (Pastin 1986, p. 219). A commitment to these ideals, almost by necessity, means avoiding the questionable activities. Below are five suggested tests for communication that should engender a spirit of honorable communication.

Discretion. Sissela Bok (1982), in her own moving and perceptive way, describes the quality of discretion:

> At its best, discretion is the intuitive ability to discern what is and is not intrusive and injurious, and to use this discernment in responding to the conflicts everyone experiences as insider and outsider. It is an acquired capacity to navigate in and between the worlds of personal and shared experiences, coping with the moral questions about what is fair or unfair, truthful or deceptive, helpful or harmful. Inconceivable without an awareness of the boundaries surrounding people, discretion requires a sense for when to hold back in order not to bruise, and for when to reach out. (p. 41)

Respect for our fellow human beings, their privacy, and their dreams require a sense of discretion.

Relevancy. Communication should be structured around the norm of relevancy. Communicators should take care that their remarks are pertinent to the purpose at hand. It means that we only collect information relevant to a specific purpose, and that we dispose of it when it is no longer pertinent. On the other hand, the norm of relevancy means that all pertinent facts are brought to bear on a decision. A manager who sugarcoats an appraisal review has not complied with the norm of relevancy. By not communicating important information, the employee does not know how to improve. Choosing what to express and what to repress involves making an ethical decision. The norm of relevancy aids the communicator in making that kind of critical choice.

Accuracy. A healthy respect for the truth provides the foundation of communication. The Biblical adage, "And the truth shall make you free," is more than a religious saying. Reliable information sets us free to make wise choices. Lies and half-truths rob people of fundamental choices. If an employee lies about the true cause of an accident, it prevents the organization from protecting others from harm. Information is sketchy enough in these situations; intended deception not only compounds the difficulty, but it may also point investigations in precisely the wrong direction (Oberg 1986). Therefore, all employees must be committed to the ethic of accuracy, even when the implications prove personally painful.

On the other hand, the communicator must be reasonably certain that the information will be interpreted in the way intended. William James once said, "There is no worse lie than the truth misunderstood." One could take this line of reasoning even further by declaring that it is philosophically impossible to be completely accurate. After all, information is inherently incomplete. Yet that takes the argument too far. Employees must strive for accuracy, even if they may never know the complete truth.

Fairness. Many questionable activities could easily be eliminated if we simply asked, "Would I want this done to me?" Lies and ambiguity meant to deceive can hardly be justified. Treating people in a judicious manner would eliminate much idle gossip, pain, and sorrow. Fair communication requires us to speak up to correct an inaccuracy, to defend someone's reputation, or to deal with impropriety. To be fair means to avoid the unjust, but it also means to do the just. It is to speak and listen only under the proper circumstances.

Timeliness. Even accurate information can be useless if communicated in an untimely fashion. Why? Just as with a lie, choice can be restricted. Every day that an employer withholds news of impending layoffs may deprive some employee of another job opportunity that comes his or her way. Likewise, if someone communicates to the press about an indiscretion before the matter has been discussed internally, the test of proper timing has been violated. By timing communication properly, one communicates respect for the individual. For instance, think about the difference between remembering a spouse's birthday at the proper time rather than a week later. Proper timing allows us not only to honor relationships, but also to build them.

A pentathlon athlete must successfully compete in all five events. The winner excels in all the events. Others do not. In the same way, an ethical communicator must run the good race on all five accounts. I can still vividly recall one cold Thanksgiving day from my teenage years. After a sumptuous meal with my family, we did what others were doing all across the land: We talked. As families do from time to time, we began to talk about various happenings and people we know. My grandmother began telling a wickedly funny story about an acquaintance of hers. We egged her on for more juicy tidbits. We all laughed. Then I said, "But Grandma, that's gossip." To which she responded: "No, it's not. It's the truth." That caused us to roar all the more. Reflecting on that incident now, I see that accuracy is not the *only* ethical criterion that should be used to judge communications. Information may well be *accurate* and even *timely,* but fail to be used with *discretion.* Each criterion must be balanced against the other. The dynamic tension in this pentad provides the challenge, compelling us to make the right tradeoffs. This requires judgment. It requires grappling with the complexity of communication. And it requires sensitivity as well as toughness. The only real losers in the pentathlon are those who fail to compete in all five events—so too with communicators.

Conclusion

Discussions of ethics seem to inevitably lead to great philosophical words, such as *dignity, freedom, fairness, right,* and *wrong.* For many, these words stay on the mind's bookshelf in the same dusty place where the Bible and the works of Aristotle and Plato reside in most libraries—untouched, unexamined, and unwelcome. But there are times when the force of circumstance or the compelling sense of place inspires one to dust off those forgotten tomes and contemplate these very words.

For me, it happened on a hot, muggy August afternoon in Washington, D.C. One marvels at the Washington monument, the Lincoln Memorial, and the White House. But there is a different and inexplicable sense upon approaching the Vietnam War Memorial. The monument does not tower; it is carved out of the earth, like a healing wound. The hard black blocks of granite shimmer. The sun gleams and glares off the names of war heroes etched on the memorial. Strangely, unlike the war itself, the names on the face of the memorial are difficult to photograph. I thought perhaps this was a reminder that even though it was the most televised war in history, no photograph could ever tell of the true horror. There were people solemnly walking by, but there were a few who knelt down, as if to pray. And then they reached out to the cold hard granite and touched the name—the life—of a loved one. They wept.

Down through the ages, men and women like these have suffered and died for freedom. Freedom of choice, freedom of speech. These were not some philosophical abstractions to be debated; they were living principles that were bought and paid for in the blood of fighters and the tears of families. One feels a tremendous obligation to not make a mockery of such sacrifice, to not abuse the freedom, but rather to use it to pursue the very best in life. We often hear of the freedom of speech, but here on that hot humid day at this touching memorial, I thought about the responsibilities of speech. Ethical communicators ponder these obligations, as well.

Notes

1. For a more detailed account of a similar event, see Benoit and Brinson 1994.

2. The English language does not have an appropriate pejorative term to describe illicit copying of information. "Theft" implies the stealing of property, but that is not quite the same as the unlawful perusal of a document.

ELEVEN

Conclusion

The distinguishing mark of managers with really fine minds is more in the questions they ask than the answers they give. They ask questions that cut to the heart of the matter. Every question has implicit assumptions that latently structure the answer. For instance, one manager asked, "What training package should we purchase to improve our communication?" The question assumes that a training package will provide the proper solution to the problem. As we have seen, there are many different types of communication difficulties that merit various intervention strategies. All too often, the *perceived* communication difficulties are not the *actual* ones. There is a more fundamental question that should be asked: How does one discern the critical communication issues that should be addressed?

A communication assessment can provide a useful starting point. The objective of this process is to discover the communication strengths and weaknesses of the organization. Then problems can be prioritized and solutions developed. After implementation, the organization should reassess to determine if the strategy was successful (see Figure 11.1).

Sometimes, managers only ask questions for which they already have answers. For instance, an organization conducts training, and then assesses the effectiveness of the training. Fair enough, but there is a broader issue at stake: Does the training address a crucial organizational need? An assessment addresses broad questions such as this by surveying employee opinions and evaluating communication practices.

Two scholars who pioneered the assessment process outlined the advantages of the exercise:

> Communication problems in the organization are not unlike the progressive development of a headache. If the initial bodily cues are ignored or not monitored, the full "throb" will hit. The result is much more time and effort lost in trying to

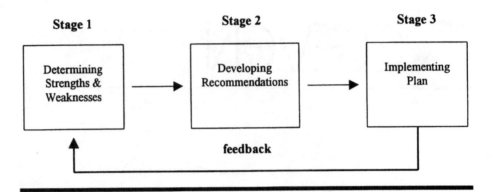

Figure 11.1. Assessment Process

correct the unbearable condition than would have been needed to prevent the situation in the first place. The communication audit can provide that initial sensoring or monitoring for the organization that will allow for a preventative stance regarding communication problems rather than the typical corrective stance. (Greenbaum and White 1976, p. 5)

The assessment not only identifies potential problems, but also communicates to employees that their opinions are valued by the organization.

The expense and time involved in collecting the information may trouble some executives. However, reputable assessors work by this creed: Gather a maximum amount of relevant information in a minimal amount of time. The other potential disadvantage to conducting an assessment involves building unrealistic employee expectations. If the organization does not plan to respond to the findings, then it is best to not collect that data in the first place. At minimum, every employee who participates in the process should receive a summary of the results.

A variety of methods can be used to conduct the assessment (Downs 1988; see also Hargie and Tourish 2000). Although each method can prove revealing, each can create blind spots for the assessor. For instance, the original version of one widely used survey contained no questions about interdepartmental communication (Downs and Hazen 1977). This blind spot might lead an assessor to conclude erroneously that such problems do not exist in the organization. If interviews are used in conjunction with the survey, these concerns might emerge. Therefore, it is wise to use a combination of methods. In other words, the best way to assess a company's position is to triangulate between three different assessment tools. Typically, I recommend using quantitative and qualitative survey questions as well as interviews to conduct a thorough assessment (Clampitt 2000). Moreover, a comprehensive assessment should examine at least the basic concerns discussed in these pages:

▷ Corporate Culture
▷ Data, Information, and Knowledge Management
▷ Channels of Communication
▷ Personal Feedback
▷ Communication About Changes
▷ Interdepartmental Communication
▷ Innovation
▷ Communication Ethics

Attaining valid results depends on proper administrative procedures. **First, carefully consider who should conduct the assessment.** In most cases an independent consultant should be used. Why? Employees are often reluctant to share their true feelings with insiders because they fear identification and possibly retaliation. Also, outside observers can be more objective in analyzing the results and less influenced by internal politics. **Second, assure all employees that their comments will remain confidential.** This will encourage employees to respond forthrightly. **Third, make sure that top management fully supports the assessment.** This will help bolster the participation rate. **Finally, recognize the inherent dilemmas in conducting any assessment.** Auditors must be able to isolate problem areas while preserving employee confidentiality. The organization is naturally interested in breaking down the results by department, job type, shift, and demographic variables in order to target corrective measures. Although it is important to do this, it is equally important to preserve employees' anonymity. As a rule of thumb, I only report results from groups larger than five persons.

After completing the assessment, the tough work really begins. The organization must grapple with a plan to address the concerns revealed. For instance, Associated Bank faced this very challenge after we conducted an assessment. Like most companies, one of the problem areas was personal feedback. But they went to work on the issue. An employee task force developed a new corporate strategy for recognizing employees. Managers participated in extensive training about how to conduct performance appraisals, and revised the performance appraisal form. They employed many other tactics that signaled a corporate commitment to an effective feedback system.

Several years later, we repeated the assessment process. The result was that employee concerns about the feedback system had almost disappeared. This is what the assessment process is all about. When managers ask the right questions, thoughtfully work through the answers, and tenaciously pursue the implications, they near the elusive goal of effective communication. And they become choreographers of organizational excellence.

APPENDIX A

Data Bank Composition

TABLE A.1 Data Bank Composition

Organization	Type	Union present?	N	% Response Rate
Auto Dealer	Service	No	44	100
TV Station	Media	No	79	75
Industrial Laundry	Service	No	62	94
Packaging Plant	Manufacturing	Yes	43	77
Hotel	Service	No	81	87
Insurance Firm	Service	No	44	90
Health Agency	Service	No	28	78
Savings Bank	Financial	No	78	93
TV Station	Media	No	24	67
Savings Bank	Financial	No	65	100
Chair Manufacturer	Manufacturing	Yes	116	98
Nuts and Bolts Distributor	Service	No	57	88
Custom Manufacturer	Manufacturing	Yes	57	90
Savings Bank	Financial	No	90	92
Bank	Financial	No	162	61
Motel	Service	No	63	65
Newspaper	Media	Yes	239	75
TV Station	Media	No	79	92
Trucking Firm	Service	Yes	29	90
Paper Product Producer	Manufacturing	Yes	54	95
Machine Maker	Manufacturing	Yes	92	99
Utility	Service	Yes	169	99
Office Supply	Retail	No	61	93
Savings Bank	Financial	No	119	87
Communication Service	Service	No	84	90
Building Supply	Service	Yes	83	94

N = 2,101 employees
Total companies represented = 26

APPENDIX B

Results of Communication Assessments

The Communication Satisfaction Questionnaire, developed by Downs and Hazen (1977), was one of the primary investigative tools used in the communication assessments referred to in the manuscript. Basically, employees were asked about their satisfaction level with various aspects of communication within the organization. This appendix contains a summary of employee responses collected from the twenty-six companies cited in Appendix A. The results are presented in three sections:

1. Table B.1 presents a list of the communication satisfaction items in descending order of satisfaction. All means are computed on a satisfaction scale of 0 to 10 points, with 0 representing *no satisfaction,* 5 representing *average satisfaction,* and 10 representing *high satisfaction.*
2. Table B.2 presents employees' reactions to factors that have an impact on their level of job performance. A 0- to 10-point scale was used, with 0 representing that the item had *no influence* on performance, 5 indicating *average influence,* and 10 indicating *high influence.*
3. Table B.3 presents the demographics of the sample.

TABLE B.1 Rank of Employee Satisfaction Levels

Rank	Mean	Standard deviation	Survey item
1	7.45	2.44	Supervisor trusts me
2	7.14	2.34	Supervision given me is about right
3	7.07	2.17	Work group is compatible
4*	6.88	2.04	My employees are responsive to downward directive communication
5*	6.81	2.04	Subordinates are receptive to evaluation, suggestions, and criticism
6	6.79	2.02	Satisfaction with my job
7	6.69	2.29	Supervisor is open to ideas

(Continued)

TABLE B.1. Continued

Rank	Mean	Standard deviation	Survey item
8*	6.64	2.12	Subordinates feel responsible for initiating upward communication
9*	6.53	2.06	Subordinates anticipate my needs for information
10	6.48	2.66	Information about employee benefits and pay
11	6.39	2.52	The extent of grapevine activity in our organization
12	6.38	2.29	Horizontal communication with other employees is accurate and free flowing
13	6.34	2.50	Information about the requirements of my job
14	6.34	2.33	Written directives and reports are clear and concise
15	6.23	2.83	Supervisor listens and pays attention to me
16	6.14	2.68	Supervisor offers guidance for solving job-related problems
17	6.13	2.28	Communication practices are adaptable to emergencies
18*	6.12	2.23	Supervisors do not have communication overload
19	6.00	2.56	Information needed to do my job is received on time
20	5.87	2.19	Informal communication is active and accurate
21	5.73	2.71	Information about company policies and goals
22	5.66	2.50	The attitudes toward communication in the company are basically healthy
23	5.62	2.73	Information about departmental policies and goals
24	5.59	2.58	Meetings are well organized, clear, and concise
25	5.56	3.25	Information on company profits and company standing
26	5.51	2.46	Personnel news
27	5.38	2.56	Company publications are interesting and helpful
28	5.34	2.31	The amount of communication in the company is about right
29	5.30	2.38	People in my organization have great abilities as communicators
30	5.27	2.86	Information about accomplishments or failures of the company
31	5.26	2.58	Conflicts are handled appropriately through proper communication channels
32	5.19	2.60	The company's communication makes me identify with it or feel like a vital part of it
33	5.18	2.60	Information about my progress in my job
34	5.02	2.63	Information about changes within organization
35	4.99	2.47	Company communication motivates and stimulates enthusiasm for meeting its goals
36	4.86	2.51	Supervisor knows and understands the problems faced by subordinates

(Continued)

TABLE B.1. Continued

Rank	Mean	Standard deviation	Survey item
37	4.86	2.80	Recognition of my efforts
38	4.56	2.71	Information about how I am being judged
39	4.53	2.60	Reports on how problems in my job are being handled
40	4.50	2.81	Information about government action affecting my company
41	4.44	2.57	Information about how my job compares with others

Note: *. Designates that only those in supervisory position answered the questions.
$N = 2,101$
$N^* = 547$

TABLE B.2 Factors Influencing Level of Job Performance

Rank	Mean	Standard deviation	Survey item
1	8.77	1.67	Feelings of personal achievement
2	8.72	1.72	Job satisfaction
3	8.68	2.14	Job security
4	7.73	2.09	Pay
5	7.70	2.81	Family
6	7.63	2.21	Immediate supervisor
7	7.56	2.59	Opportunities for advancement
8	7.18	2.13	Coworkers
9	5.91	2.71	Economic conditions

TABLE B.3 Database Demographics

Gender	Males: 49.9%
	Females: 50.1%
Age	under 21: 3.2%
	21–29: 38.9%
	30–39: 31%
	40–49: 15.7%
	50–59: 8.9%
	Over 60: 2.2%
Education	High school or less: 44.5%
	Some college: 22.7%
	Specialized professional degree: 10.7%
	Undergraduate college degree: 20.7%
	Graduate degree: 2.0%
Length of time worked for the organization	less than a year: 18.2%
	1–4 years: 33.9%
	5–8 years: 20.5%
	Over 9 years: 26.8%

REFERENCES

Adler, P. S. 1999. Building better bureaucracies. *Academy of Management Executive* 13 (4):36–49.

Allen, T. J. 1967. Communications in the research and development laboratory. *Technology Review,* October/November.

Allport, G. W., and L. J. Postman. 1947. *The psychology of rumor.* New York: Holt, Rinehart & Winston.

Alsop, R. 1999. Johnson & Johnson turns up tops. *Wall Street Journal,* 23 September, B1, B6.

Ames, B. C. 1989. Straight talk from the new CEO. *Harvard Business Review* 67 (6):132–138.

Anderson, J. A., and T. P. Meyer. 1988. *Mediated communication.* Beverly Hills, CA: Sage Publications.

Argyris, C. 1986. Skilled incompetence. *Harvard Business Review* 64 (5):74–79.

Aristotle. 1960. *The rhetoric of Aristotle.* Translated by L. Cooper. New York: Meredith.

Armstrong, D. 1992. *Managing by storying around: A new method of leadership.* New York: Double-day Currency.

Arvey, R. D., and J. M. Ivancevich. 1980. Punishment in organizations: A review, propositions, and research suggestions. *Academy of Management Review* 5:123–132.

Attempt to sue Pepsi over jet is a flameout. 1999. *Houston Chronicle,* 6 August.

Austin, R. W. 1961. Code of conduct of executives. *Harvard Business Review* 39 (5):53–61.

Avery, S. 1998. Purchasing leads desktop PC buy team to success. *Purchasing* 125 (7):104.

Barks, J. V., and K. W. Bennett. 1979. Why America can't afford to overlook. *Iron Age,* 1 October, 28–50.

Bartimo, J. 1990. At these shouting matches, no one says a word. *Business Week,* 11 June, 78.

Bate, P. 1984. The impact of organizational culture on approaches to organizational problem-solving. *Organization Studies* 5 (1):43–66.

Bateson, M. C. 1989. An interview with Mary Catherine Bateson. In *Bill Moyers: A world of ideas,* edited by B .S. Flowers (pp. 345–357). New York: Doubleday.

Battista, O. A. 1984. Research for profit: The chief executive officer connection. *Accounts of Chemical Research* 17 (4):121–126.

Baum, R. J., and A. Flores. 1978. *Ethical problems in engineering.* Troy, NY: Center for the Study of the Human Dimensions of Science and Technology.

Baumhart, R. C. 1961. How ethical are businessmen? *Harvard Business Review* 39 (4):6–21.

Bavelas, J. B., A. Black, N. Chovil, and J. Mullett. 1990. *Equivocal communication.* Newbury Park, CA: Sage Publications.

Benoit, W., and S. Brinson. 1994. AT & T: Apologies are not enough. *Communication Quarterly* 42 (1):75–88.

Benson, J. A. 1988. Crisis revisited. An analysis of strategies used by Tylenol in the second tampering episode. *Central States Speech Journal* 39 (1):49–66.

Berg, E. N. 1987. Critics fault accountant for not blowing whistles. *New York Times,* 5 July, Y3.

Bernhardt, G. 1999. Goals, teams and letting go. *Textile World* 149 (4):13.

Beveridge, W. I. B. 1980. *Seeds of discovery.* New York: Norton.

Biddle, W. 1986. How much bang for the buck? *Discover,* September, 50–63.

Boeker, W. 1989. Strategic change: The effects of founding and history. *Academy of Management Journal* 32:489–515.

Bok, S. 1978. *Lying: Moral choice in public and private life.* New York: Pantheon Books.

———. 1982. *Secrets: On the ethics of concealment and revelation.* New York: Pantheon Books.

Boorstin, D. 1983. *The discoverers.* New York: Random House.

Bott, E. 2000. Are you safe? *PC Computing,* March, 86–88.

Brockhaus, R. H. 1980. Risk-taking propensity of entrepreneurs. *Academy of Management Journal* 23 (3):509–520.

Broms, H., and H. Gahmberg. 1983. Communication to self in organizations and cultures. *Administrative Science Quarterly* 28:482–495.

Bronowski, J. 1973. *The ascent of man.* Boston: Little, Brown.

———. 1978. *The common sense of science.* Cambridge, MA: Harvard University Press.

Brown, J., and P. Duguid. 2000. *The social life of information.* Boston: Harvard Business School Publishing.

Browning, E. S. 1986. Sony's perseverance helped it win market for mini-CD players. *Wall Street Journal,* 27 February, A1, A11.

Buderi, R. 1999. Into the big blue yonder. *Technology Review,* July/August, 46–53.

Burgoon, J. K. 1982. Privacy and communication. In *Communication yearbook 6,* edited by M. Burgoon (pp. 206–249). Beverly Hills, CA: Sage Publications.

Camden, C., M. T. Motley, and A. Wilson. 1983. White lies in interpersonal communication: A taxonomy and (preliminary) investigation of social motivations. Paper presented at the annual convention of the International Communication Association, May, Dallas, TX.

Campbell, D. 1977. *Take the road to creativity and get off your dead end.* Allen, TX: Argus.

Carrns, A. 2000. Those bawdy e-mails were good for a laugh—until the ax fell. *Wall Street Journal,* 24 February, A1, A8.

Carroll, P. B., and J. R. Wilke. 1989. Calculated move. *Wall Street Journal,* 15 August, A1, A6.

Carter, J. 1976. *Why not the best?* New York: Bantam Books.

Carter, S. 1996. *Integrity.* New York: Basic Books.

Cartwright, S., and C. L. Cooper. 1993. The role of culture compatibility in successful organizational marriage. *Academy of Management Executive* 7 (2):57–70.

Casse, D. 1986. Reading and writing as an entitlement. *Wall Street Journal,* 2 September, A15.

Champy, J. 1995. *Reengineering management.* New York: HarperBusiness.

Christensen, C. 1997. *The innovator's dilemma.* Boston: Harvard Business School Publishing.

Churchill, W. S. 1931. *The world crisis.* New York: Scribner.

Clampitt, P. 2000. The questionnaire approach. In *Handbook of communication audits for organisations,* edited by O. Hargie and D. Tourish (pp. 45–65). London: Routledge.

Clampitt, P. G., and L. R. Berk. 1996. Strategically communicating organizational change. *Journal of Communication Management* 1 (1):15–28.

Clampitt, P. G., J. M Crevcoure, and R. L. Hartel. 1986. Exploratory research on employee publications. *Journal of Business Communication* 23 (3):5–17.

Clampitt, P. G., and C. W. Downs. 1993. Employee perceptions of the relationship between communication and productivity. *Journal of Business Communication* 30 (1):5–28.

Clancy, T., and C. Horner. 1999. *Every man a tiger.* New York: Putnam.

Clark, R. W. 1971. *Einstein.* New York: Avon Books.

Cohen, H. B. 1998. The performance paradox. *Academy of Management Executive* 12 (3):30–40.

Collins, J., and J. Porras. 1994. *Built to last: Successful habits of visionary companies.* New York: HarperBusiness.

Collins, O. F., and D. G. Moore. 1964. *The enterprising man.* East Lansing, MI: Michigan State University Press.

Comstock, T. 1974. *New dimensions in dance research: Anthology and dance.* New York: Committee on Research in Dance.

The culture wars. 1999. *Inc.* [20th anniversary issue], 107–108.

Cusella, L. P. 1987. Feedback, motivation, and performance. In *Handbook of organizational communication,* edited by F. Jablin, L. Putnam, K. Roberts, & L. Porter (pp. 624–678). Newbury Park, CA: Sage.

Cusumano, M. A. 1997. How Microsoft makes large teams work like small teams. *Sloan Management Review* 39 (1):9–20.

D'Aprix, R. 1982. *Communicating for productivity.* New York: Harper & Row.

Davenport, T. H. 1997. *Information ecology.* New York: Oxford University Press.

Davenport, T. H., and L. Prusak. 1998. *Working knowledge.* Boston: Harvard Business School Publishing.

Davis, K. 1972. *Human behavior at work.* New York: McGraw-Hill.

Deal, T. E., and A. A. Kennedy. 1982. *Corporate cultures: The rites and rituals of corporate life.* Reading, MA: Addison-Wesley.

Deming, W. E. 1986. *Out of the crisis.* Cambridge: Massachusetts Institute of Technology, Center for Advanced Engineering Study.

Deng, A., B. Lev, and F. Narin. 1999. Science and technology as predictors of stock performance. *Association for Investment Management and Research*, May/June, 20–32.

Dillard, A. 1989. *The writing life*. New York: Harper & Row.

DiSalvo, V. S. 1980. A summary of current research identifying communication skills in various organizational contexts. *Communication Education* 29:283–290.

Dougherty, D., and C. Hardy. 1996. Sustained product innovation in large, mature organizations: Overcoming innovation-to-organization problems. *Academy of Management Journal* 39 (5):1120–1153.

Downs, C. W. 1988. *Communication audits*. Glenview, IL: Scott Foresman.

Downs, C. W., and M. Hazen. 1977. A factor analytic study of communication satisfaction. *Journal of Business Communication* 14 (2):63–74.

Downs, C. W., K. M. Johnson, and J. K. Barge. 1984. Communication feedback and task performance in organizations: A review of the literature. In *Organization communication abstracts*, edited by H. Greenbaum, R. Falcione, and S. Hellweg (pp. 13–47). Beverly Hills, CA: Sage.

Downs, C. W., and T. Pickett. 1977. An analysis of the effect of nine leadership-group compatibility contingencies upon productivity and member satisfaction. *Communication Monographs* 44:220–230.

Downs, C. W., G. P. Smeyak, and E. Martin. 1980. *Professional interviewing*. New York: Harper & Row.

Doyle, A. C. 1978. *Sherlock Holmes*. Secaucus, NJ: Castle Books.

Drucker, P. F. 1985. *Innovation and entrepreneurship*. New York: Harper & Row.

Dubos, R. 1976. *Louis Pasteur*. New York: Scribner.

Eisenberg, E. M., R. V. Farace, P. R. Monge, E. P. Bettinghaus, R. Kurchner-Hawkins, L. L. White, and K. I. Williams. 1982. Communication linkages in interorganizational systems: Review and synthesis. Paper presented at the annual meeting of the International Communication Association, May, Boston, MA.

Eisenberg, E. M., P. R. Monge, and R. V. Farace. 1984. Coorientation on communication rules as a predictor of interpersonal evaluations in managerial dyads. Paper presented at the annual convention of the International Communication Association, May, San Francisco, CA.

Eisenberg, E. M., and M. G. Witten. 1987. Reconsidering openness in organizational communication. *Academy of Management Review* 12 (3):418–426.

Ewing, D. W. 1983. *"Do it my way or you're fired!": Employee rights and the changing role of management prerogatives*. New York: John Wiley.

———. 1989. *Justice on the job: Resolving grievances in the nonunion workplace*. Boston: Harvard Business School Publishing.

Fairhurst, G., and R. Sarr. 1996. *The art of framing: Managing the language of leadership*. San Francisco: Jossey-Bass.

Farnham, A. 1989. The trust gap. *Fortune*, 4 December, 56–78.

Feinstein, J. 1986. *A season on the brink: A year with Bob Knight and the Indiana Hoosiers*. New York: Macmillian.

Fialka, J. J. 1987. U.S. Army units win battle contests for the first time. *Wall Street Journal*, 6 July, C24.

Field, A. R. 1988. Managing creative people. *Success*, October, 85–87.

Fiorina, C. 2000. Speech to the National Governor's Association, 27 February, Washington, DC.

Fischer, C. D. 1979. Transmission of positive and negative feedback to subordinates: A laboratory investigation. *Journal of Applied Psychology* 64:533–540.

Foehrebach, J., and S. Goldfarb. 1990. Employee communication in the 90s: Greater expectations. *Communication World*, May/June, 4–10.

Foehrebach, J., and K. Rosenberg. 1982. How are we doing? *Journal of Communication Management* 12 (1):3–9.

Fombrun, C., and M. Shanley. 1990. What's in a name? Reputation building and corporate strategy. *Acadamy of Management Journal* 33 (2):233–258.

Foster, R. 1986. *Innovation: The attacker's advantage*. New York: Summit Books.

Frank, M. O. 1989. *How to run a successful meeting in half the time*. New York: Simon & Schuster.

Freudberg, D. 1986. *The corporate conscience: Money, power, and responsible business*. New York: AMACOM.

Fuld, L. M. 1985. *Competitor intelligence: How to get it—How to use it*. New York: John Wiley.

Gabor, A. 2000. *The capitalist philosophers: The geniuses of modern business—Their lives, time, and ideas*. New York: Times Business.

Galante, S. P. 1986. More firms quiz customers for clues about competition. *Wall Street Journal,* 3 March, A17.

Garton, L., and B. S. Wellman. 1995. Social impacts of electronic mail in organizations: A review of the research literature. In *Communication yearbook 18,* edited by B. Burleson (pp. 440–441). Thousand Oaks, CA: Sage.

Gerbner, G. 1956. Toward a general model of communication. *Audio-Visual Communication Review* 4:171–199.

———. 1990. Personal communication, 5 March.

Geyelin, M. 1989. Fired managers winning more lawsuits. *Wall Street Journal,* 7 September, B1.

Gilchrist, J. A. 1982. The compliance interview: Negotiating across organizational boundaries. In *Communication yearbook 6,* edited by M. Burgoon (pp. 653–673). Beverly Hills, CA: Sage.

Gilder, G. 1981. *Wealth and poverty.* New York: Basic Books.

Gill, B. 1981. *John F. Kennedy Center for the Performing Arts.* New York: H. N. Abrams.

Goldhaber, G., M. Yates, T. Porter, and R. Lesniak. 1978. The ICA communication audit: Recent findings, background, and development. *Human Communication Research* 5 (1):81–84.

Golen, S., D. Lynch, L. Smeltzer, W. J. Lord, J. M. Penrose, and J. Waltman. 1989. An empirically tested communication skills core module for MBA students, with implications for the AACSB. *Organizational Behavior Teaching Review* 13:45–57.

Gopnik, A. 1999. The return of the word. *New Yorker,* 6 December, 49–50.

Gray, B., and S. S. Ariss. 1985. Politics and strategic change across organizational life cycles. *Academy of Management Review* 10 (4):707–723.

Greenbaum, H., and N. D. White. 1976. Biofeedback at the organizational level: The communication audit. *Journal of Business Communication* 13 (4):3–15.

Greenspan, A. 1995. Talk show. *Business Week,* 3 July, 6.

Grimes, B. 1999. Lessons from MindSpring. *Fortune,* 21 June, 186(C)–186(G). Available on-line at <www.earthlink.net/about/mission.html>.

Grinder, J., and R. Bandler. 1976. *The structure of magic II.* Palo Alto, CA: Science & Behavior Books.

Hamel, G., and C. K. Prahalad. 1994. *Competing for the future.* Boston: Harvard Business School Publishing.

Hammarskjöld, D. 1978. *Markings.* New York: Knopf.

Hample, D. 1980. Purposes and effects of lying. *Southern Speech Communication Journal* 46:33–47.

Haney, W. V. 1979. *Communication and interpersonal relations: Text and cases.* Homewood, IL: Irwin.

Hargie, O., and D. Tourish, eds. 2000. *Handbook of communication audits for organisations.* London: Routledge.

Hart, B. H. L. 1967. *Strategy.* London: Faber & Faber.

Hart, M. H. 1978. *The 100: A ranking of the most influential persons in history.* New York: A & W Visual Library.

Ho, C. Y., R. W. Powell, and P. E. Liley. 1974. Thermal conductivity of the elements: A comprehensive review. *Journal of Physical and Chemical Reference Data, Supplement* 3:1–244.

Hoerr, J. 1988a. Privacy. *Business Week,* 28 March, 61–68.

———. 1988b. Work teams can rev up paper-pushers, too. *Business Week,* 28 November, 64–72.

Hofstadter, D. R. 1979. *Godel, Escher, Bach: An eternal golden braid.* New York: Vintage Books.

Holbrooke, B. 1983. *Gossip: How to get it before it gets you and other suggestions for social survival.* New York: St. Martin's Press.

Holy bible: New international version. 1978. Grand Rapids, MI: Zondervan Publishing House.

Hudson, R. L. 1987. Scientific saga: How two physicists triggered superconductor frenzy. *Wall Street Journal,* 19 August, A1, A10.

Humes, J. C. 1980. *Churchill: Speaker of the century.* New York: Stein & Day Publishers.

Iansiti, M., and A. MacCormack. 1997. Developing products on Internet time. *Harvard Business Review* 75 (5):108–117.

Ilgen, D. R., C. D. Fischer, and M. S. Taylor. 1979. Consequences of individual feedback on behavior in organizations. *Journal of Applied Psychology* 64:349–371.

Ingrassia, L. 1990. How secret GE recipe for making diamonds may have been stolen. *Wall Street Journal,* 28 February, A1, A11.

Jablin, F. M. 1987. Organizational entry, assimilation, and exit. In *Handbook of organizational communication,* edited by F. M. Jablin, L. L. Putnam, K. H. Roberts, and L. W. Porter (pp. 679–725). Newbury Park, CA: Sage.

Jacobson, G., and J. Hillkirk. 1986. *Xerox.* New York: Macmillan.

Janis, I. 1982. *Groupthink: Psychological studies of policy decisions.* Boston: Houghton Mifflin.

Jassawalla, A. R., and H. C. Sashittal. 1999. Building collaborative cross-functional new product teams. *Academy of Management Executive* 13 (3):50–63.

Judson, H. F. 1979. *The eighth day of creation.* New York: Simon & Schuster.

Kanter, R. M. 1983. *The change masters.* New York: Simon & Schuster.

Kaplan, A. 1963. *The conduct of inquiry: Methodology for behavioral science.* San Francisco: Chandler.

Kaplan, R. S. 1984. Yesterday's accounting undermines production. *Harvard Business Review* 62 (4):95–101.

Keidel, R. W. 1988. Going beyond "I'm o.k., you're o.k." *New York Times,* 27 November, F2.

Keller, R. T., and W. E. Holland. 1981. Job change: A naturally occurring field experiment. *Human Relations* 34 (12):1053–1067.

Kennan, G. 1993. *Around the cragged hill.* New York: W. W. Norton.

Kiesler, S. 1986. Thinking ahead. *Harvard Business Review* 64 (1):46–60.

Kissinger, H. 1979. *The White House years.* Boston: Little, Brown.

———. 1982. *Years of upheaval.* Boston: Little, Brown

Kleinfield, N. R. 1986. The whistle blower's morning after. *New York Times,* 9 November, C1, C10.

Koepp, S. 1986. Honda in a hurry. *Time,* 8 September, 48–49.

Kotter, J. P., and J. L. Heskett. 1992. *Corporate culture and performance.* New York: The Free Press.

Kubler-Ross, E. 1969. *On death and dying.* New York: Macmillan.

Labich, K. 1989. Hot company, warm culture. *Fortune,* 27 February, 74–78.

Laird, A. 1982. A rules approach as a supplement to organization communication research. Paper presented at the Central States Speech Association Convention, April, Chicago, IL.

Laird, A., and P. G. Clampitt. 1985. Effective performance appraisal: Viewpoints from managers. *Journal of Business Communication* 22 (3):49–57.

Langley, M. 1986. Generous juries. *Wall Street Journal,* 29 May, A1, A20.

Larson, J. R., Jr. 1986. Supervisors' performance feedback to subordinates: The effect of performance valence and outcome dependence. *Organizational Behavior and Human Decision Processes* 37:391–408.

———. 1989. The dynamic interplay between employees' feedback-seeking strategies and supervisors' delivery of performance feedback. *Academy of Management Review* 14 (3):408–422.

Lasswell, H. D. 1948. The structure and function of communications in society. In *The communication of ideas,* edited by L. Bryson (pp. 37–51). New York: Harper & Row.

Lawrence, P. R. 1969. How to deal with resistance to change. *Harvard Business Review* 47 (1):4–8.

Lawrence, P. R., and J. W. Lorsch. 1969. *Organization and environment.* Homewood, IL: Irwin.

Lawson, J. 1980. *The principles of classical dance.* New York: Knopf.

Lengel, R. H., and R. L. Daft. 1988. The selection of communication media as an executive skill. *Academy of Management Executive* 2 (3):225–232.

Levinson, H. 1970. Management by whose objectives? *Harvard Business Review* 48 (4):125–134.

Locke, E. A. 1976. The nature and causes of job satisfaction. In *Handbook of industrial and organizational psychology,* edited by M. D. Dunnette (pp. 1292–1350). Chicago: Rand McNally.

Lopez, F. M. 1968. *Evaluating employee performance.* Chicago: Public Personnel Association.

Lynch, P. 1989. *One upon Wall Street.* New York: Simon & Schuster.

Maccoby, M. 1999. Building cross-functional capability: What it really takes. *Research Technology Management* 42 (3):56–58.

The Macintosh design team. 1984. Interview. *Byte,* February, 58–80.

Mackenzie, K. D. 1994. Some real world adventures of a bench scientist. In *Producing useful knowledge for organizations,* edited by R. H. Kilmann, K. W. Thomas, D. P. Slevin, R. Nath, and S. L. Jerrell (pp. 100–118). San Francisco: Jossey-Bass.

Manchester, W. 1983. *The last lion: Winston Spencer Churchill.* Boston: Little, Brown.

Mardesich, J. 1999. The web is no shopper's paradise. *Fortune,* 8 November, 188–198.

Markides, C. 1997. Strategic innovation. *Sloan Management Review* 38 (3):9–23.

Martin, J. 1997. *Miss Manners' basic training: Communication.* New York: Crown.

Martin, R. G. 1983. *A hero for our time.* New York: Macmillan.

Mayfield, H. 1960. In defense of performance appraisal. *Harvard Business Review* 38 (2):80–85.

McConnell, M. 1987. *Challenger: A major malfunction.* Garden City, NY: Doubleday.

McCormick, J. 1989. Taking stock of employee ownership plans. *USA Today,* 30 May, B3.

McFarlin, D. B., and J. Blascovich. 1981. Effects of self-esteem and performance feedback on future affective preferences and cognitive expectations. *Journal of Personality and Social Psychology* 40 (3):521–531.

McGill, D. C. 1989. A "Mickey Mouse" class—for real. *New York Times,* 27 August, F4.

McGregor, D. 1972. An uneasy look at performance appraisal. *Harvard Business Review* 50 (5):133–138.

McKinnon, S. M., and W. J. Bruns, Jr. 1992. *The information mosaic.* Boston: Harvard Business School Publishing.

Metcalfe, B. 1999. Invention is a flower, innovation is a weed. *Technology Review,* November/December, 56–57.

Meyer, A. D., and J. B. Goes. 1988. Organizational assimilation of innovations: A multilevel contextual analysis. *Academy of Management Journal* 31 (4):897–923.

Mikulecky, L. 1990. Basic skill impediments to communication between management and hourly employees. *Management Communication Quarterly* 3 (4):452–473.

Miller, J. 1978. *The body in question.* New York: Random House.

Miller, K. I., and P. R. Monge. 1985. Social information and employee anxiety about organizational change. *Human Communication Research* 11 (3):194–203.

Miller, M. W. 1985. Productivity spies. *Wall Street Journal,* 3 June, A1, A15.

Mirel, B. 1990. Expanding the activities of in-house manual writers. *Management Communication Quarterly* 3 (4):496–526.

Mitchell, R. 1989. Master of innovation. *Business Week,* 10 April, 58–63.

Moorhouse, B. 2000. Personal communication, 12 January.

Morgan, G. 1986. *Images of organization.* Beverly Hills, CA: Sage.

Morris, E. 1979. *The rise of Theodore Roosevelt.* New York: Coward, McCann & Geoghegan.

Morrow, L. 1981. The morals of gossip. *Time,* 26 October, 98.

Morton, J. A. 1971. *Organizing for innovation.* New York: McGraw-Hill.

Moscinski, P. 1979. *The appraisal system in American business and industry.* Unpublished master's thesis, University of Kansas.

Motley, M. 1990. On whether one can(not) not communicate: An examination via traditional communication postulates. *Western Journal of Speech Communication* 54 (1):1–22.

Nadler, D. A., and M. L. Tushman. 1989. Organizational frame bending: Principles for managing reorientation. *Academy of Management Executive* 3 (3):194–203.

Near, J., and M. Miceli. 1995. Effective whistle-blowing. *Academy of Management Review* 20 (3):679–708.

Nelson, E., and E. Ramstad. 1999. Hershey's biggest dud has turned out to be new computer system. *Wall Street Journal,* 29 October, A1, A6.

Newman, B. 1986. The tilting train: Movable monument to British persistence. *Wall Street Journal,* 7 April, A1, A9.

Nights of the garter are over. 1989. *Wall Street Journal,* 25 August, B1.

Nohria, N., and R. Gulati. 1996. Is slack good or bad for innovation? *Academy of Management Journal* 39 (5):1245–1264.

Nutt, P. 1999. Surprising but true: Half the decisions in organizations fail. *Academy of Management Executive* 13 (4):75–90.

Oberg, J. E. 1986. Soviet secrecy may cost future lives. *Wall Street Journal,* 5 May, A15.

Oberg, W. 1972. Make performance appraisal relevant. *Harvard Business Review* 50 (1):61–67.

Oech, R. 1983. *A whack on the side of the head.* Menlo Park, CA: Creative Think.

Ono, Y. 1978. Sick of meetings? Then ODS is not the place for you. *Wall Street Journal,* 12 September, A1, A11.

O'Reilly, B. 1990. Quality of products. *Fortune,* 29 January, 42–43.

———. 1999. The mechanic who fixed Continental. *Fortune,* 20 December, 176–186.

O'Reilly, C. A., J. A. Chatman, and J. C. Anderson. 1987. Message flow and decision making. In *Handbook of organizational communication,* edited by F. M Jablin, L. L. Putnam, K. H. Roberts, and L. W. Porter (pp. 600–623). Newbury Park, CA: Sage.

Organizing for productivity. 1981. *Industry Week,* 9 February, 55–60.

Ornstein, S. 1989. The hidden influences of office design. *Academy of Management Executive* 3 (2):144–147.

Ouchi, W. 1981. *Theory z.* Reading, MA: Addison-Wesley.

Oxford English dictionary. 1989. 2d ed. Edited by J. A. Simpson and E. S. C. Weiner. Oxford: Clarendon Press.

Pacanowsky, M. E., and N. O'Donnell-Trujillo. 1982. Communication and organizational cultures. *Western Journal of Speech Communication* 46:115–130.

Pace, W., and R. Boren. 1973. *The human transaction.* Glenview, IL: Scott Foresman.

Pastin, M. 1986. *The hard problems of management.* San Francisco, CA: Jossey-Bass.

Paul, W. J., K. B. Robertson, and F. Herzberg. 1969. Job enrichment pays off. *Harvard Business Review* 47 (2):61–78.

Paulos, J. A. 1998. *Once upon a number: The hidden mathematical logic of stories.* New York: Basic Books.

Peace, W. H. 1986. I thought I knew what good management was. *Harvard Business Review* 64 (2):59–65.

Pearce, W. B., and V. E. Cronen, 1980. *Communication, action, and meaning.* New York: Praeger.

Pearce, W. B., L. M. Harris, and V. E. Cronen. 1982. Communication theory in a new key. In *Rigor and imagination,* edited by C. Wilder and J. H. Weakland (pp. 149–194). New York: Praeger.

Pereira, J. 1989. L. L. Bean scales back expansion goals to ensure pride in its service is valid. *Wall Street Journal,* 31 July, B3.

Peters, T. J., and R. H. Waterman, Jr. 1982. *In search of excellence.* New York: Harper & Row.

Pfeffer, J., and R. I. Sutton. 1999a. Knowing what to do is not enough: Turning knowledge into action. *California Management Review* 42 (1):83–109.

———. 1999b. The smart-talk trap. *Harvard Business Review* 77 (3):134–144.

Pierce, J. R. 1983. *The science of musical sound.* New York: Scientific American Library.

Pierce, J. R., and M. Noll. 1990. *Signals: The science of telecommunications.* New York: Scientific American Library.

Pinchot, G. 1985. *Intrapreneuring.* New York: Harper & Row.

Pinder, C. C. 1984. *Work motivation.* Glenview, IL: Scott Foresman.

Polmar, N., and T. B. Allen. 1982. *Rickover: Controversy and genius.* New York: Simon & Schuster.

Prahalad, C. K., and G. Hamel. 1990. The core competence of the corporation. *Harvard Business Review* 90 (3):79–93.

Prokesch, S. E. 1997. Unleashing the power of learning: An interview with British Petroleum's John Browne. *Harvard Business Review* 75 (5):146–168.

Pullum, G. K. 1991. *The great Eskimo vocabulary hoax and other irreverent essays on the study of language.* Chicago: University of Chicago Press.

Putnam, L. L., and C. E. Wilson. 1982. Communicative strategies in organizational conflicts: Reliability and validity of a measurement scale. In *Communication yearbook 6,* edited by M. Burgoon (pp. 629–673). Beverly Hills, CA: Sage.

Reddy, M. J. 1979. The conduit metaphor: A case of frame conflict in our language about language. In *Metaphor and thought,* edited by A. Ortony. Cambridge, England: Cambridge University Press.

Reed: Reflections on a culture clash. 2000. *Fortune,* 20 March, 28.

Reinhardt, A. 1999. The man who hones Cisco's cutting edge. *Business Week,* 13 September, 140.

Rivette, K. G., and D. Kline. 2000. Discovering new value in intellectual property. *Harvard Business Review* 78 (1):54–66.

Robichaux, M. 1989. Teens in business discover credibility is hard to earn. *Wall Street Journal,* 9 June, B1–B2.

Rogers, E. M. 1995. *The diffusion of innovations.* 3d ed. New York: The Free Press.

Rogers, F. G. 1986. *The IBM way.* New York: Harper & Row.

Sanders, W. C. 1986. Important and unimportant organizational communication: Public employee freedom of speech after Connick v. Myers. Paper presented at the annual convention of the International Communication Association, May, Chicago, IL.

Schank, R. 1990. *Tell me a story: A new look at real and artificial memory.* Menlo Park, CA: Crisp.

Schank, R. C. 1984. *The cognitive computer.* Reading, MA: Addison-Wesley.

Schmidt, E. 2000. Speech to the National Governor's Association, 27 February, Washington, DC.

Schramm, W. L. 1954. How communication works. In *The process and effects of mass communications,* edited by W. Schramm (pp. 3–26). Urbana, IL: University of Illinois Press.

Schwadel, F. 1985. Burned by mistakes, Campbell Soup Co. is in throes of change. *Wall Street Journal,* 14 August, A1, A15.

Scott, C., D. Jaffe, and G. Tobe. 1993. *Organizational vision, values and mission.* Menlo Park, CA: Crisp.

Shannon, C., and W. Weaver. 1949. *A mathematical theory of communication.* Urbana: University of Illinois Press.

Shapiro, B. P., V. K. Rangan, and J. J. Sviokla. 1992. Staple yourself to an order. *Harvard Business Review* 70 (4):113–122.

Shook, R. L. 1988. *Honda.* New York: Prentice Hall.

Shulman, S. 2000. Software patents tangle the web. *Technology Review,* March/April, 68–76.

Smith, K. K., and V. M. Simmons. 1983. A Rumpelstiltskin organization: Metaphors on metaphors in field research. *Administrative Science Quarterly* 28:377–392.

Sobek, D. K., A. C. Ward, and J. K. Liker. 1999. Toyota's principles of set-based concurrent engineering. *Sloan Management Review* 40 (2):67–84.

Sobel, R. 1999. *When giants stumble.* Paramus, NJ: Prentice Hall.

Solomon, J. 1989a. As firms personnel files grow, worker privacy falls. *Wall Street Journal,* 19 April, B1.

———. 1989b. Managing: Old culture behavior. *Wall Street Journal,* 17 August, B1.

Solzhenitsyn, A. 1978. A world split apart. *Vital Speeches,* 1 September, 678–684.

Sproull, L., and S. Kiesler. 1986. Reducing social context cues: The case of electronic mail. *Management Science* 32:1492–1512.

Staw, W. 1988. Music videos in its contexts: Popular music and post-modernism in the 1980s. *Popular Music* 7 (3):247–266.

Stepanek, M. 1999. How fast is net fast? *Business Week [On-line],* 1 November. Available at <www.businessweek.com/reprints/>.

Stewart, T. A., A. Taylor, III, P. Petre, and B. Schlender. 1999. The businessman of the century. *Fortune,* 22 November, 111.

Storck, J., and P. A. Hill. 2000. Knowledge diffusion through "strategic communities." *Sloan Management Review* 41 (2):63–74.

Suchan, J., and R. Colucci. 1989. Analysis of communication efficiency between high-impact and bureaucratic written communication. *Management Communication Quarterly* 2 (4):454–484.

Sullivan, J. J. 1988. Financial presentation format and managerial decision making. *Management Communication Quarterly* 2 (2):194–215.

Szilard, L. 1961. *The voice of the dolphins.* New York: Simon & Schuster.

Templin, N. 1990. Johnson & Johnson "wellness" program for workers shows healthy bottom line. *Wall Street Journal,* 21 May, B1.

Trachtenberg, J. A. 1988. *Ralph Lauren: The man behind the mystique.* Boston: Little, Brown.

Tracy, K., D. VanDusen, and S. Robinson. 1987. "Good" and "bad" criticism: A descriptive analysis. *Journal of Communication* 37 (2):46–59.

Trevino, L. K., R. L. Daft, and R. H. Lengel. 1990. Understanding manager's media choices: A symbolic interactionist perspective. In *Organizations and communication technology,* edited by J. Fulk and C. Steinfield (pp. 71–94). Newbury Park, CA: Sage.

Tropman, J. 1996. *Effective meetings: Improving group decision making.* Thousand Oaks, CA: Sage.

Tufte, E. R. 1983. *The visual display of quantitative information.* Cheshire, CT: Graphics Press.

Turek, R. 1985. Interview with Rosalyn Turek by W. F. Buckley [with Schuyler Chapin and Tim Page]. *Firing line,* Southern Educational Communications Association, 17 July.

U.S. Department of Commerce. 1984. *How plain English works for business.* Washington, DC: U.S. Government Printing Office.

Useem, J. 1999. Can these marriages be saved? *Fortune,* 8 November, 102–110.

Usow, B. 2000 (January 15). Personal interview with author.

Wald, M. L. 1990. Whistle-blowers in atomic plants to be aided. *New York Times,* 11 March, Y13.

Wang, A. 1986. *Lessons.* Reading, MA: Addison-Wesley.

Ware, B. L., and W. A. Linkugel. 1973. They spoke in defense of themselves: On the generic criticism of apologia. *Quarterly Journal of Speech* 59 (3):273–283.

Watson, J. D. 1968. *The double helix.* New York: New American Library.

Watzlawick, P., J. Beavin, and D. Jackson. 1967. *Pragmatics of human communication.* New York: Norton.

Weisman, A. 1986. Interview by Morley Safer. *60 minutes.* CBS News, 9 March.

Welles, E. 1999. Mind gains. *Inc.* December, 112–124.

Wenger, E., and W. Snyder 2000. Communities of practice: The organizational frontier. *Harvard Business Review* 78 (1):139–146.

Westin, A. F. 1980. A profile of Bank of America's privacy experience. In *Individual rights in the corporation: A reader on employee rights,* edited by A. F. Westin and S. Salisbury (pp. 226–243). New York: Pantheon Books.

Wiio, O. 1978. *Wiio's laws—And some others.* Espoo, Finland: Welingoos.

Williams, F. 1987. *Technology and communication behavior.* Belmont, CA: Wadsworth.

Williams, M. L. 1976. Equivocation: How does it affect receiver agreement and recall? Paper presented at the annual convention of the Speech Communication Association, November, San Francisco, CA.

Winch, P. 2000. Personal communication, 10 January.

Wood shows signs of defensive ability. 1984. *USA Today,* 1 August, C2.

Wriston, W. B. 1986. The world according to Walter. *Harvard Business Review* 64 (1):65–80.

———. 1990. The state of American management. *Harvard Business Review* 68 (1):78–83.

Wurman, R. S. 1989. *Information anxiety.* New York: Doubleday.

Zuboff, S. 1984. *In the age of the smart machine.* New York: Basic Books.

Index

ABOUT THE AUTHOR

Phillip G. Clampitt, Ph.D., is a Professor of Organizational Communication and Information Sciences at the University of Wisconsin—Green Bay. His work has been published in a variety of journals, including *Management Communication Quarterly,* the *Journal of Business Communication, Communication World,* the *Journal of Broadcasting,* and the international *Journal of Communication Management.* He is also a recognized expert on communication assessments, having conducted over 100 communication audits and written chapters on the subject for *Handbook of Communication Audits for Organizations,* edited by Owen Hargie and Dennis Tourish, and *Communication audits,* by Cal Downs. In addition, he founded MetaComm, a communication consulting firm that has worked with many companies, including TWA, Appleton Papers, Schneider National, Medalcraft Mint, Dean Foods, and Boldt Construction. His firm specializes in assessing, analyzing, and resolving communication problems in organizations (see *www.imetacomm.com*).